*Additional praise for*

# WHAT I LEARNED IN THE MIDST OF KAOS

"Dr. Shields uses his life story to offer a compelling look into the obstacles and barriers that prevent so many from achieving their full potential. This book challenges the reader to seek a higher sense of purpose and make a difference in the lives of others."

– Dr. Ronn H. Johnson
Superintendent, Lawnside School District

"LaMarr uses his personal story as a tale of caution and triumph and shares with us how he made it through and how his survival can be a potential roadmap for bringing others through. He is interested in the whole story of the boy and offers a way where so many see no way. Although some of the lessons offered in this book speak directly to Black boys, the love, support, and compassion that all humans need to thrive are found in these pages. LaMarr is very generous with this book. Experience his gift."

- André Robert Lee
Director, *The Prep School Negro*

"*What I Learned in the Midst of KAOS* provides the reader with insights on life and leadership that LaMarr has been communicating and modeling for at least 20 years. His efforts have helped many youth and adults recognize the lessons of childhood and the importance of strengthening and sustaining one's community through all of one's actions. His dynamism and energy jump off every page in the same way that is evident to audiences when he lectures, to youth when he teaches, and to anyone who has ever had the privilege of sitting around a table and talking with him."

- Dr. Philip J. Leaf
Professor, Johns Hopkins University
Bloomberg School of Public Health
Director, Center for the Prevention of Youth Violence

"In his latest work, Dr. Shields gives us not only his memoirs, but also insight into the inner workings of Black and Brown boys growing up in America. As a prevention researcher, I can see the great benefits of this book to many of us who work with this population. It helps us understand and deconstruct at a deep level some of the trends we see in the statistics. As a mother of two boys, I can also see this book as a powerful tool to open up dialogue between us as a family. This book is poised to make an impact for years to come."

- Dr. Nadine Finigan-Carr
Research Assistant Professor
University of Maryland, Baltimore School of Social Work

"Quite an inspiring read that provides the ingredients for uplifting the spirit and for empowering young people who are living in a state of powerlessness and hopelessness."

> - Dr. Frances Staten
> Professor of Sociology and Psychology
> Grambling State University

"This book is a must-read for anyone who has had personal setbacks and triumphs. *What I Learned in the Midst of KAOS* is relatable and will serve as an excellent roadmap for anyone searching for a glimpse of hope while in the midst of his or her own personal chaos."

> - Jeff "Jazz" Jones
> Supervisor of Juvenile Probation Officers
> Las Vegas Department of Juvenile Justice Services

"It isn't often that we are given the opportunity to speak from the deeply rooted places of our souls with a chance to positively impact the lives of others. Many are bound by a posture of "playing it safe" for the sake of projecting a respectable image. LaMarr Darnell Shields has always had the gift conveying his personal stories with vulnerability while managing to encourage others to do great things. He does so because he knows the stakes are high for a generation of youth who struggle with self-identity. *What I Learned in the Midst of KAOS* courageously advances Dr. Shields' life-changing work to enhance the lives of young people who might otherwise be left behind. This is an admirable achievement."

> - Dr. Derek S. Hicks
> Assistant Professor of Religion and Culture
> Wake Forest University
> Author of *Reclaiming Spirit in the Black Faith Tradition*

"In his new book, Dr. Shields captures the experiences and journeys of millions of boys of color from the lens of his own life. Shields' transparency in recounting his journey from childhood to adulthood provides opportunity and hope for others. Many educators have heard LaMarr speak multiple times, but this unique text opens new opportunities for all educators - whether familiar with LaMarr's work or not - to think critically about how to approach this phenomenon we call "teaching and learning." I encourage any educational stakeholder to put this book on their reading list."

> - Dr. Roger Cleveland
> Associate Professor, College of Education
> Eastern Kentucky University

# WHAT I LEARNED IN THE MIDST OF KAOS:
## THE MAKING OF AN UBUNTU TEACHER

### By Dr. LaMarr Darnell Shields
with Dr. Marina V. Gillmore

FULL CIRCLE PRESS

Cambio Books

Published by Full Circle Press in association with Cambio Books

Printed in the United States of America

FULL CIRCLE PRESS

700 E. Redlands Blvd, Suite U #293
Redlands, CA 92373

Cataloging-in-Publication data for this book is available from the Library of Congress

ISBN 978-0-9890453-4-6

Copies of this book are available at special discounts for bulk purchases in the U.S. by schools, non-profit organizations, and other government and private agencies. For more information, please contact the Special Markets Department, Full Circle Press at 700 E. Redlands Blvd, Ste U #293, Redlands, CA 92373 or at www.fullcirclepress.org.

Cover design and layout by Laura Stephen.

This is an educational narrative of creative nonfiction. The events are portrayed to the best of the primary author's memory and have been enhanced by information gleaned from informal conversations and interviews with people in the author's life whose experiences have overlapped with his. In cases where the primary author could not remember the exact words used by certain people or the exact descriptions of certain items, he filled in the gaps as best he could. Otherwise, all characters, incidents, and dialogue are authentic and while all the stories in this book are true, some names and identifying details have been changed to protect the privacy of the people involved.

# WHAT I LEARNED IN THE MIDST OF KAOS:
## THE MAKING OF AN UBUNTU TEACHER

*Ubuntu means my humanity is caught up, is inextricably bound up, in yours. We belong in a bundle of life. We say, "a person is a person through other persons." It is not, "I think therefore I am." It says rather, "I am human because I belong, I participate, I share."*

- Desmond Tutu, No Future Without Forgiveness

# DEDICATION

*Dedicated to the memory of Dr. Wayne W. Dyer, whose example of how to live a life of peace and purpose and how to write with truth and integrity have inspired our individual and collective work both within and beyond this project in more ways that we could put into words. Thank you.*

*And for all of the students who have given
me an opportunity to serve, thus fulfilling my calling.
- LDS*

*And for all the ones I tried to save, but couldn't.
I get it now. You were never mine to save.
- MVG*

# TABLE OF CONTENTS

# PREFACE : ON INSPIRATION

*If you bring forth what is within you, what you bring forth will
save you. If you do not bring forth what is within you, what
you do not bring forth will destroy you.*

– Gospel of Thomas

I came up with the idea for this book nearly a decade ago. I wanted to write about
the love that I had received from my childhood friends and how these friendships
and bonds had shaped me. I wanted people to intimately see what this type of
friendship had meant to a group of boys, many of whom did not have strong
men in their lives. We called ourselves the KAOS crew and we were inseparable. I
wasn't even thinking when I first started writing about how all these formative
experiences had shaped me as a teacher, an artist, a father, a husband, and a
man. I just wanted to remind myself, my boys, and the world of how strong we
were and how together we were able to overcome so much.

A decade is a flash of lightning and a decade is a forever journey. A lot has changed
in my life and perspective since I first conceptualized what this book would be. In
many ways, the core group of us who formed KAOS has been weathered a bit by
the passing of time. Love, losses, marriages, careers, children and age have taken
their toll on the fiber of our friendship, rendered it a bit weaker in places.

And yet our collective sense of hope, drive, redemption, accountability and
vulnerability has remained. The awareness that we belonged to others so
completely has traveled with us wherever we have gone.

When I speak, I often introduce myself as that little Black and Brown boy from
the South Side of Chicago, because in many ways I am still that boy. And as I
travel, I carry each person from the KAOS crew with me. I share their hopes and
dreams, and sometimes their misfortunes. I'm honored to represent them in their
absence.

Just as you are an accumulation of the earliest experiences that shaped you, so
am I. Just as you carry with you the stories closest to your heart – those filled
with pain and those filled with love – so do I.

If you're willing to read my story, my hope is that you are also willing to acknowledge the power in your own. If you're willing to learn about how one little Black and Brown boy paved a way – through his own intentions and through the love, support and belief of some of those closest to him – to become an Ubuntu teacher and, in so doing, has given voice to some of those most marginalized by our educational and judicial systems, my hope is that you'll be willing to look at the young men who sometimes are so quickly reduced to statistics and – in really *seeing* them – will bring some humanity back to the conversations about what our young people need to succeed.

When I first saw the cover mock up for this book, I was *so* excited – not for myself, but for all my boys in KAOS. Of all of us who might write a book about our experiences, I don't think it has surprised any of us that I was the one to write this one. Because I was there through it all. From the very beginning. And just seeing the book cover with the word *KAOS* so bold, I knew that this book would take me and my boys back to a different place in time. Wow! We've done some amazing things. And the fact that I've survived to tell it, and to use it as a testimony of what is possible, humbles me beyond measure.

When I thought about who could help write this book, I considered not only who had the writing experience, but also – and more importantly – who shared and understood my beliefs and would protect my story. After leading several retreats with Marina and observing firsthand her authenticity, I knew she'd be able to help bring what was in my head and heart onto these pages. I wanted to work with someone who would challenge me to do my best work, someone who cared about the things that matter most to me. We read the same books and both care deeply about the fate of America's most vulnerable and marginalized children and the adults who work with them. There was no one else I felt could do it. And although it hasn't always been an easy journey, here we are.

*- Dr. LaMarr Darnell Shields*
*Baltimore, Maryland*

---

I'll never forget when LaMarr first asked me to help him with this project. I said yes immediately and then tried to come up with a million excuses as to why I couldn't do it, but the only excuse that really held any weight was that I was scared. I was afraid of the enormity of what this project would entail and of the responsibility of getting it right. Because I knew from the beginning that, of all the writing projects I'd ever tackled, it was really important to get this one right.

I challenged LaMarr a bit at the onset. I said that even though everyone has a story (or two or 10) to tell, not everyone's story is the making of a book that will actually *mean* something to anyone besides the author's mom. I had a hunch that this story would be different, but I have to admit that I didn't really know in the beginning. Now, I do know. And it is different.

My hope is that I've helped tell LaMarr's story in a way that honors all the places he's been and everyone who has crossed his path. My hope is that whether you knew him intimately at 16 years old, or 22 years old, or never at all, you'll connect with something in the pages that follow and say to yourself, *Yeah, I get that. Now I understand.*

I hear my teaching story in LaMarr's story and I hope, if you're reading this as an educator, that you will too. I hope you will see the universality of what binds us as teachers who care very deeply about the young people we're charged to serve. I also hear the lives of so many of my students in his story – the countless young men in my own teaching career who looked different than me and with whom, sometimes more successfully than others, I was able to bridge the vast sea that lay between us.

If there's any disclaimer I want to make about this book, through my lens as a white female social justice advocate navigating a world in which many people I work, write, teach and engage with come from backgrounds that look and feel different from my own, it's that this is not a simple "bootstraps" story of a successful Black man who has made it out of the South Side of Chicago. It's not a simple lesson in *See, if he can do it, so can you!* with the often accompanying thoughts of *What's YOUR problem? What's YOUR excuse?* This story, this life, this book – if I've played any small part in doing it justice – is infinitely more complex than that. If you read it as a simple bootstraps story, I challenge you – wherever you may be on your own journey – to do a bit of self-examination of your beliefs about what it takes to make it in this world.

In the short but intense time that LaMarr and I have been working with each other, we have traveled some miles together. Our families have shared meals, we've run up a mountaintop or two together, and we've flown back and forth across the country to collaborate on projects that we hold close to our lives and senses of purpose. Although we come from such different worlds, in so many ways our values, worldviews and interests are closely aligned.

I share this because it's important for the reader to know that I don't believe I could have helped to tell his story in any way that might be considered objective. The pages that follow are full of my own bias, my own belief that of all the educators I've worked with throughout the years, of all the social justice advocates I've collaborated with and stayed up late with working through some of the most complex of our society's ills, of all the intelligent minds I've picked apart in order to better understand my own place in this world, LaMarr is among the very best.

So I've helped to tell his story in the same way that you might help to tell the story of your own brother – someone who, although complex and wildly irritating to you at times, is nonetheless a part of your life's narrative in a way that renders objectivity neither possible nor desirable. If you're looking for the objective version of this story – the one not colored so much by LaMarr's own perceptions of the ways things were or my own interpretation of the legacy his life will one day leave, then you'll have to look elsewhere. But if you're looking for a story told with as much love and respect as you might want the stories of those closest to your own life to be told, then I hope you find that story here.

*- Dr. Marina V. Gillmore*
*Palm Springs, California*

---

The idea that a little Black and Brown boy from the South Side of Chicago and a little red-headed white girl from Southern California would grow up and co-author a book that tackles some of the issues that we've addressed here is a testament to the fact that – in ways both large and small – our society and our world are making some progress. And yet here we are, in a time with so much work left to be done, so many educational and racial issues left unresolved.

There is significance to the journey we've taken in writing this book that we hope shines through in the pages that follow. It's been both a labor of love and a challenge to meld the experiences that have shaped the author's life with a level of reflective insight that will encourage even the most seasoned of educators, parents and youth service providers to stop and give thought to what we're doing for our boys of color in this country today and how and why we need to do better.

We have intentionally worked to write in such a way that if you are reading these words as a boy or young man, wondering if and how you'll navigate your way out of the chaotic and seemingly hopeless situations in your life, you'll see this as a map of sorts. Not your map, because we all have to pave our own ways, live our own truths, follow our own compasses, but a map that says *Here you go. It's possible. You don't have to wonder if you can make it out alive. You can. You will. You're not alone.*

In crafting a book like this, we had to make many decisions along the way regarding our use of language and which details to include and which to omit. With both the Spanish phrases that appear throughout the book and the references to terminology that might not be familiar to all readers, we were very deliberate about what we explained within the text, what we referenced in the Notes section, and what we left to the you, the reader, to figure out on your own. Likewise, there was an intentionality to how we shaped certain stories – the details we've included and what we've chosen to leave out.

We come from different worlds in many ways, but we do share a passion for asking difficult questions, telling stories honestly, and helping others communicate their truths. We have in common a deep love for education, and we believe with our whole hearts that a more equitable and just system is possible in our lifetimes. We like a good challenge and we both possess the inherent hope that things can be better than they are. We believe that if we look a little deeper, reflect a little more honestly, and give a little more freely of ourselves, the world will reward us with ample opportunity to make a difference in the lives of others. And it's often in these opportunities, in these times when we are being of service, that we journey back to the deepest hopes of our own lives.

What follows is a story of perseverance, curiosity, optimism, hope, discipline, abandonment, love and support. It's a coming of age story of a young boy from the South Side of Chicago, rooted in a time and place of unique significance. And yet it's also a story of universal themes, timeless lessons, and hopeful connections. It's a story of the strong link between student and teacher, boy and man, son and father, novice and expert. It's a story of one and of many. Whatever you came looking for when you first held this book in your hand, flipped through its pages, and questioned its significance, we hope you find it in the chapters that follow. And we hope that just maybe this will inspire you to share your own story – big or small, triumphant or difficult, joyful or filled with sorrow. They all matter in some way.

*With Gratitude,*
*LaMarr & Marina*
*October 2015*

# PROLOGUE

*I'm just doing better than what everybody projected*
*Knew that I'd be here so if you asked me how I feel*
*I'mma just tell you, it's everything that I expected.*

- Big Sean

"Baba, tell me about the photo again." His 6-year-old eyes look up at me expectantly, beautiful in their wonder and constant inquisitiveness.

This inquiry from my son Mosiah-Sekou – whose name means "anointed learner" – isn't unusual. He frequently asks me about how I felt at his age and what I did. *Baba, do you miss your father? How did you feel when your dad died? When you were young, what did you think life would be like as an adult? What does it take to win? Why are people mean to others? Why are there bad people in the world? What was it like growing up without a dad? Are there TV shows out now that were out when you were young? How does it feel to be the youngest in your family? What were you allergic to when you were younger? How does it feel when there are crowds of people waiting to hear you speak?*

Just recently, his mother wanted him to spend time with his two older sisters and he told her that he's so glad he has a dad who knows what it feels like to be a boy. When my wife Meshelle recounted this to me, it reinforced in me the importance of telling my story here – which in a real sense is my son's story as well.

In a way, this entire book is a letter to Mosiah, filled with all my memories that I hope one day he'll understand – memories of what it was like when I was a boy, memories of a childhood that was complex, but not hopeless.

I know there are things he might not fully comprehend until he's older, if at all. And I'm mostly okay with that. Growing up in a two-parent household in a middle-class Baltimore neighborhood as a vegan, his day-to-day experiences look a lot different than those of my childhood in many ways.

And he's unique in his own right – he's more talkative than I was as a child and he doesn't know what it's like to grow up in a fatherless house. He loves school. He cares a lot about looking good. He's not a sickly kid like I was at his age. In other ways, though, I see myself in him every day. He's introspective like me. He doesn't want to see people suffer. He's very well-liked among his peers and loves sports. He has a lot of friends and will try new things without hesitation. And like me, he questions everything. And I mean everything.

What I do hope he understands is the complexity of the struggle and wonder of growing up as a young man of color in America. I hope he recognizes that all the work I have done throughout my career with Black and Brown boys has been both an attempt to understand myself better and also a way to pave a different future for him than might have otherwise existed. I hope he sees the congruence in my life and my work and recognizes that at the same time I'm pouring into him, I'm also pouring into all the young men I work with. I want there to be no gray areas. I want my life and work to make sense to him. It's hard for me to separate who I am from what I do, and I hope that he learns that there's beauty in this sometimes difficult struggle of caring so much.

And I hope that my work is a reflection of what he sees when he looks at that picture of himself he asks about so often – opportunity, optimism, and a belief in a future that is bright. The photo in question, the one Mosiah asks me about frequently, immortalizes a moment in my own life that I'll never forget.

I'm standing at the threshold looking in. The room seems foreboding to me, but seeing the young boy, holding a shiny red apple in his hand, looking up with wonder at the man kneeling down in front of him, you would almost think the boy thought he was home. Both the man and the boy are dressed in nearly matching navy blue blazers and patriotic red, white and blue ties. And even though I cannot see the man's face, I can see vividly – in the same way that is now commemorated in a photo of the moment that hangs in my home – the wonder, trust and excitement so transparent on the boy's face. The boy is my then 3-year-old son. And the man is the 44th President of the United States. They're in the Oval Office. And I can't help but wonder how I – a boy from the South Side of Chicago with a rocky past – ended up here, in the White House, bearing witness to this moment between my son and our President. A man who looks like us. A man who knows the challenges of having a large amount of melanin in your skin. I mean, these things just don't normally happen to kids who came from where I did.

*How did I get here? How did we get here?* I wonder. My mind wanders. I know that there is a reason for it all, but that putting the pieces of this story together, connecting the dots from my childhood to here, is going to take some work. But before we go back to where it all started, let's talk about the day at the White House – a day that in and of itself was quite a journey.

It was a cold morning in February of 2009. My wife Meshelle, our three children – Hadiya, Sameera and Mosiah – and I sprinted as fast as we could through the five inches of snow that covered the ground from the parking lot to the White House gates. We ran because we were late for a very important meeting with the President of the United States.

A few weeks prior, a writer from the Washington Post had interviewed me and had asked if I could provide her with the names of any young people who could articulate their perspectives on having an African American president. I supplied her with a short list of names, including a friend's son, Khalil, and my eldest daughter Hadiya, who I had known could handle the interview.

When the reporter had spoken with Hadiya and had asked her how she felt about having the first African American President of the United States, Hadiya's response had left her floored: "I think the first African American president is great, but I'm more excited that there are two little girls who look like me named Sasha and Malia growing up in the White House."

Hadiya's comments were included a couple of days later in the article that ran in the Washington Post. Soon after, I received a call from the White House informing me that President Obama had read the article and that he wanted to invite the families of the children featured to the White House for a visit.

Needless to say, our entire family was excited about the news. We spent the day before the visit preparing – haircuts for me and Mosiah, salon visits for the girls, and a trip to the mall for new dresses and suits. After all, we were going to the White House!

The morning of the visit, as I buttoned my 3-year-old son's white shirt, I thought back to the night when then Senator Barack Obama was elected President of the United States. I remember being filled with emotion as my family and I watched the new First Family – a mother, father, and the two little Black girls my daughter had referenced in her interview – walk out on a platform to address a sea of people in my hometown of Chicago. I had watched this man's political star rise – from community activist, to senator, to president – and had told my family on inauguration night that one day we would meet President Barack Obama. I didn't know how or when, I just knew that one day I'd make good on this promise. Little did I know that the visit would come on the shoulders of my 8-year-old daughter's insightful comments.

We were finally all dressed and ready to head to Washington, D.C., only to open the front door of our house and see snow – *lots* of it. I looked at my family, then back out at the white blizzard beginning to swirl around us. In all of our excitement and preparations the previous day, we had forgotten that a Nor'easter was barreling toward the state threatening to dump more than two feet of snow on the entire East Coast. "I don't care what else happens today," I told my family with a mixture of confidence and apprehension. "We *are* getting to the White House."

Meshelle and I loaded the kids into our blue Ford Expedition and skidded to the highway. Traffic was at a crawl once we merged onto I-295 heading south toward D.C., but I was determined. As a Chicagoan, I am a skilled driver in the snow, unlike many folks in Maryland who are known to crawl along at 10 miles an hour and somehow manage to still turn the highway into a sea of bumper cars.

"Drive on the shoulder," my wife instructed. I looked over at the emergency lane and then back at her. She had a point. No one was driving there, and we would be able to pass the traffic and hopefully arrive at the White House in time for our visit.

"What happens if we get pulled over by a state trooper?" I questioned as I maneuvered toward the free lane.

"Just tell them we're going to the White House!" she replied.

"What if the state trooper is a Republican?" I asked with a laugh.

I wove in and out of traffic until I made my way to the emergency lane, praying I wouldn't crash or be pulled over by Maryland State Highway Patrol.

---

This wasn't my first invitation to the White House. In 1996, while President Clinton was in office, I had received a call from Marietta English, President of the Baltimore Teachers Union.

"LaMarr, we have selected you to represent Baltimore City Public Schools at the White House," she informed me. "They want you to provide insight on your experiences teaching in an urban setting."

I was stunned. I had only been teaching high school Spanish for two years at Baltimore City College when I received the invitation. Immediately, I thought, *Me? What would this young man of color, from the South Side of Chicago with only a couple of years of teaching experience, say to the President of the United States about the profession?* I didn't have the answer, but I did know that I was not about to turn down what I thought then was a once-in-a-lifetime opportunity.

The day of that trip, I rode to the White House with two women who were part of the Baltimore Teachers Union. Though it was just a 30-minute drive from

Baltimore, I had only been to Washington, D.C. a few times since migrating to Maryland and had never been to the White House, so it was a big trip for me.

Teachers from around the country converged on the nation's capital for the single-day event and I was excited and honored to be among them. After parking, we got out of the car and approached the first check-in station. My name was not on the list.

*Shields, why are you here?* I asked myself, echoing a question that had haunted me ever since my high school Spanish teacher, Señor Hogan, had shouted it at me one day before putting me out of his class. It's like even though I knew I had an invitation to the White House, I could not help but question if I belonged or if it was just a giant mistake. I feared that I was going to be turned away right then and denied admittance. After checking the list numerous times, the White House security team called the second check-in station. My name was on that list. I breathed a sigh of relief and let that haunting question fade back into the background of my mind. I *did* deserve to be there.

After receiving full clearance at the second checkpoint, the first person I saw was ABC political correspondent Sam Donaldson.

"Excuse me, Sir," he greeted me as he extended his hand. "Are you one of the teachers the White House invited to speak?"

"Yes, I am," I responded, thinking no one I knew would believe where I was and who I was meeting, especially since I had left my camera at home. We talked for a moment before I was ushered to the West Lawn.

The program began, and as I stood listening to the educators' discussions, President Bill Clinton walked out of his office, came over to me, and struck up a brief conversation. *Wow! I thought! I'm at the White House. Talking to the President. About education.* Two years into my teaching career, and here I stood on the West Lawn with President Clinton sharing my upbringing in Chicago, education at De La Salle Institute, training through Teach For America, relocation to Baltimore, and thoughts on teaching in an urban environment. The President listened intently as I spoke, thanked me for coming, and moved on to the next teacher.

Though that visit to the White House was special, this second visit with my family was going to be even more meaningful, mainly because the reason we were going had nothing to do with me at all, but with my daughter.

We finally arrived at 1600 Pennsylvania Ave. nearly 90 minutes after we'd left home. We were late, but we had made it. My wife and I ushered our children out of the car and the five of us ran as quickly as we could to our assigned entrance. It felt like we were moving in slow motion, though, as we trudged through all that snow. We got to the security gate and, unlike my last visit to the White House, my name was on the list this time. We were screened by Secret Service and then escorted to the group already deep into a White House tour.

There is nothing like being inside of the White House. That day our guide, who was also from Chicago, showed us photographs of the First Ladies, presidential artifacts, and the Green Room with stretched-silk walls designed by Jackie Kennedy. Our guide even took us to the space that had been set up for the President's Super Bowl party before walking us into a room with red carpet where the president normally addresses the nation.

Suddenly, Khalil – one of the other children interviewed for the Washington Post story – stopped and asked our guide, "Where does the President live?"

"Upstairs," she answered.

"Can we go up there to see *that*?" he inquired hesitantly.

"Now, would you want someone coming to your house unannounced?" she asked.

He replied with a sheepish, "No."

"Well, we don't want to frighten the First Lady by doing that, so we'll just stay down here and finish the tour."

Khalil looked at his mom, Kim, and then nodded his head slowly in agreement.

At one point during the tour, I stopped to gaze out a window at the snowstorm brewing outside. I have always loved watching the snow fall. It has a way of making everything peaceful and quiet, of turning even ugly things beautiful.

"You're looking at the West Lawn," the tour guide interrupted my thoughts. Wow! Just 12 years ago, I had stood on those very grounds speaking with the President of the United States. All I wanted was for my family to have a similar experience and somehow get to meet this President. I knew he was in town because I had followed his movements throughout the week, but I didn't know if we were going to meet him. All I could do was hope.

Our tour guide asked us to put on our coats so we could transition from the White House to the West Wing. As we walked, we saw a Marine standing guard outside the building. A huge smile spread across my face because I knew Marines only stand outside when the President is on the premises.

"See that?" I whispered to my wife as I pointed discreetly to the Marine at his post. "President Obama *is* here."

Once we entered the West Wing, a notable senior government official I recognized immediately walked out of an office screaming and cursing with another official-looking gentleman. I looked at him and questioned sternly, "Don't you see these kids here with us?" Immediately, he apologized, greeted the children on the tour and then returned to the office.

Our tour guide then led us to a room where we removed our coats before another woman walked in to ask if she could take the children with her. My wife and I were nervous because we knew Mosiah, who was barely 3 years old at the time, might need a little guidance to help him contain his energy.

"He's only 3 and may need a little more attention than the other kids," I informed the woman.

"He will be fine," she smiled as she grabbed his hand. I let her take him, but to where, I did not know.

It wasn't until after our children left that we realized we were standing in the Roosevelt Room, the very space where President Obama met with his Cabinet and signed documents. We marveled that we were in the room where major national and international decisions were made. The chairs were pushed in at an oval-shaped, mahogany wood table, with the President's seat at the head of the table a good 2 or 3 inches above the others. My wife walked over to that chair and raised prayers of protection over it.

Soon after, we heard a door open. Khalil's mom, Kim, hit my back.

"Darnell, there's the President," she exclaimed. "There's the President!"

I turned around to find our President standing in the doorway leading to the Oval Office. He looked around the room, smiled, and then welcomed us in.

Kim shook with excitement, my wife was stunned speechless, and my mouth gaped open at the thought that we had just been invited into the President's personal quarters.

We walked in a single-file line into the Oval Office. Inside, our children had made themselves at home. My son was eating a huge red Washington apple. Later he would tell me that the President had given it to him.

President Obama greeted each of us in turn. As he spoke to the other parents, I stood preparing what I was going to say. I knew it was going to be something so intellectual, so mind-blowing that he was going to think, *Wow, this guy is sharp!*

I was still planning my words when he turned to me and extended his hand. I looked at him and said, "Homeboy!" and immediately thought to myself, *No I did not just call the President of the United States "homeboy!"* Without delay, my wife tapped me on the back and whispered through gritted teeth, "Did you just call the President *homeboy*?"

A huge grin spread across President Obama's face and his eyes softened, "You must be from Chicago!" I immediately breathed a sigh of relief and nodded.

"You know, I was just talking to my wife Michelle about how Chicagoans drive in the snow," he shared. "I couldn't believe that Sasha and Malia's school closed because of the snow today."

"But, Mr. President," I said. "This *is* a lot of snow."

"Yes, but you and I know how to drive in this snow because we're from Chicago."

I agreed.

As we drove home that day, I reflected on how this experience had change our lives forever.

———

Meeting the President with my family that day really defined for me the significance of making connections in two important ways. Although my wife may have thought I was crazy when I called the leader of the free world "homeboy," by following up that greeting with comments centered around our shared experiences – we were both from Chicago, both married to beautiful women with similar names, and both raising two daughters – we were able to quickly delve into a deep conversation about the possibilities that exist in our world. Yes, we shared the immediate connection of both being African American men, but by seeking other points of connection quickly, we were able to take our conversation into a deeper place than might have otherwise been possible in such a brief meeting.

In my work, teachers often tell me they fear that they will never be able to connect with their students, especially if the students look differently than they do. But the thing about connection is that there are so many complex elements of our identities and experiences through which we can connect. All we have to do is take the time to get to know one another and to foster relationships, ask questions, and – quite often – let go of our preconceived notions of disconnection. As educators, we have to appreciate and accommodate the similarities and differences among our students. We have to pay attention to the varied ways in which students navigate their own ways of learning. As we talk about engaging and connecting with diverse learners, transparency becomes so important in our work. Not transparency in that we overshare or try to build inappropriate connections – no one wants to hear about the teacher who is down the hall trying to connect with students by sharing that he, too, used to smoke a blunt on the way to school every morning – but transparency in so far as we disclose when we need help engaging, when we don't understand where our students are coming from, and when we need to learn a bit more about our students' social-emotional, academic, and cultural competencies before we forge ahead blindly and pretend to have it all together when we don't.

The other way my family's visit to the White House powerfully illustrated the importance of connections lies in how a series of seemingly unrelated events led up to this meeting in ways that I could never have predicted. My life, like everybody's in some way, has been about making connections between moments that often seem so random until we are able to see them through the wisdom that comes with hindsight. As the late Steve Jobs said, "You can't connect the dots going forward; you can only connect them looking backwards. So you have to trust that the dots will somehow connect in your future."

So if I reflect honestly about *why* I ended up at the White House watching my young son look up at our President with so much wonder, I'd have to say that it went back to that election night when I told my children that somehow, we'd get to meet President Obama one day. I honestly had *no* idea how that was going to happen, but I believed deeply that it would. And it did.

And on the day of our family White House visit, despite what my initial greeting to the leader of the free world might otherwise have indicated, I was *ready* for that moment. Life, with all of its chaotic twists and turns, had prepared me well.

One of the things I teach often is the importance of believing in things before you see them. At the time of my second visit to the White House, I had been reading the Wayne Dyer book, "You'll See It When You Believe It," that explores deeply the meaning of the Bible verse "blessed are those who believe without seeing," and here I was living out what that really meant in my life. There were times between my first and second White House visits when my faith was tested in some *big* ways. But everything somehow transpired exactly how it was meant to in some of the most unlikely of ways. During my first visit to the White House, I wasn't really prepared. But the second time, it all felt a little different. And I had my entire family right there by my side.

# AMIDST THE KAOS

My momma gave birth to me, but momma didn't raise me.
I was lost to the streets, so I grew up a little crazy
With other bastard seeds and babies
That the mean streets cuddled and showed love not received in the cradle.
A bad baby boy, but none to the fault of my own,
I was brought up in what some would describe as a broken home.
I learned far more than most my age, I knew too much.
I learned of gangs, guns, sex, drugs, drug dealing and such.
School couldn't motivate me. The streets gave me a rush.
My faith was in the wrong place. I was chasing the bucks.
I still hear tales of lives lost in the streets and I feel fear,
And think it's amazing that I'm still alive, that I'm still here.
But I had my brothers, the only real friends that I've known.
We fought to get through school. At times we had to fight to get home.
Sometimes we did things and knew they were wrong.
But overall we were each other's brother's keeper, so we kept each other strong.
And everywhere we'd go, rest assured we'd leave no doubt,
We liked to let the people know that "KAOS was in the house."
We lost a few friends along the way –
Kerroy, Derrick, Curt, and Dre –
Bonds from my past that keep me strong today.
Now I'm older.  Baby boy has grown into a man.
And everything I own, I've earned with my own two hands.
Amidst the KAOS, somehow it all came together.
Experience is what makes a man, and mine have made me better.
I'm now a husband, and a father, and a teacher of youth.
My simple message: Be a seeker of TRUTH!

- Steve Williams, Original KAOS Member

# INTRODUCTION

*Chaos (n): complete confusion and disorder; a state in which behavior and events are not controlled by anything*

*KAOS (n): my saving grace; my brotherhood; the circle in which we fought, prayed, laughed, cried and buried those of us who didn't make it*

Storms are preceded by calm and followed by chaos. When a massive natural disaster strikes, relief agencies descend upon the hardest hit areas to reach those in immediate need. Humanitarian officials' first priority is to establish emergency medical service sites, distribute food, and sanitize water as needed. They assess the damage, seek funding, and arrange transportation. They coordinate with local government personnel to discuss such daunting tasks as how to register displaced people, where to disseminate donated items, and when to take precautions against epidemics. For all those involved, issues of management and logistics dominate. After all, time is of the essence. The chaos needs to be managed.

Every chaotic situation contains within it the possibility for something powerful – an opportunity, a lesson, a chance for growth. It's how we view the chaos that matters most. If we can see our lack of resources as an advantage, we can be challenged to be more inventive with the little we may have. Dr. King said that "the measure of a man is not where he stands in moments of comfort and convenience, but where he stands at times of challenge and controversy" and it's these times of challenge that often present the best opportunities to prove others, and even ourselves, wrong.

In my own life, I've never thought of the obstacles I've faced as mistakes. I've always called them lessons. And boy have I had my fair share of them. I learned early on in life that you can't stand still in the midst of chaos. You cannot wait for a better moment to make a decision, to move forward, to exercise hope. My mother always taught me that what doesn't kill you makes you stronger. I must admit though, in the difficult moments, seeing this lesson as truth has often been easier said than done.

This book is in part a coming-of-age story about how I responded to the chaos in my life, first as a young man and student growing up on the South Side of Chicago, then as a college student and community leader, and finally as a man who became an Ubuntu teacher. The stories that follow also juxtapose my years as a student at De La Salle Institute, the Catholic high school from which I was expelled, with my time at Grambling State University, where I first traveled to a Spanish-speaking country and found my voice as an activist and youth mentor. They detail my years as a Teach for America corps member and classroom teacher and chronicle my journey to becoming a social entrepreneur through co-founding the Urban Leadership Institute and then later the Cambio Group. And then the stories explore where I am today in my life and work and where I hope to be in the years to come, both within and beyond my role as an Ubuntu teacher.

The connection between my evolution as a teacher and the brotherhood that defined my teenage years is a tight one. KAOS, pronounced chaos, was a fitting word to describe a group of Black and Latino boys trying to find their place in the world, while causing a bit of chaos on the streets of Chicago, in our classrooms, and in our homes along the way. Our bond helped us navigate the segregated and gang-ridden streets of the South Side of Chicago and the racism that governed our Catholic high school. KAOS was the saving grace that inspired us to work harder and stand up for what was right. It taught us the value of community and of the ties that bind. Together, we fought, prayed, laughed, and buried those of us who didn't make it.

Now, don't get it twisted – some of us were Catholic school boys, but we attended these schools on a hope and a prayer. Our parents could only just afford the tuition and we often barely toed the line to stay enrolled. So even though we attended Catholic school, we came from in and around the roughest neighborhoods in Chicago. We dared anyone to make fun of us or challenge us because of where we spent our days. It was like we almost invited some dude to try to get in our faces and tell us we were weak because we attended Leo, De La Salle, Luther South, Mendel or Brother Rice. We were known, if the need arose, to be able to kick some serious ass. Other KAOS members went to some of the most violent public schools in Chicago. Their fights within those school walls were fights of a different sort than those of us at private school endured. But in both cases, the chaos we experienced outside of our circle was all relative to our internal bond. KAOS became our benchmark for most everything – it was definitive, and helped shape who we were as young people and who I'd become as an Ubuntu teacher.

During my first years of teaching, I had an opportunity to travel to Africa as a chaperone for D.C.'s Union Temple Baptist Church's Rites of Passage program. While in Africa, I constantly heard this term *Ubuntu*, but I never really understood the word's exact meaning. When people used it, they were usually referencing someone who had dedicated his or her life in service to others, but even with this understanding I was still a little unclear as to why people used this particular word with such strong conviction.

I wanted to know more about its origin and meaning, so I asked the South African mother of one of my high school students at the time about it. She told me Ubuntu comes from the Nguni language, that it's one of those well-loved, elemental words that defies simple translation. The closest English equivalent is "humaneness," or "the quality of being human." A proverb common across Africa expresses the Ubuntu ideal: "a person is a person through other people."

"It actually describes *you*," this mother went on to tell me. "I watch how you pour into your students and parents. It's really nice to watch. And from someone so young. It's a word that comes with *big* responsibilities."

I thought to myself at the time, *I don't need any more responsibilities. Trying to keep these wild animals in check is enough for me.* And yet here I am now, so many years later, writing a book about my own journey to become an Ubuntu teacher.

An Ubuntu teacher is an educator who values community and recognizes the symbiotic relationship between a community's different members. He or she recognizes the inherent humanity in all of us and understands that dignity, respect, acceptance and trust are not conditional sentiments to be given and taken at will, but inherent rights to which everyone is entitled. An Ubuntu teacher is prepared to not only give these things to students and colleagues, but also to request them in return.

An Ubuntu teacher is not separate from the community in which he or she serves, but is an intricate part of this community and values each member within it, including him or herself, for all of their uniqueness. He or she recognizes that a community doesn't require that everyone be the same, but that all members be safe to thrive in an environment where diversity is celebrated alongside shared ideals and a common vision for a better future.

An Ubuntu teacher recognizes that he or she cannot go it alone in solitary isolation, but must reach out and embrace community. Interdependence is an important tenet of an Ubuntu teacher's philosophy and way of working in the world.

Some of the elements of the Ubuntu philosophy that guide an Ubuntu teacher's pedagogy include understanding, empathy, tolerance, compassion, sympathy, sensitivity, sharing, solidarity, communication, cooperation and kindness.

An Ubuntu teacher teaches with passion and heart, understanding that teaching is not restricted to four walls. He or she seizes opportunities to teach anywhere, at any place and time. An Ubuntu teacher is skilled and has a working knowledge of pedagogy and the fundamentals of the content in which he or she teaches. He or she is adept at combining those two elements to create a vibrant, meaningful and transformational classroom experience for students.

Finally, an Ubuntu teacher is shaped by experiences, both personal and shared. He or she is secure in who he or she is and is comfortable playing the roles of both teacher and student, sometimes listening rather than instructing, knowing when to push students and when to let go.

In my more recent work, I've labeled the way I work, live, and collaborate with others the Shields' Way, which complements the above definition of an Ubuntu teacher. The Shields' Way framework guides both how I move through my work and how I lead others to navigate through theirs. The tenets of this framework include being both patient and persistent, having a clear vision for our work and life, leading by example, asking tough questions, and fostering strong relationships based on trust.

Whenever I've asked myself why these tenets are so important to my work, I've always come back to many of the stories that you'll read in the pages that follow. Because my work has evolved from my life – from the hopeful, triumphant, challenging and chaotic experiences I've lived.

You may be asking why I've chosen to write a book on education and youth development when many have already been written, when the topic has been debated so often, and when it seems every possible angle on education has already been explored. My response is that I don't think the conversation is over. There are issues still to address, perspectives left to examine. There is so much more work to be done. So much good, honest conversation to be had. So many young lives to be saved.

For much of my early career, I thought it was me, LaMarr Darnell Shields the teacher, writing lesson plans, leading discussions, grading papers, advocating for youth, and holding parent-teacher conferences. But, in actuality, it was Darnell, that inner student who still lived inside of me – trying to be heard, longing to learn, and excited to solve problems. These are the voices I want people to hear in the pages that follow, the voices that helped make me an Ubuntu teacher.

A fair part of the work I do these days is centered around boys of color and the adults who work with them. I hear often the trite phrase "boys will be boys," and whenever I hear this phrase, I can't help but think: *What in the hell does that even mean?!* Sometimes, I think this thought aloud. And the responses I get are mixed.

Much has been made of the complex social arrangements that girls and women navigate, but little scholarly or popular attention has focused on what friendship means to boys and men. Based on what some research claims, one might deduce that boyhood friendships are not strong or bound to last. But my experience was different. My friends and I supported each other deeply. We had one another's backs. If we felt one of us was lying, we would say, "Put it on the K," representing a sworn oath to each other to tell the truth. For example, if one of us said, "I just saw your girlfriend with someone else" and another KAOS member thought we were lying, we'd only have to say, "Put it on the K – I saw your girlfriend with someone else" and we'd all know the truth was being told.

As Seron, one of my KAOS brothers, stated so well: *Our support mechanism, the way we really supported each other no matter what we did, was amazing. There was no animosity, no jealousy. We always felt joy for everybody's success. We also felt each other's pain. If there was a need, we were there to fill it. We did it collectively... we made sure that we went out of our way for one another. That unconditional love and bond was always there.*

This support and connection, this internal trust that we fostered amongst ourselves, is something that I believe strongly has a place in the conversations today about how we're meeting the needs of our youth.

In contrast to my own experience, I have noticed that many of the boys I've worked with through the years tend to become more distrustful, lose their friendships, and feel increasingly isolated and alone as they approach manhood. This observation has left me with a lot of questions, some of which I've chosen to explore in this book.

My interest in boys' development grew out of both trying to make sense of the chaotic experiences of my own youth and also listening to my younger cousins and the boys I met while mentoring in college and then later as a new teacher. I became fascinated by the discrepancy between stereotypes of boys and what I observed some boys actually saying and doing. I wanted to explore more deeply their social and emotional developments, particularly during adolescence – the age during which boys are most heavily stereotyped as stoic and only interested in sex. I started to discover that while boys do play into the stereotypes at times, they also often implicitly challenge them, especially in the context of their closest male friendships.

I've never claimed to be an expert. I have, however, made a shift from looking for the answers in these chaotic situations in my life and work to looking at the questions. I've learned a lot from the model espoused by the great Socrates, who lived his life's work through asking tough questions, who wasn't afraid to die for his convictions.

———

One of my hopes is that if you are a young man of color reading this book, you see me not as an international teacher but as someone just like you, who's faced some chaos and made it to the other side. I hope you see me as a possibility. Will Smith said it well when he explained, "I don't want to be an icon... I want to represent an idea, I want to represent possibilities, I want to represent magic." I also hope that you are able to identify with some of the characters, based on real people in my life, who have so graciously allowed us to highlight their stories. And through these stories I hope you learn to never give up, to see your way out of whatever chaos you're facing. Because there's always a way out.

And I hope that these words will instill some optimism in those who are still concerned about how we might help some of our most disenfranchised young people. Many of the stories in the pages that follow center around serving others, learning from mistakes, and peeling back some of the mystery and mystique of what it took to get from where I started to where I am now. So if you are reading this as a teacher, principal, professor, college student, mother, father, grandmother, grandfather, police officer, social worker, or any other change agent, I hope you leave with some tools and some renewed faith in the promise of our youth.

This is not a memoir in the traditional sense of the word. It's an educational narrative where my personal stories serve as the conduit for discussing the challenges, issues, and hopeful avenues for change that I've witnessed firsthand. There's hope inherent in a map, and the only map I can really provide comes from the road that I myself have traveled. Memories breed lessons and I hope the lessons of my own life can teach someone in some way.

One of the quotes that kept playing over and over in my mind as Marina and I were finishing this introductory chapter comes from Henry David Thoreau, who wrote that "It's not what you look at that matters, it's what you see." I want you to see the beauty in my story – not to critique my life, but to use my life as one example of what can happen when you stay focused on serving people and a mission far greater than yourself.

# PART I

EVERYWHERE WE GO, WE LET THE PEOPLE KNOW

# CHAPTER 1

# FROM GREEN STREET TO SOUTH MICHIGAN AVENUE

*Peace before everything. God before anything.*
*Real before everything. Home before any place.*

– Mos Def

I get up before dawn, well before my children and wife wake and the house fills with the familiar sounds of our family's morning routines. I walk into the small room adjacent to my office and sit down in front of my altar to begin my day – the candles, affirmations, and other small inspirational items that surround me here give me a sense of peace. I meditate and read. This morning, I look at the two books in front of me, the "Tao de Ching" and "A Course in Miracles," and pick up the latter. The day's reading is on how God is in everything I see. I soak in the words one by one, reading over the passage a few times until I feel like I'm ready to face my day with purpose and intention. I pick a card from my affirmation deck and commit it to memory. Then I leave my quiet space, wake up each of my three children, help get them ready for their days, and somehow manage to load them all up in the car and get them to school on time.

I'm very meticulous about my morning rituals and work to remain mindful of the sounds around me, the altar that I set up, the music and words that pour into my soul. It all matters.  Growing up, I was just as meticulous – although my routine looked a bit different than it does now.

---

At 14 years old, I did the same thing every day – got up at 6 a.m., brushed my teeth, washed my face, and took time to make sure my fresh cut was still tight. I had an image to uphold, after all. I put on my Ralph Lauren polo button-down shirt and tan slacks – adhering to the dress code of the De La Salle Institute – and made sure my tie was tucked away in my Eddie Bauer portfolio before heading downstairs to the kitchen for breakfast. Unlike most kids I knew, I ate grits instead of cereal because I was allergic to milk. Once I scraped the bowl clean, I grabbed my Sony Walkman and my Hip-Hop and House tapes and was out.

My home at 7914 S. Green St. was situated in the legendary South Side of Chicago. Green Street was an extremely close-knit community. We were surrounded by some serious gang activity, but we had strong police officers and community activists on our block who served as a sort of buffer against the outside world. Our block was especially protected by four police officers who lived there. Officers Pamon, Martin, and Lemon were all tough men, but our favorite was Commander Joe P. Mayo, who lived across the street from me and was like my uncle. He didn't take mess off anybody. No matter the time of day or night, he greeted everyone with "Morning" as he walked by. What we didn't know at the time was that Officer Mayo was the Commander of the Chicago Police Department's Youth Division and that he later served as Interim Chief after many of us had traded Green Street for college campuses. His very presence in our neighborhood gave many of us who didn't have fathers in our homes a small glimpse into what real manhood looked like.

There wasn't a day that passed when I didn't see someone outside mowing grass, gardening, or making repairs under the hood of a car. On our block, homeowners took great pride in their manicured lawns and didn't want us boys making winning touchdowns in their yards. Our neighbors sat on their front porches, greeted everyone who walked or rode by, and didn't have a problem telling our parents what we were doing while they were at work. Green Street was a neighborhood where kids hired themselves out to mow lawns, rake leaves and shovel snow. It was a neighborhood that watched young couples move in, start families, cheer on their babies taking first steps, teach them years later how to ride bikes, and then kiss them goodbye as they packed them up to leave for college. Green Street was more than a community. It was a family.

Before it became known as one of the most prominent neighborhoods for African Americans in the city, the South Side was a haven for wealthy white Protestants, Irish Roman Catholics, German Jewish families, and European immigrants from Poland, Lithuania, Czechoslovakia, Slovenia, Scotland and Scandinavia. Chicago's Black population soared during the Great Migration, the period between 1915 and the late 1920s when African American southerners relocated to Northeastern and Midwestern cities. They fled deplorable living conditions, lack of employment, inadequate education, and the Ku Klux Klan. By 1919, the population of African Americans in Chicago had reached 109,000.

Despite having moved from the South, most of the African American transplants found themselves subject to even more intense levels of racism, institutional segregation and violence in Chicago than what they had faced in the Southern states from which they came. Chicago was already a hotbed for culture clashes between immigrant gangs. The city's first gangs were notorious for harassing people on the streets, committing both petty and violent crimes, stuffing ballot boxes, and participating in voter intimidation. Though these German, Italian, Irish and Polish gangs fought amongst themselves, they banded together in groups called "Mickies" to terrorize South Side Blacks.

Despite Chicago's racial turmoil, however, African Americans were able to create decent lives for themselves and their families. Many found employment as domestic workers and manual laborers, while others took up work in the city's steel mills and factories. Some even won elected office seats in local and state government.

In the South Side, the Bronzeville neighborhood became known as the "Black Metropolis" for Black Chicagoans. It was the cultural, economic and social hub for African Americans of all socioeconomic levels from which businesses, music venues, and places of worship all sprouted. The Chicago Defender, the South Side newspaper that chronicled accounts of racial injustice nationwide, became Black America's newspaper. The neighborhood also gave birth to Chicago's Black Renaissance and writers like Richard Wright, Gwendolyn Brooks, Elizabeth Catlett, Gospel's crown jewel Mahalia Jackson, King of the Blues Muddy Waters, photographer Gordon Parks, boxer Joe Louis, and countless others whose work and lives reflected the vibrancy of Chicago's South Side.

Post-World War II saw an expansion in highway development in Chicago. In the late 1940s, the city began construction on Chicago's first urban expressway. The Eisenhower Expressway, originally named the Congress Expressway, opened in sections between 1955 and 1960. The Eisenhower divided the African American residents on the South Side from Chicago's white citizens to the north.

In 1955, Cook County Chairman Dan Ryan wrote a bond issue that directed millions of dollars toward building another urban expressway. The planned route for that expressway, his namesake, ran through the white working-class section of the South Side as a way to funnel people from the suburbs into downtown Chicago.

When the mayor at the time, Richard J. Daley, realized that the proposed Dan Ryan expressway would divide his beloved childhood neighborhood of Bridgeport, he ordered city planners to change the direction of the expressway. They acquiesced, and shifted the new route to run along the State Street corridor, forming a border between the white community of Bridgeport to the west and the African American community of Bronzeville to the east. The construction of both the Eisenhower and Dan Ryan Expressways boxed the African American migrants into one area of Chicago, destroyed businesses, displaced residents, and decimated much of the community. Many believe that the Dan Ryan highway was built specifically to segregate Blacks and whites further. Ironically, Dan Ryan was an alumnus of the same high school I attended.

The South Side suffered further devastation after the Civil Rights Movement when affluent African Americans seized the opportunity to relocate into other more up-and-coming communities, leaving the poor and unemployed behind to fend for themselves.

---

But I didn't know any of this history growing up. *My* Chicago was the Sears Tower, Lake Shore Drive, the Cubs, and the greatest basketball player of all time, Michael Jordan. My Chicago was the route I took to and from school each day, which was a journey in itself.

Most days I walked to the bus stop with my boy Willie Stewart. He was the only cat I knew who was cock diesel at 14 – with a much stronger and more muscular build than most of us – and who wore vests with no shirts before it became a style. Willie made my 5'4" frame look small when we stood next to each other, but I could take him down if I wanted to. The two of us had a lot in common. We were both athletic – I ran track while he played football – and we both loved girls.

Willie spent most of his childhood in the Ickes. The Harold L. Ickes Homes was a Chicago Housing Authority (CHA) public housing project in the Near South Side neighborhood on the South Side of Chicago. It was bordered by State Street and Federal Avenue and Cermak Road and 25th Street. The Ickes was part of the State Street Corridor, which included the neighboring projects of Robert Taylor Homes, Dearborn Homes, Stateway Gardens and Hilliard Homes.

If you visit this area today, all the housing projects have been demolished and replaced with high-end condos. As in many areas, the poor Blacks were all pushed out to the suburbs, leading to the creation of suburban ghettos. Crime started to spike in these south Chicago suburbs just about the time that Blacks were being relegated from their homes by the gentrification of the area.

Nearly 30 years after the construction of the housing projects, Willie's mom and dad, tired of raising their children in what had become a violent environment, packed their bags and moved to my neighborhood on Green Street.

Willie Stewart was brilliant, but he was also wild. He stole his brother's car so we could go driving with girls and did other crazy stuff that got him into trouble. Whenever I was in a fix, I knew I only needed to call Willie and he would come ready to take everybody on. Willie used to pop lockers, meaning that he would take a screwdriver and break into the lockers in the halls of Dunbar High School where he spent his days. I remember being up at the school watching him break these locks and even though sometimes I'd participate, I felt like my mind was always somewhere else. It was as though being a student at De La Salle Institute, a private Catholic high school, gave me a level of consciousness about the larger world that Willie just didn't have access to.

When De La Salle Institute was founded in 1889 by Brother Adjutor of Mary, it was only a two-year commercial Roman Catholic school for poor and working-class boys. The school educated its students regardless of race or religion. Brother Adjutor was part of the De La Salle, or Lasallian, Roman Catholic religious teaching congregation of lay brothers founded in France by Saint Jean Baptiste de la Salle in 1680. The Christian Brothers came to North America in the latter part of the 19th Century to open schools and further their mission of educating youth.

Though located in Bronzeville, from its inception De La Salle belonged to the white community. Many poor, working-class school-aged boys would travel from Bridgeport to De La Salle to receive a solid education. In addition to having graduated five different mayors, De La Salle boasted the fact that its alumni included several men in local and national political seats, professional baseball and football figures, television journalist brothers Greg and Bryant Gumbel, and many local police officers and city workers.

I was an eighth-grader at St. Leo Catholic School when I heard about De La Salle Institute. Unlike most of my classmates, I had never wanted to attend Leo Catholic High, the majority African American Catholic school known more for the students' athletic prowess than for their academic achievements. After attending a high school fair at De La Salle, I fell in love with the school's architecture, the state-of-the-art gym, and the immaculately groomed grounds that were so green they didn't look real.

I knew that all I had to do was pass the entrance exam to get in, which I did with ease. It never occurred to me how difficult the test was until I spoke with some of my friends who took the exam and told me how hard it was for them. They didn't get in. I did.

So along the journey to Dunbar High School and De La Salle, Willie and I talked about music, girls, the next party that was jumping off, and girls again. Sometimes, we talked about school. What we discovered when we spoke was that even though we lived in the same neighborhood, the schools we attended were *worlds* apart. We were learning such different things! When I heard some of the stuff Willie was working on, I would stop and say, "Man, we way past that! Why ya'll so far behind?" Willie could never answer the question, and neither could I.

Looking back on it now, I don't think at the time I fully understood the weight of this question about the educational inequities that we were facing in our respective schools. Here Willie and I were, traveling from the same neighborhood on the same path every day, and – because we exited one stop apart and attended different schools – our educational experiences led to vastly different opportunities and potential paths to future aspirations. We came from similar socioeconomic backgrounds, but the differences in opportunity became apparent when we walked through our separate school gates – Willie's school was wrought with a cycle of low expectations and my school, with all its faults, was still a place that fostered a high level of academic expectations as a whole. I developed a consciousness, even if it was a forced consciousness, that Willie just didn't have access to. I was brought to believe that there was something greater to strive toward than the chaotic situations of our surroundings – a notion that college was an option, that leaving the South Side of Chicago was possible, and that dreams were worth fostering. Willie's school experience, and by extension his life, was so full of turmoil because he just couldn't shake the streets. Dunbar High School was near the projects where he grew up, so even though he moved out of the 'hood onto Green Street, he'd travel back and reconnect with his old neighborhood friends on a daily basis at school.

Much of my work today centers around inspiring diverse groups of educators and other change agents to work to mitigate the educational injustices that exist in our curricula, standards, and teaching pedagogies. My passion for challenging educational inequities comes from those I saw so clearly in my own life, even if I couldn't name them at the time. The questions I now raise about why some are afforded so much and others have to struggle for even the most basic of educations are just another incarnation of the question I'd ask Willie about why we were learning such different things in school.

I've become focused in my work on this idea of equity pedagogy, of educational justice praxis and a commitment to positively teaching with equity as a *primary* goal, because my heart as a teenager just didn't *feel* good about the different paths that Willie and I were on.

And I've remained focused on helping to equip teachers with the tools they need to reach all students because I witnessed Willie not getting what he needed academically. I knew that we both deserved the opportunity to not only enter the race, but to make it to the finish line – wherever we deemed that finish line to be. I've stayed committed to conversations centered around how we engage our young men of color because I wish some adult in Willie's life had been able to talk with him about what he wasn't getting out of his own education and why. I wish some adult had been able to give him some tools so that he could have advocated on his own behalf and, in so doing, found a way out.

I've also focused in my work on naming the inequity and claiming it for what it is so that we can help students empower *themselves* to see a way out of the chaos, out of the fog. Once I began to open my eyes, I started to get upset. And once I started to get upset, I started to realize that change might be possible. And this awareness is something that all of our young people deserve.

Once we help our youth become aware, I believe that it's our responsibility to help them deal with the onslaught of questions similar to those that began to ring in my own mind about why I had access to something that Willie didn't, and *why*, even with this access, I still faced so many obstacles at every turn. Because if we can teach our young people to question their own circumstances, we can begin to create empowerment from within. And if we believe that every child deserves educational excellence, then we have to do a better job of putting some heft behind our ideals.

So, getting back to our daily journey to school, Willie and I had to catch the bus to 79th Street and the Dan Ryan stop, where we'd catch the L for the next phase of our trip. Catching the bus was always a bit tricky, because even though we had the money to pay the fare, we wanted to use that money for other things. So most days we rode to school courtesy of Chicago taxpayers. This worked best on the days when the bus was packed because no one noticed us sliding past debarking passengers to hop on at the back exit. We would squat behind standing passengers or sit on the exit stairs to ensure that the bus driver couldn't see us through his rear-view mirrors. From our free seats, we heard kids cussing and being rude to the elderly passengers, watched other kids scrambling to finish homework, and listened to Chicagoans of all ages talk about the Bulls, Da Bears, the White Sox and the Cubs. If anyone noticed that we didn't pay for our ride, they never said anything to us about it.

Once we arrived at the Dan Ryan stop, it was on. The L terminal was the place where hundreds of people from all walks of Chicago life met to travel to their final destinations. As we joined one sea of people exiting the bus, another crowd rushed to get on. Professionals who wanted to avoid the headache of commuting by car waited on the platform next to school-bound kids who stood next to homeless people looking for a place to rest their heads.

Most days, Willie and I arrived at the Dan Ryan just in time to hear people yelling, "There's the L! There's the L!" We jumped off the bus and hopped the turnstile to get to the platform in time to catch the train. If we had time, we would tear dollar bills in half and pay for our fares with them. The machine didn't know the difference. We'd jump on either the A or B train toward 35th Street and Comiskey Park, the same stop where the Chicago White Sox played. On days when the L was crowded, we walked from car to car to find a place to sit only to be harassed by vendors selling incense, ID wallets with the phone books in them, peanuts, barrettes and socks. On days when it was really hot, we sat between the cars, catching the breeze to cool off. We didn't realize then how dangerous that was.

The train ride was rough because one moving boxcar contained a mix of kids from all walks of life sizing each other up and making determinations about who was king, and who was not. We could identify what type of school kids attended by the clothes they wore. The Catholic school girls wore short skirts and knee-high socks, accessorized with Coach duffle bags and Laura Biagiotti sunglasses, commonly referred to as LBs. The private school boys like me wore slacks, button-down shirts, and sneakers that we swapped for dress shoes when we got to school. We always kept our ties tucked away until we entered the school gates. And then there were the public school kids. They had the flyest gear and accessories – Eddie Bauer portfolios, snakeskin hats, Starter jackets, and Jordans. But the public school girls were even more on point. They wore riding boots, Treetorn sneakers, Coach belts, Guess jeans, and Levi cords when it got cold. And I can't leave out the Salt-N-Pepa asymmetrical hairstyles, topped off with chocolate lipstick by Chi-Town's own Fashion Fair. Even though those of us who attended Catholic school had to adhere to a certain dress code and you could usually identify where we went to school based on how we were dressed, on the way to and from school we accessorized ourselves to blend in as much as possible. Dress shoes off, ties off. Hats and sneakers on point.

There were six stops on the L between where Willie and I got on at Dan Ryan and 79th street, or the "9" as we called it, and where we got off at 35th Street. As we entered the L, kids were getting off to get to Chicago Vocational School (CVS), South Shore, and rival schools Simeon and Hirsch. Next, was 6th for the Maria and Robeson kids. At 63rd, Harper, Englewood, Mt. Carmel, High Park and St. Rita students exited, while the 55th stop, otherwise known as "the Boulevard," was home to Lourdes and Hales and Kenwood, where some of the finest and smartest girls went to school. 47th was the exit for Tilden, DuSable and Chicago's basketball powerhouse, King High School. Some of the NBA's future most noted players attended school there. Next was 43rd Street where students from Phillips de-boarded.

Only De La Salle and Dunbar High School kids were left on the train by the time the 35th Street exit came. Dunbar was a typical athletic powerhouse school. Most of the Dunbar kids lived in either the Robert Taylor Homes or Stateway Gardens, and they caused the most ruckus on the train. Nobody else on my Green Street block went to De La Salle, but by the time we got off at the 35th Street exit, a lot of my boys had jumped on the L at one of the other South Side stops.

We had an unspoken pact where we'd wait for each other before leaving the L station, because walking alone that last leg to school made all of us easy targets. We made sure as we exited the L that our hats were straight and we were on high alert, just in case we ran into any gang members itching for a fight along the way. Each of us had our own bop that let everybody know we were not to be messed with. Though we joked with each other as we walked, we stayed constantly aware of our surroundings.

Leaving the L station, we traveled east to walk the final three blocks to De La Salle. To the west were Comiskey Park and the South Side's Bridgeport neighborhood. Bridgeport was a haven for Irish immigrants who settled there in the 1830s. Originally named Hardscrabble, Bridgeport was patrolled by neighborhood gangs and had developed a reputation for being one of the most racist neighborhoods in the country. African Americans were often terrorized if they crossed the neighborhood boundary on Wentworth Avenue, and Harlem Renaissance poet Langston Hughes recounts being beaten by gang members after accidentally crossing into the all-white neighborhood on his first Sunday in Chicago.

The racial complexities of Bridgeport hadn't changed much by the time I was a teenager in the mid-1980s. In fact, sometimes I think things had grown worse. We all were careful not to be in the area after the city-mandated evening curfew of 10:30 p.m. because we knew that instead of taking us to our homes, or even the police precinct, Chicago cops would drop boys who looked like us in the middle of Bridgeport and let the neighborhood gangs deal with us.

Bridgeport was also home to five of Chicago's mayors, including De La Salle Institute alum Richard J. Daley and his son, Richard M. Daley. The senior Daley was known for various acts of political corruption, including allegedly stuffing ballot boxes and rigging votes in the 1960 Presidential election that put John F. Kennedy in office. He created a political machine that ran Chicago with an iron fist for 21 years. He was responsible for the construction of the O'Hare International Airport, the Sears Tower, the University of Illinois' Chicago campus, and major subway and expressway projects.

"Da Mare", as many of his supporters called him, was unapologetic about not doing anything to integrate Chicago. In fact, in 1966 when Martin Luther King, Jr. attempted to introduce the Civil Rights Movement to the city, Daley met with King and drafted, signed, and then ignored an agreement between the city of Chicago, King, and other community leaders to foster open housing in segregated areas. Daley stated after the fact that the agreement was not legally binding. During the 1968 race riots, Daley ordered the police to "maim...cripple...and kill" rioters and looters, angry African Americans he deemed "potential murderers."

His Gestapo-like tactics were broadcast on national television during the 1968 Democratic National Convention when Daley ordered police to attack any Vietnam War protester who disrupted the Convention. What ensued was a barrage of beatings of not just the non-violent protesters, but also men, women and clergy who had nothing to do with the protests. People around the country were outraged by footage of the police beatings on their television screens, but in an interview between Daley and CBS's beloved news anchor, Walter Cronkite, "Da Mare" supported his police officers and claimed they were protecting themselves, fellow convention attendees, and Chicago citizens from violent protesters. Daley died of a heart attack while in office in 1976.

---

So the crew and I crossed Wentworth before walking beneath the viaduct where the Illinois Institute of Technology (IIT) – one of the country's most prestigious universities – loomed high above us on one side. IIT's sprawling campus stood on what Chicagoans labeled the coldest corner in the city. In the winter, the tall campus buildings provided a perfect crossway for the wind, or "the hawk" as we called it, to come right at us and nearly split us in two. IIT, with its unique architecture and winding bike paths, stood in stark contrast to the projects surrounding it. Directly across IIT on State Street was Stateway Gardens. Like the Robert Taylor Homes and the infamous Cabrini-Green projects, Stateway Gardens was run by gangs. Crime, poverty and desperation were the norm. Turf wars abounded and we were the last crew of Catholic school boys who wanted to get caught up in them.

We weren't afraid to fight the guys in the projects, but we tried to avoid trouble on the way to school. We weren't crazy. Well, let me take that back – we tried not to be *too* crazy while en route to school. So each morning our strides quickened a bit to get to South Michigan Avenue, where De La Salle sat, to avoid hearing *it*. *It* was the whistle that let us know that the gang members knew we were walking across their territory. If we heard the whistle, then we knew we needed to get our asses to South Michigan Avenue real quick, or else suffer getting our stuff stolen and said asses beat.

It was like we had to fight everywhere. On the street, it was "Nigga, you think you're better than us, going to that private school." And then we entered the school and it was the white boys saying, "You don't belong with us. You're just here on scholarship. Who's paying your tuition, anyway? The only reason you're here is because you're good at sports." I was fighting in two different worlds, both of which I needed to belong to. I didn't have the option not to try to fit in in the projects or I'd risk getting beat up. And then I had to try to fit in at school because I was fighting to get an education that – despite what my behavior in class might have sometimes indicated – I knew I needed if I ever wanted to create a different type of life for myself.

And all this meant that I had to code switch quite a bit just to get from the front door of my house to school every day. We KAOS members who attended Catholic schools had to let people know that even though we were private school boys, we had as much street sense as anyone else. It wasn't about selling out so much as it was about protecting who we were and minimizing the number of times that we'd get into altercations. The reality was that even though I could hang with the guys in the projects and had family and friends who lived in the projects, I didn't live there. And yet I still had to be able to fit into this environment. I had to code switch as a means of both protection and survival. And then when I got to school, I had to code switch right back to fit in with my classmates.

In all my work with boys, I've found that so many of them don't know when and where to code switch. So I teach them about the importance of being able to blend in and out of different environments when it comes to both the way they dress and the way they speak. I remind them that they don't have to be hard all the time. They don't have to walk into church with mean mugs on their faces. And they don't have to talk with their teachers the same way they talk with their best friends. I also speak with parents of color about the fact that their children won't always be around kids who look like or who were raised like them, and so being able to code switch is a valuable skill to learn early on. Perceptions are powerful. A recent study by a University of Buffalo professor found that Black girls who demonstrated stereotypically urban attitudes and behaviors when at predominately white high schools were viewed as "loud" or "ghetto," while their male counterparts were viewed as "athletic" or "cool" by their peers. Despite this finding, we know that boys are still not off the hook because even though their peers might see their language as "cool," it still makes them a target in the classroom. From my experience, code switching works both ways. Some kids have trouble when they're switching into more structured settings and others, like my own three children, have a harder time adjusting to and code switching in urban environments.

I share with the boys I work with that I've carried this ability to code switch with me throughout my life. These days, when I'm walking around the campus of Johns Hopkins University as a professor, I walk with my head up. I speak with my colleagues in a particular way. I carry a certain type of confidence because I know I'm qualified to be there. I understand what an honor it is to be at this great institution. But I still have to work hard, even after all this time, to look like I belong. When I leave campus and enter the streets of Baltimore City, I'm simultaneously more relaxed and guarded. I'm rocking a backpack and not a briefcase. My jaw drops, my face gets a bit harder. I'm code switching into the environment around me and I do it seamlessly. I've had a lot of practice through the years. Maybe I do it because it's necessary, because the physical threat off campus if I'm caught slipping is a real one, but other times maybe I do it because in my mind I'm right back in high school, knowing that if I don't master this code switching thing, I might not – literally – survive the journey.

Once we arrived on De La Salle's campus, we were funneled through the main gate just in time to see school buses and expensive cars rolling in from the suburbs of Chicago. The buses and cars carried De La Salle's wealthier white students who were shuttled daily from the front doors of their homes to the front door of the school, oblivious to the fact that we'd just hopped the bus, rode the L, and walked – sometimes sprinted – past Stateway Gardens to get to the same school each morning.

Officials at De La Salle took pride in the school grounds and wanted to see them protected from the outside elements – the violence and mayhem taking place just steps away from their front door. The school's perimeter was surrounded by metal gates, and within those gates stood stately tan buildings atop green manicured lawns. The campus was also protected by an invisible shield that was the Bridgeport police. Even though De La Salle wasn't located in Bridgeport, a lot of kids from that neighborhood attended our school and it was important that they arrived and stayed protected while on campus.

The gates were guarded by a retired Chicago police officer we called Officer Old Man because the dude looked about 100 years old. He reminded us of someone from an old western movie, with his hat cocked at an angle, slightly stooped gait, hands in his pockets like he was always ready to draw a piece. He didn't actually police the grounds, but he always looked like he was ready to go if something popped off.

My boys and I walked into the foyer of the school each morning, where large glass cases filled with athletic trophies loomed all around us. On the walls above the trophies hung framed photographs of the different classes that once roamed De La Salle's halls. Spanning the nearly 100 years of the school's existence, the photographs were filled with white boys being prepared for life after high school. Faces like mine only appeared in the photos of those graduating classes of the 1970s and beyond. *What would all those white boys think of us being here now?* I thought to myself as I caught my reflection through the framed glass.

From the foyer, we walked down to the lunchroom. Every morning we had the same routine. After giving each other dap, we took our seats to change into our black loafers and rummage through our Eddie Bauer bags for our ties. Once our outfits were up to the school's dress code standards, we read, talked about sports and girls, finished homework, cracked jokes, and grabbed a quick bite to eat before the bell rang and our day began. As with many lunchrooms in schools across America, De La Salle's was segregated not only by race, but also by athletic sport, school club and socio-economic class. In her book "Why are All the Black Kids Sitting Together in the Cafeteria?" Beverly Tatum explores whether this segregation, which is a common phenomenon not just in school cafeterias, but also in college gathering places and workplace settings, is a harmful and self-imposed separation or a positive coping mechanism people use to find allies. She points out that we usually only question the phenomenon when it's people of color sitting together and that maybe we need to ask ourselves why we do this. Ultimately, she posits that the first step to understanding racial complexities and how they play out in observable behavior is to be able to discuss them openly and to acknowledge their existence instead of ignoring what's sitting right in front of us in school lunchrooms throughout the country.

From our morning routine in the lunchroom, the school days unfolded with a mix of predictability and uncertainty. We could almost bet that in Mr. Hopkins' history class someone from the crew would try to trip him up and call out "discrimination" just to get under his skin. And yet we never knew when things were going to get really deep, like the day the class engaged in a debate about Black history. I remember when one of my white classmates balked at the notion of having an entire month devoted to African American history, and Mr. Hopkins reminded the student, in front of us all, that white men – himself included – had the other 11 months of the year pretty much devoted to the history of those who looked like them.

We could also almost bet that Señor Hogan, our Spanish teacher, would get all red in the face and scream at one of us about something – although the impetus for these outbursts was often unpredictable. I don't remember much of what he yelled about most days, but there was one such eruption that followed me for years. This is how it happened.

The heat in Señor Hogan's Spanish II classroom was so oppressive it sometimes made you feel like you had to fight for every breath you took. It didn't matter whether it was summer or winter in Chicago, his room always felt like a sauna and that particular day was no exception.

My classmates and I climbed three flights of stairs to get to Room 306, found our assigned seats and waited for the Spanish drill to begin. Señor Hogan towered over us like a linebacker. His platinum blond hair and pale skin were in such contrast to my own, and the military-like precision with which he led his class demanded that we fall in line, do what we were told, not ask questions. We complied, except of course on those days when our testosterone and need to assert ourselves got the best of us.

Like the rest of us, El Profesor wore the standard De La Salle Institute uniform – button down shirt, dark tie and slacks. But I remember distinctly that he wore short-sleeved button downs to accommodate the heat in his classroom. I hated those shirts – that never made any sense to me, why you'd wear a dress shirt with short sleeves. He was a muscular dude with slicked-back hair and when he'd get angry and pound on his desk his face would turn a shade of red that will forever be etched in my memory.

"Hola clase!" he bellowed from the seat behind his desk. Outside of writing notes on the chalkboard or responding to an occasional outburst, nothing much brought Señor Hogan to his feet.

"Hola," we responded in unison. *La clase había comenzado.* Class had begun.

"Raul!" Señor Hogan called out. At the beginning of the school year, he had given all of us Spanish names that we used during class, and sometimes elsewhere when we were clowning around. Leonardo was my name.

"Que dia es hoy?"

Raul responded by telling the maestro, our teacher, what day of the week it was. "Hoy es viernes, Señor."

"Muy bien," Señor Hogan praised. "Diego Dos, qué hizo en sábado?"

"Ummm, what did I do on Saturday?" Diego Dos asked, repeating El Profesor's question in English before formulating his response. "Voy a pasar el tiempo con mis amigos."

"Hmmmm! Hanging out with your friends?! Asegúrese que hace su tarea," he replied.

I sat in my third-row seat, thumbing through my textbook. Although Diego Dos hadn't understood Señor's sarcastic response, I did, and it made me feel frustrated, disappointed, and upset with the lack of care from this man who was supposed to be teaching us. Wasn't it a teacher's job to praise us for our participation and engagement? Guide us to greatness? Inspire us?

"Not to do homework with those friends, I assume," he said before moving on to drill Julio. Señor Hogan was notorious for making smart comments like that, most of which flew by many of the boys in our class. I wasn't the best student, but like most of my 15-year-old classmates, I was smart and surprised myself by how much Spanish I understood, even though Señor Hogan didn't know it.

El Maestro completed the drills and moved on to assign us some workbook pages that I burned through, finishing far ahead of most of my classmates. *Nada es demasiado difícil para mí* – nothing too difficult for me. When I finished, I sat and scanned the room. I don't know what I thought I'd see, as Señor Hogan wasn't big on classroom decor. There were no maps of Spanish-speaking countries, no pictures of food, beaches or musicians. Nothing to even indicate that we were in a place where we might talk or learn about other cultures, countries, languages. The walls were just white and bare.

"As you all know," he said, interrupting my musings and the other kids' classwork. "The school year is coming to a close and I need to let each of you know whether or not your grades have earned you a coveted spot in the next level of Spanish class."

I sat up in my seat. *This* had my attention. My mom had recently told me that colleges wanted to see more than two years of foreign language on high school transcripts. Moving on to Spanish III was my chance to explore in more depth a language I was beginning to respect and love. It was also an opportunity to prove how capable I was. Señor Hogan knew me as a jokester, not as a serious student. I was ready to change that perception.

He picked up his grade book and walked down the rows of the classroom.

"Juan," Señor Hogan said as he looked down at his grade book, scanning over the numbers that he had somehow equated with our significance, our academic promise, our worthiness to move on to the next level. "Si, I encourage you to move on to Spanish III." Juan nodded his blond head and smiled at the news.

"Jesus," Señor said, "Si, I encourage you to move on to Spanish III."

"Gracias, Señor," Jesus said before slapping five with Juan.

I waited anxiously as El Profesor made his way up and down two more rows, delivering our *suerte*, our fate, before he got to me.

"Ahhh Leonardo," he chuckled before looking at me over the rim of his glasses. My heart thumped in my chest, but my eye contact with him didn't waver.

His sarcastic response to the question of me moving on to the next level of Spanish was, *"Cuando las gallinas meen!"* – When hens pee!

"Dang! That's really bad," one of my classmates said, laughing at the news Señor had just shared in front of the entire class for all to hear.

All I could hear was the blood rushing in my ears. I was embarrassed. I was mad. I was disappointed. *This is not fair!* I thought to myself. *This man was supposed to help me to be successful, not clown me in front of my classmates. Hell, my mom is paying his salary to teach and guide me, not discourage me from excelling.*

"You know what?" I said as I stood up, pushing my chair into the desk behind me. Señor Hogan stopped speaking to *mi compañero*, my classmate, and shifted his gaze my way.

"Si, Leonardo?"

"To hell with this damn class! I don't need it anyway!"

Blood rushed to Señor Hogan's face, turning it that beet red. He slammed his hand down on my classmate's desk in front of where he stood, causing my classmate to nearly jump out of his seat, and yelled, "I don't condone that type of language in my classroom! Besides, I don't even know why you're here in the first place! Get your stuff and get out!"

I grabbed my books, and my bruised ego, and stormed out of the room.

And so it went. As I moved through high school, things seemed to grow increasingly chaotic both inside and outside of the classroom. The stabilizing force in all of it, though, was KAOS.

# CHAPTER 2

# KAOS

*Everywhere We Go*
*We Let the People Know*
*That KAOS is in the House!*

- KAOS Crew Chant, circa 1987

*I'm so Chi I'm bashful.*
- Kanye West

This is how it all began. Steve, Curtis and Dion sat in the back row of religion class our sophomore year at De La Salle counting the minutes until the bell rang. Steve says he was daydreaming when the name for our crew hit him. KAOS.

For weeks, we had been discussing coming up with a name to describe us. By "us" I mean the original five members of KAOS: Steve, Curtis, Dion, Rich and me. Though the five of us had started vibing at the lunch table at De La Salle our freshman year, we really became tight sophomore year when we all got our driver's licenses. The day Steve and Curtis got theirs was also their shared 16th birthday, so we decided to celebrate by going out to the show, Chicagoans' term for the movies. From then on, we were inseparable. The Original Five.

Before long, our crew of five quickly expanded to over 30 brothers, including Marlon, Maurice, Marlon M., Rich, Dion, Mike, Clarence, Lance, Wood, Rod, Larry, Darnell (aka "Hen"), Kerroy, Bill, Derrick, Jerry, Wayne, Kelvin, Cory, Frenchie, Andre, Mike G., George, Troy, Desmond, Seron, Marcus and Walter (who called himself "Buff"), among others. A lot of us came into KAOS with deep connections – Jerry and Darnell were related to me, while others like Steve, Lance and Kerroy had been friends since elementary school. The majority of us had either competed against each other in neighborhood football, basketball or softball games, had childhood friendships with some of the other crew members, or remembered each other from around the way when we ate 25-cent hamburgers in the parking lot of Chins, a neighborhood restaurant near St. Sabina school, an institution made famous by Father Michael Pfleger, a progressive white priest known for his leadership in advancing causes of racial, social and economic justice.

There were no leaders in KAOS, but we did divide our troop into two groups: the Seniors, who were the older sect of our crew, and the Juniors. The Original Five were all Seniors. There was no real initiation to become a member of KAOS. If one of us believed a cat fit into what we were doing and held the same ideals as the crew, then we respected our brother's choice and brought that person into the fold. It was that simple.

Though the majority of KAOS went to De La Salle, some of us attended other schools in Chicago's South Side. Jerry, Kevin, Mike and the twins, Marlon and Maurice, were juniors at Leo, where George, Mike G., Troy and Julio were all seniors. Hen and Derrick B. went to South Shore. Andre, Marlon M. and Frenchie were at CVS. Wood and Rod attended Brother Rice. And some of the other crew members attended South Shore and Luther South, to name a few. It really didn't matter where we went to school, though, because we came together every waking moment we could. We were a crew of wild cats who had each other's backs, supported each other academically, and became as close as family.

The reality was that many of us didn't have strong male role models in our homes and so our KAOS brotherhood became that male role model, that influence that prepared us to take on the world. Together we experienced tragedy, celebrated triumphs, sometimes parented one another, and helped each other develop the layers of skin we were going to need to navigate a world whose goal – we truly believed – was to destroy boys that looked like us.

As Seron, one of my KAOS brothers, stated: *I was growing up in a household by myself. I had siblings, but they didn't live with me. In KAOS, we were all heading in the same direction with similar goals and aspirations. We had a pride in school, our heritage, our shared history. Beyond just being a crew of guys, KAOS became an extended family.* He went on to say that all of our homes were each other's homes, and that we competed, but we uplifted each other and challenged ourselves and each other to become better.

Lance, another KAOS member, echoed a similar sentiment and shared that he, too, grew up in a household without brothers. He said that when he found KAOS, it made him more responsible: *We kept each other accountable. We couldn't go out and commit crimes – we had accountability to and for each other.*

I grew up in a very strict, loving, one-parent household as the youngest of four, with two older sisters and an older brother. I was the only one of my siblings who grew up without the memory of my father at home. My mother reminded me often that I was just too young to remember when he was there in the house. But in all my family memories of museum visits, piano recitals, sporting events, theatre trips, and family vacations, I don't remember my dad being there for any of it.

He was a police officer with the Chicago PD and would drop in from time to time, but never long enough for me to feel like we had any real connection. My relationship with my father was mostly transactional at this point – he'd stop by, give me money, drop off some new shoes, take me to a baseball game – but we never formed the deep bond that I needed.

I'd even go to stay at his house every so often, but the only memories I really have of being there have to do with my feeling like it wasn't where I was supposed to be. In my young mind, I felt that at his house there wasn't the structure I craved, there wasn't enough conversation happening, there weren't any rituals to ground me. My junior year in high school, my mom – who felt like I was getting a bit out of control – sent me to live with my dad. But it didn't last long. He couldn't give me what I needed. Before I knew it, I was back home where I belonged.

Thanks to my boys in KAOS, though, we were somehow able to fill in the gaps of what many of us weren't getting from our fathers. Wayne joined our crew kind of late, but he feels like KAOS – literally – saved his life: *If it wasn't for the brotherhood, I probably wouldn't be alive today. It taught me something greater in life than what I was used to. It gave me impact – I went to college because of these guys. I didn't want to be left home alone. I wasn't even thinking about going to college, but they showed me that there was something more positive in this world than what I was used to. I learned how to be a better man, a better brother, because of our brotherhood. It taught me how to love. I didn't know nothing about love until I started hanging out with these guys.*

---

The love we felt from each other didn't really extend to the broader context in which we spent our days, though. Things at De La Salle were rough for us. There was nothing more embarrassing than sitting in class and hearing your name called over the intercom system.

"Mr. LaMarr Shields, please come to the main office immediately."

I cringed because I knew what time it was. My mother hadn't paid my tuition. I gathered my books and walked out of class as quickly as possible, feeling the eyes of my white classmates boring into the back of my head. As soon as I stepped into the hallway, I exhaled and got my stuff out of my locker. Damn. Here we go again.

This was not unusual at De La Salle. I, like most KAOS crew members attending the school, knew the route to the Dean's office with my eyes closed. None of our parents could afford to send us to the private Catholic school, but they pulled together whatever money they could scrape up to pay our tuition anyway. In their minds Calumet, King, Robeson, Hirsch, Dunbar, and many of the other public and even private schools in Chicago were not an option. Our parents' main desire was to provide us with an opportunity to receive a quality education that would be the avenue for us to go to college and make something of our lives. They knew that most of Chicago's elite were De La Salle alumni, and that was the legacy they wanted for us. If our parents had to work extra shifts, get second jobs, fill out financial aid paperwork, or otherwise scramble to pay tuition, then that's what they did. But sometimes real life, unexpected bills, or emergencies disrupted their plans, eating up the hard-earned money they'd allotted for tuition. So while they sat at work and agonized over how to pay for our schooling, we were made to face their financial woes with the school administration in person.

Although De La Salle was chartered under the pretense of Christian character and brotherly love, the school had little love for parents who could not pay tuition. We represented the population of students whose parents were not De La Salle alumni and who didn't have political connections, old money, or pedigree. For us, the school adopted a rigid "no pay, no finals" policy. If our tuition wasn't paid, then we were not allowed to take finals, which wreaked havoc on our GPAs. As teenagers, we didn't understand that business and school policy trumped our feelings of whether or not the rules were fair.

Truth be told, De La Salle was a very white school even at the time I attended. Aside from one African American typing teacher who was only there our freshman year and who we all thought was mean as hell anyway, there weren't any adults of color in the building. We lived in what many had labeled the most segregated city in the country at the time, and that fact was reflected in the halls of our private school every day. But we were never encouraged to discuss anything about race, as the school administration and teachers wanted us to believe we all coexisted equally under the banner of Christianity. Those of us in the KAOS crew knew that anything resembling equality didn't have our names on it.

We were singled out a lot by teachers for being who we were. One of the things that drove us crazy was when the teachers would call us a gang. We were not a gang and we thought it so derogatory whenever they would refer to our brotherhood as such. The Chicago gangs we were familiar with were hanging outside school walls, selling drugs, creating mayhem, and waiting to wreak havoc on us as soon as we left the school gates. And here we were, sitting in class, harmlessly yelling out "KAOS" every time one of our crew members answered a question. We always got in trouble for doing this, as teachers and administrators told us we couldn't express our gang affiliations in school. I don't know why we felt it necessary to disrupt class in this way, but I do know that the more we were called a gang by the adults in the building, the more intent we were on making our identity as a crew known on campus. We were KAOS, and everywhere we went, we wanted people to know we had arrived.

My childhood friend Ramon, who was not himself a member of KAOS, described our crew as follows: *KAOS was the way for kids to team up and have each other's backs. It was definitely not a gang thing. You know, Chicago's got a gang culture, so there needed to be groups like KAOS when we were kids. That was a good thing. A lot of my family members were in gangs, so for me it was pretty much an obligation to have gang associations growing up. In my own particular situation, I dealt with a lot of gang activity because of my association with the gangs in my family – people trying to beat me up and kill me and stuff like that. Guys like LaMarr, guys who I went to high school with, showed me there were other ways of life. You didn't have to belong to a gang, didn't have to run in that circle. In a lot of ways, the KAOS guys were true to me. In high school, you know, they showed me there were more ways of life than what I was accustomed to, what I grew up in.*

There was another crew made up of the few other Black and Brown boys at De La Salle. They called themselves the Lost Boys, and even though we didn't have any animosity toward them inside of the school walls, when we left the school building we were always fighting. We felt compelled to assert our own identity as a crew and back up some of our non-De La Salle KAOS members who had some beef with the Lost Boys. This always bothered me – the way that we could be enemies outside of school and yet walk through the school gates and somehow co-exist so well. What were we trying to prove to each other by fighting so often before and after school, and what unspoken rules kept us bonded together peacefully while on campus?

During our freshman year, an African American named Harold Washington, who had held the seats of U.S. Senator and U. S. Representative of Illinois, announced his run for mayor. The prospect of Chicago being run by an African American in a city where Daley had employed his racist agenda for decades was radical enough. Washington's subsequent election further divided Chicago and angered many of the city's white residents. The South Side celebrated Washington's elevation to mayor because after decades of abuse, racial violence, and governmental disparities, we felt vindicated that one of our own finally sat at the city's helm.

The administration and teachers at De La Salle forbade us from even discussing Mayor Washington at school, and when he died on November 24, 1987 the school made no mention over the intercom of his untimely heart attack. The school officials may have been reluctant to discuss the mayor's death, but the white students were not. Many of them expressed themselves quite vocally, making snide remarks about his passing: "Who cares about this man dying? He wasn't that great of a mayor anyway." Those comments, coupled with the fact that the school turned a blind eye to so much of the racial conflict on campus, weighed heavily on us because we didn't have many adult allies at school who we felt saw the world through our eyes. We didn't have many adults guiding us through the maze of racially-charged minefields in which we so often found ourselves.

The only person at De La Salle who really advocated for me, and many of us in KAOS, was Brother Tim. We called him "Brother" because he was part of the Christian Brothers order, not because he was a "brotha." I always saw Brother Tim as a strong ally. A lot of the other guys in KAOS didn't want to be around him because they thought that perhaps he was gay and it made them uncomfortable. What you have to understand is that for a group of boys who were already dealing with a lot of phobias in general, the thought of him being different in yet another way made them panic a bit. I really didn't care about any of the rumors about him – I just knew that he had my back and that was enough. He was a staunch advocate later on when I faced expulsion, when no other adult in the building seemed to care about my future too much.

Brother Tim's office felt like a chapel. It was warm and he always had soft chamber music playing in the background. The walls were adorned with typical religious renditions of Jesus with long wavy hair, a thick beard, and milky-white skin, a Jesus who looked nothing like me. Next to the Jesus pictures hung college posters advertising all of the Ivy League schools. I never saw any pennants from schools that were on my radar, historically Black colleges and universities (HBCUs) like Grambling, Tuskegee, Morehouse or Howard. Even in a place like De La Salle, I still somewhat expected to see posters from these familiar schools alongside those advertising Harvard, Yale and Princeton. Maybe I should have known better.

Shaun Harper talks about getting Black boys into college and his research notes that the majority of Black boys report that their guidance counselors didn't talk to them much about college and, when they did, the conversations were often more discouraging than encouraging. What's interesting to me looking back on it is that my boys and I never visited the counseling office to talk about college. So I saw these college posters and pennants hanging on the walls, but I don't once remember any adult in the building, including Brother Tim, engaging me in a conversation about my college aspirations. We were too busy talking about what it would take to keep my insubordinate behind in school to even begin to talk about what I might want to do once I got out of that place.

"LaMarr, do you *want* to be here?" Brother Tim asked every time I walked through his door. My visits to his office were frequent because I was always being sent out of class for playing the clown, for being insubordinate, for not toeing the line. As with most boys, it was hard for me to answer his questions about why I chose to do the things I did in class.

What I couldn't share with Brother Tim at the time was that I was reluctant to talk to him because he was white. Before my interactions with him, I had never been in a room with a white dude where I was supposed to spill my guts about what was going on with me internally. I felt that he would never understand what if felt like to be me, an African American boy from the South Side who literally had to fight just to get to school, and then to wrestle with the underlying racial tension inside De La Salle that no one seemed to want to acknowledge. I thought Brother Tim wouldn't be able to relate to the fact that I sat in those classrooms every day feeling the disdain that teachers like Señor Hogan had for me, and walking in the hallways with students whose parents taught them to feel the same. Brother Tim never had to guess where his place was in the fabric of the Catholic school because he saw himself reflected in the people, the school's vernacular, and even the Jesus he had nailed to his wall.

But instead of telling him these things, I would just shut down and let him lead the conversation until he was satisfied enough to let me leave. In the end, I continued to act out in class and he continued to try to do what he could to reach me. Not much was ever accomplished. It was strange being a young man of color having someone who didn't look like me being my only advocate. Like many Black and Brown boys, I was so *desperate* to have someone who looked like me to talk to and to advocate on by behalf. But when you look around and *nobody* looks like you, you take what you can get. I remember always wondering *why* Brother Tim was doing anything for me, not realizing that it was his job to do so.

There are so many layers of pain wrapped up in this – here I was at a school where I felt like none of the adults in the building were in my corner except this one man. I was uncomfortable with the fact that he was trying to save me and didn't know why it made me so uneasy. Looking back on it, I think I was recoiling against the whole "white savior" concept before I could even put a name to it. If you've been to the movies in the last half-century or so, you've probably been exposed to this concept more than once, whether you've realized it or not. It's an idea common in the catalogue of films – "Dangerous Minds," "Freedom Writers," "The Blind Side," "Fresh" and "Radio," just to name a few – that features white people single-handedly rescuing people of color from their plights. A criticism of such films is that their story lines often insinuate that people of color are somehow unable to rescue themselves. Additionally, the films often serve the dual purpose of both making white audience members feel good about themselves – as benevolent messiahs – and also making people of color feel helpless and indebted to their white "saviors."

The documentary "Prep School Negro" discusses how, among other issues connected to racism, white privilege, and cultural clashes, some Black and Latino student coming out of prep schools feel like they owe white people so much for seeing them through, for helping them create an avenue out of the life they knew.

The issue is further compounded when there are so few people of color in an environment, especially a school. In a panel discussion held after a screening of the aforementioned documentary, a prep school graduate talked about how she felt like she was expected to be the almanac on young people of color for all of the white folks with whom she interacted, like she was supposed to hold all the answers, all the secrets, to an entire race and culture. The pressure of this can create a feeling of both responsibility and resentment that is hard for young people of color to navigate on their own.

As a young man of color, I remember not wanting to feel like I owed anyone anything, especially white people. I also remember thinking about my exchanges with Brother Tim and what we were both really getting out of the interactions. In some ways, we were both being selfish. Brother Tim's interests were served through helping me because it gave him the satisfaction of doing his job well, even if none of the other adults around him were stepping up to the plate. And then I was being selfish in that I so desperately wanted and needed to be helped. But even within this dynamic, I still questioned his motives so often: *What do you want from me? Why are you going out of your way to try to save me when I don't deserve saving? When I'm not even willing to save myself? When I can't even get adults who look like me and are related to me and live around me to fight for me?*

The questions often brought me to a painful place because I began to question who the real enemy was. I wanted to hate Brother Tim, but if I looked at it honestly, he was one of the only adults in the school building who was showing up day in and day out to try to help me and others like me. And how could I really hate him for that?

It often takes a bit more self-reflection than we're comfortable with to recognize ourselves in the stories of others, but if you're reading this as a change agent, my hope is that you're able to really reflect on *why* we do what we do. What motivates us when it comes to advocating for our youth, and if we find that our motives are less than altruistic how do we rectify that with the other parts of our hearts that really are committed to doing the most good? I don't have the answers, but I do believe it starts with honestly turning the lens on ourselves for a minute.

So being in an environment like De La Salle and not having a single advocate in the whole place who looked like me was painful. But if I'm honest with myself, I have to admit that I had more than what many students do because I did have Brother Tim in my corner.

Once I became a teacher, I tried to advocate for all of my students, but despite my best efforts, I knew there were students I missed and days when my lesson objectives overshadowed the young people sitting at the desks in front of me. In "This We Believe in Action," the Association for Middle Level Education notes that in order for students to be engaged learners, they need teachers who clearly communicate with them that they are cared for, appreciated, respected, and welcomed into the school without exception.

Most of the teachers at De La Salle, with a few notable exceptions, weren't transparent or culturally sensitive enough to build any sort of connection. As my friend Ramon described it: *Some De La Salle teachers were borderline, no let me just go ahead and say it – they were racist. My English teacher was very racist. He would say things in the classroom that I'm sure would raise eyebrows today. But a lot of our teachers were products of Bridgeport, Chicago, which historically has always been a racist area.*

Outside of Brother Tim, one of my greatest positive influences at De La Salle was probably Mr. Duzrak, who I credit with first instilling in me a love for British Literature. I became a closet reader, but I didn't want people to know that I was identifying with these quirky kids from a different time and place. Mr. Duzrak introduced me to Keats and Mary Percy Shelley. Maybe I loved his class so much because it exposed me to a genre of literature that took me out of my own environment and put me into a world where I could imagine the possibilities in life. Maybe through this exposure to literature I began to dream a little more freely.

Mr. Duzrak wasn't anything like I *wanted* him to look or sound like, but he had such a love for literature that it was contagious. He was also a lover of all people. I remember thinking he was such a hippie, but he was so authentic that I just connected deeply with him, even if I didn't want to at first. As young people, we can be so brutal when we're judging our teachers or other adults charged with helping us, but we have to be able to see beyond our own initial judgments and prejudices. We can't just leave it to the adults to be the only ones forging connections.

There's a paradox I discuss often in the work I do now with educators – this idea that connections can and should be built across racial lines between teachers and students while also acknowledging that Black and Brown youth need more educators who look like them in the classroom. We have to be able to look past differences in race that separate us in order to build connections and points of shared interests. I think that the more we help young people tune in to their own hearts, the more likely they'll be to build connections with the adults in their lives who they might otherwise view as the "other." It's about acknowledging that feeling of disappointment without letting it limit you or the potential for relationship.

When we transfer this concept to other environments – foster homes, youth detention centers, group homes, after school agencies – we can see how any adult working with any youth in any context can find a point of connection if he or she is willing to show up with authenticity, share a bit, and learn a little more about the deep complexities of the youth with whom we work. I so rarely *felt* this kind of bond and remember hating how the disconnection felt, even if I didn't have the emotional vocabulary to explain it as such.

Carrying this memory into my work, I didn't want a single young person I worked with to *ever* feel like they couldn't connect. So building connections, and helping the adults who work with youth do the same, has become central to my work as an Ubuntu teacher. In her TED Talk "Every Kid Needs a Champion," long-time educator Rita Pierson talks about the importance of teachers building relationships. She explains that kids won't learn from people they don't like, that every single kid needs a champion, and that it's up to us as teachers to answer that call.

The quote "I am not what I think I am. I'm not what you think I am. I'm what I think you think I am" exemplifies why it's essential for schools to provide an adult advocate for every student. Because our students are paying attention to how we feel about them. And they each deserve to have at least one adult at school who they know believes in them and wants the best for them.

But this work of connecting can't just be left up to the adults. Building relationships can and should be a two-way street. As a young man, I wish I had understood more directly this idea that I needed to find my *one* person, even if he wasn't the one I liked or related to the most. It's often more about finding the person who is going to have your back no matter what. Sometimes when we recognize who our *one* is, it might force us to humble ourselves a bit. Maybe it's the teacher we just cursed out last week, or the mentor we've been ignoring because we just didn't think he was *down* enough to understand where we were coming from. Maybe it's the old white dude down the hall who cares so deeply, but we don't even notice he's trying to help because we're so caught up in why our dads aren't there or why the one Black male teacher in the building just doesn't *get* it like we think he should.

The interesting thing is that even though I had these issues with all these white people, I did have a couple of teachers, Mr. Duzrak included, who I held in high esteem. And yet I still always wanted it to be someone else who was there for me, someone who looked like me. It was like I felt the pain of seeing in another man all the things I *wanted* to see in my father, but never really did.

So many layers of pain. So many hopeful avenues out of the pain. So much opportunity for growth. And yet there I was, not feeling like I was growing at all. Not feeling like I was getting what I so desperately needed.

---

Even though my KAOS brothers and I struggled with male role models and mentors in our lives, we were really focused on each other and our growing crew. Once we formally chose the name KAOS, we decided we needed gear to properly accessorize ourselves. We already had a song, so why not add in some accessories? We'd chant "Everywhere we go, we let the people know that KAOS is in the house." We didn't recognize the literal truth to what we were chanting – that many of us were living in homes with their fair share of chaos – but we did recognize the mark we wanted to leave on the world. And we wanted to be visible.

"We have to choose our own colors," I told the crew one night. "The last thing we need is to get caught up wearing gang colors."

We decided on blue, and the Kansas City Royals baseball team gear was perfect because the team's colors and initials matched those of our crew. So the next day, we took the L to Maxwell Street's open-air flea market to purchase some jackets. Maxwell Street, which ran from the south side of the Chicago River to Blue Island Avenue, was inhabited first by Irish immigrants but eventually became the gateway neighborhood for Greeks, Bohemians, Russians, Germans, Italians, African Americans and Mexicans. After the Great Migration, southern African Americans moved into the area and brought the blues to Maxwell Street.

From the 1880s to the 1920s, Russian Jews established the Maxwell Street Market to help sustain the community. The open-air pushcart market extended from Halstead to 16th Street and was at the time of my childhood the largest open-air market in the United States. It was the place where merchants of all races and ethnicities came to make money, and where Chicago's poor came to spend money on clothing, food, cars, appliances, tools – anything they needed, legal or illegal, to sustain their homes. Anyone approaching the market would know it was close because of the strong and distinct smell of Polish hot dogs and onions. The market looked chaotic, but actually had a lot of order to it.

Though most Jewish families moved out of the area in the 1920s, they still owned the majority of the shops in the market. For this reason, most folks on the South Side called the market Jew Town. For South Side Chicagoans, Jew Town was our one-stop shop to get everything from Easter clothes to those Eddie Bauer portfolios, snakeskin hats, Starter jackets, Jordons, Treetorn sneakers, Coach bags, Girbaud jeans and Levi cords, Gazelles, and Laura Bigotti sunglasses we all wore.

Maxwell Street was gritty and dirty, but white Chicagoans were still proud of the notoriety that bandleader and clarinetist Benny Goodman, polish sausage sandwiches, and the television show "Hill Street Blues" brought to the neighborhood. Those of us on the South Side were hyped because, inside the gym of St. Ignatius High School, right around the way from Maxwell Street, a well-known basketball player by the name of Michael Jordan was photographed gliding, legs spread-eagled, through the air toward a basketball net. That image of basketball's all-time reigning champion became the branding force behind a shoe company called Nike. And to think that the inspiration for that iconic logo happened so close to where we all hung out filled us with pride.

Once we got off the L, we entered the market and began surveying the many vendors selling Kansas City Royals Starter jackets to find who would sell the gear to us at the cheapest price.

"Hey yo! Yo, homeboy!" yelled out one of the Asian merchants in his broken English. "I got real herringbone for you. Cheap price!" All of us stopped walking to watch the little Asian man take a lighter out of his pocket, flick the thumb-wheel, and then put the flame up to the thin herringbone necklace.

"See. No burn. Real gold," he bragged. "I sell to you for 10 dollars."

We looked at him and laughed. "A'ight!" one of us said, before we all pulled $10 bills out of our pockets, bought our herringbones, put them on, and then walked away in search of the rest of our gear.

It didn't take us long to find our jackets. The shimmering blue caught our eyes right away, and the KC lettering popped. Nobody was going to be able to miss us now! Each of pulled out $50 cash that we had somehow scraped together – I must have had to get on my hands and knees to beg my mom for that money – and handed it to the merchant in exchange for our new prized possessions. With our herringbones and KC jackets, nobody could tell us we weren't the shit.

---

If KAOS was known for anything, it was for our parties. As we grew in both age and number, we began to throw bigger and better parties. Everyone wanted to be down.

The first unofficial KAOS party occurred during my sophomore year. I collected $3 dues from every KAOS member each week to book a spot. Rob's cousin Marlon got us a room at the Travelodge that was so small we had to move the beds into the bathtub to make adequate space for us to party. We didn't care. We thought we had arrived.

Every New Year's Eve, one of my mother's friends would host a party downtown at the Westin Hotel next door to the John Hancock building. So New Year's Eve of 1986, Mom and her friends partied in the ballroom, which left the room she'd paid for upstairs unoccupied. She didn't want her money to go to waste, so she told me and my cousin Darnell we could use it. In no time at all, KAOS was 25 deep in that small hotel room, and, as one would expect, we were loud. Security kept appearing to tell us to be quiet, and before the night ended all of us, Mama included, had gotten ourselves kicked out.

New Year's Eve of 1987 we went upscale. My cousin Sandra, who was in her 20s at the time, booked a suite for us at the Barclay Hotel. Everybody we knew showed up and even paid a cover charge to get in. We had music, food, and a bathtub filled with liquor. When we saw all of the girls who had come to the party that night, we *really* thought we had arrived.

Senior year we knew we had to step up our game, so we set our sights high. We wanted the Palmer House. We paid cash for a suite, which was much bigger than the one at the Barclay. This time we also got rooms for those of us who had girlfriends. And for a $5 cover charge, our guests got all the food they could eat, all the liquor they could drink, and all the beats they needed to dance all night long. KAOS' own DJ Rod's House music kept the party going.

Girls, girls and more girls came to this party, which was cool, especially when our girls – the Posse – arrived. The Posse was a group of public school girls mostly from Kenwood, Lindblom, Longwood and Corlis. The Posse was KAOS' female counterpart and, just like us, the Posse girls liked to drink, hang out late, and fight. Some girls from the Catholic schools came too, but they didn't capture our attention like the Posse girls did.

We had a ritual when it came to selecting girls. If we liked a female, we would ask another member of KAOS to sign off on her in a very particular way. If a girl was fine, we said nothing except, "Man, whatever you do, get the poo." But if she wasn't that attractive, we would signal to leave her alone by scratching our heads. The harder we scratched, the uglier the girl was, and there was no way we'd allow our fellow members of KAOS to get with some girl who wasn't fine. The Posse girls passed the test, and we used those parties as our time to get as many girls as we could.

The New Year's Eve bashes were so successful that we decided to start throwing Memorial Day parties too. Because it was so hot by May, we moved these parties outside to the Dan Ryan Woods on 83rd and Western. Rod and Orlando, the "Big O," were our DJs. We had food on the grill, all types of liquor on ice, organized softball and volleyball games, and water gun fights. We did everything you can imagine that a group of unsupervised kids could do. The Posse girls, and many others, came out in their short shorts and bikini tops and drank all the wine coolers they could. Never once did the police, or any other adults for that matter, question us, scold us for drinking, tell the girls to get dressed, stop us from having sex, or make us leave the premises. We were KAOS, and we believed we were untouchable.

When you look at what we were doing from an organizational perspective, it's easy to see where my leadership skills were first groomed. If you ask members of KAOS today, most of them will share how I became one of the central members of the crew – because of where my house was located geographically, because of my ability to motivate people around me and build consensus, and because of my vision.

We weren't just throwing parties – we were organizing complex cultural events. We'd meet about where a party was going to be, how it was going to be funded, how we'd market it, what food we'd serve, and other logistical items. We built upon these same skills when we went on later to establish our own scholarship fund in honor of our KAOS crew members who had died. I was the one who managed the financial resources of whatever it was we were doing, and looking back on it I'm impressed with the underlying level of trust that existed among our band of brothers – they trusted *me* to take care of their cash, and this total trust laid an important foundation for much of the work I'd do years later.

KAOS was also known to crash parties all over the South Side, but the night we all showed up at a huge party at the Navy Pier in our KAOS Santa Claus hats was legendary. We rolled up 12 deep and turned that party out. We danced, drank, and even had the girls up in the air. Literally. We didn't care that it was cold as hell that night, we just knew we were KAOS, and everyone wanted to know who these cats with the Santa Claus hats were. Yep, they wanted to be down, too.

If our crew wasn't partying, we were fighting, and there wasn't a brawl we'd back down from. KAOS was so tight-knit, so connected, that we almost sensed when trouble was in the air, and mobilized like Voltron to defeat whomever came at us. Outside of girls, we fought over everything, especially when we believed one of us had been disrespected. The location of the fight didn't matter. We'd walk into gang territory at Stateway Gardens to fight over the smallest of things. Which, of course, seemed like big things to us at the time. It was an age when boys were killing each other over Starter jackets and sneakers, but we thought we were invincible. We wore those Starter jackets everywhere. I think my mom was afraid I might somehow get killed over mine, but lucky for me the worst thing that happened was that it got stolen.

Kanye West's mother, who was raising her son in Chicago at the same time that I was coming up, spoke about the violence that was breaking out over sneakers and Starter jackets. She wouldn't even let Kanye ride the L because she feared for his life. So she'd drive him wherever he needed to go. It's easy to look at this and think she was just an overprotective mother overreacting to something that might have been no big deal. But the article discussing Kanye's mother also referenced a Sports Illustrated article from 1990 that noted a Chicago police sergeant's report that his district had approximately 50 reported incidents of violence over the jackets and more than a dozen reported incidents involving shoes. In a single month.

So when my LA Lakers Starter jacket was stolen, which I wore on days that I wasn't in my KC jacket, my KAOS boys and I rolled through the projects looking for someone wearing that jacket. I wonder now what the heck we would have actually done if we had found the thief, but at the time I don't believe we were thinking that far ahead at all. We were teenage boys, caught up in a time and a place, sometimes not acting nearly as smart as we actually were.

One night, Dez and Jerry and I were out when some cats jumped on Dez. The fight had been precipitated by a previous altercation with some guy we had fought one night in De La Salle's parking lot after a party. This time, Jerry and I were able to fight them off enough to get Dez out of their grip and make it to our car. Dez was hurt, though. He was hit in the head with something. I remember hopping into the passenger seat and looking behind me to see him bleeding all over the back seat of the car.

Once we got back to George's house, I made one phone call and all of KAOS showed up ready to go into the projects to battle. It was before the time of cell phones, but somehow we were able to mobilize our whole crew in a matter of hours.

Another time, Rich's mother's purse got snatched on Indiana Street. We were not having that, so Rich called the crew and all 25 of us came to his house ready to find those cats who took it.

One Friday night, we went to a basketball game at St. Rita's, one of De La Salle's rival schools. All of us had been together most of that afternoon at Jew Town getting our Gazelles for cheap. That night, we thought we were the shit when we rolled up at this mostly white Catholic school to support De La Salle's basketball team.

After the game, we walked outside trying to figure out which party we were going to crash when these dudes from St. Rita's came over to us talking smack.

"Why don't you niggers go back to your side of town?" one short Italian cat with thick black hair yelled in our direction. This was our first wake-up call as a collective group that racism was not only real, but that it extended far beyond the walls of the classrooms where we spent our days. And we were both angry and hurt.

Immediately, Rich and Steve picked the kid up and slammed him down on a car. Lance turned and started to whoop another dude's ass. When other St. Rita students saw what was happening, they ran over to us in attack mode. Before I knew it, I couldn't see anything except fists flying and arms swinging. And I couldn't hear anything except the sound of expletives in the frigid winter air as we mopped those cats.

After the fight was over, we jumped in our cars and made our way to Dion's house. It was Dion's birthday, but he had had to work that day and, as a result, had missed out on all the action. Once we got out of the car at Dion's, we noticed Derrick's swollen hand.

"Yo, what happened?" I asked him.

"Man, this dude was just about to hit you, Nel," he said, pacing back and forth while holding his swollen hand close to his chest. "So I punched him in the face, forgetting I had my Gazelles in the same hand."

"Damn, man," I commiserated. "Let me see your hand." It wasn't bleeding, but we could tell his hand was messed up. We knew we couldn't take Derrick to the hospital, and we definitely were not going to tell his mother what had happened. So, we did the next best thing.

"Go get him some ice!" somebody yelled.

All of us hung out at Dion's place most of the night rehashing what had happened, trying to figure out why those dudes picked a fight with us and how a day that had started out as so amazing for us – we were with all our friends, headed to a basketball game, looking forward to just *kicking* it together – had ended up such a mess.

On a personal level, that day was a wake-up call that this life wasn't going to be easy, even if I attended one of the best high schools in Chicago, even if I was surrounded by a group of friends who always had my back. The altercation that day was racially motivated, and I realized at a deeper level than I had ever before that I was going to be judged no matter what, for reasons that existed way beyond my control or sphere of influence.

---

Monday morning, we KAOS crew members who went to De La Salle arrived at school a little nervous. Because the fight happened on St. Rita's campus, we were pretty sure our school administrators had heard about it. We just had no idea how they were going to respond. We didn't have to wait too long after first period began to find out.

"Will the following students please report to the office immediately: LaMarr. Steve. Dion. Bill. Kerroy. Marcus. Richard. Clarence. Lance. Larry. Derrick. Kelvin. Curtis."

*Damn!*

I left my class and walked anxiously down a flight of stairs to the long corridor leading to Mr. Bartholomew Yuncer's office. The Dean of Students was a stocky dude who reminded me of Bart Simpson. *Is he going to believe we didn't start this fight?* I wondered.

I walked into the waiting room outside of Mr. Yuncer's office and glanced over at his secretary. *Damn!* I thought. *Here I am. Back in this office with this woman who, like always, smells funky as hell.* But this visit, I knew exactly why I was there

– and looking around and seeing all of KAOS deep in the room, I knew that the secretary's poor hygiene was the least of our concerns.

"Wassup?" I said as I made eye contact with the crew. Some of us looked concerned, others looked like they were trying to build themselves up in preparation to combat what was coming. Whatever was about to happen in that office and whether we got suspended or not, we knew we had defended ourselves Friday night. Nothing more. Nothing less.

Mr. Yuncer ushered us into his tiny office.

"What happened at St. Rita's Friday night?" he asked as he closed the office door, all of us piled in there on top of each other.

We were silent for a moment before we all started talking at once.

"Man, they started it."

"It wasn't us."

"We went there to watch the game."

"All I know is we were trying to leave when they tried to move on us."

We were on the defensive from the moment we heard our names called over the intercom, and it was showing. I remember just sitting there listening to it all, still in disbelief that we were even in that office having to defend ourselves at all. It was disorienting for reasons that at the time I couldn't explain.

"OK, hold it!" Mr. Yuncer yelled. "One at a time."

"Mr. Yuncer," Curtis began calmly, "We were leaving the game at St. Rita's when these guys approached us trying to instigate a fight."

"And when they threw the first punch," I chimed in, "we had to fight back."

Everyone else started telling bits and pieces of the story, until we were able to rehash the entire event.

When we finished, Mr. Yuncer leaned back in his chair and took a deep breath.

*Here we go! Now how am I going to explain to my mom that I just got suspended?* I thought to myself.

"Look, guys. I found out this was a set up," Mr. Yuncer began. "The Dean from St.

Rita's called to tell me that some of the kids confessed. He said the boys planned to start a fight with you guys just to get you in trouble."

We looked at Mr. Yuncer, blinking and saying nothing until Curtis asked, "So, what does that mean for us?"

"It means," Mr. Yuncer explained as he stood up and walked toward the door, indicating that the meeting was over, "that I'm not suspending any of you. You were defending yourselves. But don't let this happen again. I won't be so lenient next time."

The KAOS crew had nothing to say. All of us stood there dumbfounded that Mr. Yuncer had acknowledged that we had acted in self-defense. And we were blown away that we weren't all getting suspended. For once, the De La Salle coat of arms had protected us.

As time went on, though, we learned that this protection didn't follow us out into the street. I remember one distinct moment of clarity that came when I realized that the rules of the game were changing. We were walking away at the end of a fight when shots rang out. I knew in that moment that this wasn't the life I wanted to live. Once guns came into play, I no longer trusted all the unspoken rules that had always governed our street fights. As someone in the crew once said, "These fools are now popping tools." I wanted to live. I valued my life.

I remember another time when a kid was dragged off a bus and stomped in the street. What happened was that the crew was just leaving Denis, a store notorious for selling liquor to minors, when they saw a guy from Leo named Chris just walking down the street with two girls. They watched him get jumped on by two other guys, so Seron jumped in first and then the entire crew joined in as well. During the fight, one of the guys who had originally jumped on Chris tried to escape by hopping onto the bus, but he was eventually dragged back out onto the street by some of the guys in KAOS. As Seron recounted it, *We were being advocates. We couldn't let Chris get beat down.*

George and I didn't witness the event because we were working that day. We both had jobs by then at the Traffic Jam, a bar that was owned by a Chicago Bears player. But hearing about the fight secondhand was more than enough for me. I was actually glad I had a job because it forced me to separate myself from some of the madness. And it really did feel like things were starting to get a little crazy.

---

Much has been said about our parties and our fights, but not many who knew the

KAOS crew had any idea that we were budding philosophers as well. On nights when we weren't out in the streets, we were either at Rich's or my house. Rich's mom was a nurse who often worked the night shift, so his house was usually the spot we brought our girlfriends to have sex because there were no adults home to supervise us. But on nights we didn't want that, we hung out at my place for some deep conversation.

We talked about everything, from college and careers to marriage and how many kids we'd have when we grew up. We talked about the men we would become, the kids we would save, and the lives we would create for ourselves, our families, and the world.

We watched "Mississippi Burning" and saw every Spike Lee movie together. We talked about race, politics, and our place in the world. Those conversations made us contemplate our future as African American men on a deep level. Some of the cats we knew were beginning to get caught up in gangs, and plenty of them weren't making it to their 18th birthdays, let alone older adulthood. We knew we didn't want to go that route and vowed we'd do everything we could to ensure we all stayed on the right path. We took our bond in KAOS seriously.

"There's a college fair happening Thursday night in the city," Rich disclosed one night during our junior year when we were just cooling out.

"Oh yeah?" Curtis interjected. "We should go. You know there's gonna be a whole lotta girls there."

Two nights later, we walked into the McCormick place on Lake Shore Drive. The massive convention center was buzzing with energy, and we looked around wide-eyed to see college recruiters from Harvard, Duke, Stanford, USC, Ohio State, Yale, and other big name universities standing behind tables covered with college flyers, pennants and as much information as we could ever want about college. We decided immediately that we needed to split up to get a better lay of the land.

"Damn, there's a lot of people here," I noted to Curtis as we walked up and down the aisles. We turned a corner to enter another, smaller room where we saw recruiters that looked like us. They represented the HBCUs – the historically Black colleges and universities built by African Americans for people of color to receive a quality education. There was Florida A & M, Tuskegee in Alabama, Howard in Washington, D.C. and Hampton in Virginia. There was Grambling in Louisiana, and Clark, Spelman and Morehouse in Atlanta. We'd seen Spike Lee's "School Daze," but none of us had realized that the school in that movie was based on life at a real school, filled with kids who looked like us.

"Young scholars," we heard a voice address us. "Stop over here. Let me talk to you." The recruiter who stopped us stood next to a table with the words MOREHOUSE COLLEGE printed on a maroon tablecloth. He wore tan slacks, a white button down shirt with a tie, and a maroon blazer with the Morehouse crest on the breast pocket.

"Have you ever heard of Morehouse College?" he inquired.

"Yes," we replied in unison.

I knew about Morehouse because my man Steve Pamon was a freshman there. He wasn't in KAOS, but he was one of my closest friends on the block, along with Dave, Gerald, Dre, Al, Kevin, Mani, and my cousin Jerry. Steve would share some cool stories with us about going to school in Atlanta and all the fine girls at Spelman, Clark, and Morris Brown. I remember Steve talking about Freaknik and how girls from all over the country would attend this huge Black college festival. All the top music artists of the time would be there, from Tupac and TLC to Run DMC. The list just went on and on. Curtis and I were like, "Anything that has *freak* in the title, we're down!"

Steve's mother, Mrs. Pamon, was a teacher who really inspired me. Looking back on it now, I can see that she had a lot of Ubuntu characteristics. I would watch her bring kids home from school so they could experience a different type of community than they were exposed to daily in their violent neighborhoods. All the kids loved her. I remember thinking early on in my teaching career that if I could learn to be half the teacher that Mrs. Pamon was then I would be alright.

"Ahhh, perfect," the college admissions officer remarked with a smile. "Well, let me tell you a bit more! As you may know, Morehouse College is a historically Black college that was founded in 1867. It's the only all-male HBCU in the country."

"All *Black* dudes like us?" Curtis asked. Because of De La Salle, we were used to the all-male environment, but the idea of going to an all-male school with all African Americans amazed us.

"Yea, man," the recruiter replied. "But don't worry. Spelman, an all-female HBCU, is right across the street." All three of us looked over at the Spelman table to see their recruiter talking to some of the Catholic school girls we knew. We smiled.

We talked to the Morehouse recruiter for nearly half an hour before we moved on – gathering application packets, brochures, pennants, and other collateral materials from the other HBCU recruiters at the college fair.

By the time all of KAOS had gathered back at the entrance of the building to head home, our lives had changed. The door to higher education had swung wide open and we were ready to run, full force ahead.

# CHAPTER 3

# WHERE DO WE GO FROM HERE?

*And just when it seemed that the game is hopeless,*
*we arranged some things for a dose of dopeness.*

- Kid Cudi

Though KAOS usually rolled as a crew, we sometimes split into smaller groups. There was a subset of KAOS that liked to smoke weed, and since they knew most of us weren't into that they would schedule their own "meetings" outside of the full group to do what they did. Of course, the Original Five also hung tight, as did those who went to the same schools.

Curtis was my best friend. He was a lil' dude with a high-pitched voice who called himself "Too Sweet." He, like all of the crew, called me "Nel." We were partners in crime. When you saw me, you saw Curtis. We spent the night at each other's houses all the time and had deep conversations about family, relationships, and our dreams for the future. Curtis and I made a pact that we would go to Morehouse together, and we liked to muse about how many Spelman girls we'd get when we got there. Sometimes we dated a pair of friends, and if I had a girl and he didn't, then I had to hook him up with my girl's best friend. That's just how it was, and we loved it.

The summer before junior year, KAOS suffered its first tragedy. Curtis' mother was found brutally murdered in her car outside the family home and it was Curtis who found her. The experience decimated Curtis.

It was 10 a.m. on a cloudy Wednesday morning when my phone rang.

"Yo, Nel! My mother is dead," Curtis' shrill voice cut through the morning air. My 15-year-old, sleepy brain couldn't process what he was saying. *What? How can Ms. Williams be dead?*

Curtis and I had kicked it the night before, just rolling around Chicago looking for something to get into. When we didn't find a party, Curtis had decided to drive around racing, making mini-jumps over railroad tracks. When we were tired of doing that, Curt had dropped me off and driven to his home on 71st and Cottage Grove.

Curt lived with his mom in a typical Chicago 20-unit building that sat across the street from a police station and the infamous Oak Woods Cemetery. The 783-acre cemetery opened in 1853, and after the Civil War between four and six thousand Confederate soldiers and prisoners were buried there. Oak Wood was also the final resting place of some of Chicago's most notable African American citizens, including Civil Rights and anti-lynching activist Ida B. Wells-Barnett, the "Father of Gospel" Thomas A. Dorsey, Chicago Giants Negro League pitcher and outfielder Charles Johnson, Olympian Jesse Owens, and Mayor Harold Washington.

"Curt, stop playin'!" my voice shook nervously as I desperately hoped that what he was saying wasn't true. Ms. Williams, a beautiful, petite, brown-skinned lady who stood not much taller than her son, was one of the sweetest women I knew. No one would guess by looking at their modest home that Ms. Williams was moderately wealthy. She worked at the Chicago Stock Exchange and splurged on one thing – her only son, Curt. He always had the flyest gear and kicks, and more importantly than that, he had a mother who would do anything for him.

"Nel, I'm not playin'," he said. "My mother is dead. She's dead." I knew by the tremble in his voice that he was serious.

"Curt, what?" I asked again, still in disbelief.

"Man, I don't have time for this!" Curtis exclaimed.

He was about to hang up the phone when I stopped him. "Curt, wait!" I yelled through the phone, trying to keep him on the line. "What happened?"

"I went outside and found her in her car out back," he began. His voice was calm now.

"Dude," I muttered, picturing in my mind her two-door burgundy Grand Am with the leather front-end bra, still trying to comprehend what he was telling me. "What is going on?"

"Nel, the police are on their way here now," he continued. "My mother's fiancé is here. I called him and Leroy right after I found her." Leroy was Curtis' older cousin. His parents owned a convenience store on the bottom floor of the building where Curt and his mother lived.

"What do you need me to do?" I asked him, wanting to help any way I could.

"Nothing right now. I'm gonna call you back." As soon as I hung up with him, I called Steve, Rich and Dion to tell them what had happened and to ask if one of them would come get me once I heard back from Curt.

"We all should ride together," Steve offered. "I'll pick everyone up."

Three excruciating hours later, my phone rang.

"Meet me at my father's house. 10131 Charles St.," Curt directed and then hung up. *Father?* In all the time we'd spent together, Curtis had never mentioned his father. I didn't even know he had a relationship with him.

I called Steve back and told him Curt had called and told me where he wanted us to meet him. When Steve picked me up, Rich and Dion were already in the car. That car ride was filled with nothing except the heavy silence of our confusion and fear.

We rolled into Beverly, a beautiful and very affluent community of Chicago, and found Curt's father's house at the address Curt had given me over the phone. All of us were blown away by the pristine neighborhood, the large manicured lawns, and the quiet. This was nothing like most of the neighborhoods we were used to.

All of the houses in Beverly had driveways, and Curtis' father's house at 101st and Charles was no exception. In that driveway sat Curtis' mother's car, which we recognized immediately. We parallel parked on the street in front of the house and got out of Steve's car. As we walked up the driveway, we couldn't help but notice the blood on the bra of the car.

"You see that?" I whispered to Steve. "How did blood get *there?*" He shrugged his shoulders, speechless.

We all slowed down when we noticed that the windows of the car were open. We looked inside and saw more blood pooled on the front seat and the floor. Steve, Rich and Dion looked at me, eyes wide and filled with questions. I knew from what Curt had told me on the phone that he had been the one to find his mother, but he hadn't fully explained her state. In that instant, I knew that what he had seen would probably haunt him for the rest of his life.

Dion rang the doorbell. A little girl who couldn't have been more than 10 years old swung the door open. "May I help you?" she asked in an articulate voice that seemed far too grown up for her age.

"We're Curtis' friends. Is he here?" Dion spoke for us all.

She nodded, stepped back, and ushered us inside. "He's downstairs," she said as she closed the front door behind us. "My name is Kim. Follow me."

Each of us took a quick survey of our surroundings as we followed Curtis' sister down a long hallway. The house was expansive, but the walls were white and bare and the furniture was sparse. It was hard to believe that people actually *lived* here, especially people related to Curt. Through the large living room windows we got a glimpse of a deck with a grill overlooking a huge backyard.

On the way to the basement, we saw two other children – a girl and a boy – quietly playing. *How did I never know that Curtis had siblings?* I thought to myself. We stopped at the kitchen door where a woman was storing snacks on top of the refrigerator.

"Mom," Kim said. "These are Curtis' friends."

The heavy-set woman, who wore a short natural and glasses, briefly stopped what she was doing to glance our way and I remember thinking that Curtis' stepmother looked to be the total opposite of his mother. "Nice to meet you," she greeted us.

"Nice to meet you, too," we mumbled in unison.

At that moment, Curtis' father entered the kitchen. He was built similarly to Curtis – short, stocky and strong – and appeared to be much older than his wife. But unlike his wife, he didn't acknowledge our presence with any type of greeting. He didn't say a word, although he did look directly into each of our faces as we passed.

Kim took us to a set of stairs leading down to what we would soon discover was a large, finished basement. The first thing we saw when we entered the basement were our reflections in the huge color television. There was also a bar with stools, a pool table, and a bathroom. I picked the cue stick up off the pool table and started shooting. The sound of the clacking balls seemed inappropriately loud. I stopped the eight ball from rolling into the pocket and put the stick down. Even my teenaged mind understood that this wasn't the time for pool.

"What happened, Curt?" I asked as I walked over to a stool near where he sat. Rich, Steve and Dion sat at the bar facing Curt, waiting in silence for him to say something, anything, to better explain the horrific scene in the car that we had walked by just a few minutes before.

"After I dropped you off, Nel, I drove home and went to bed, but something woke me up. I can't remember what," he told us in a whisper. "I called for my mother, but she didn't answer. So I put on my shoes, walked down the stairs, and headed out back to the alley."

He stared at the floor as he spoke, "I approached her car on the driver's side and when I opened the door, that's when I found her lying with her face down on the steering wheel." He stopped talking for a moment, trying to fight back tears. We sat in silence not knowing what to say. *What would we have done in his situation?* I wondered.

"I could see the stab wounds. Blood was everywhere and I knew she was dead," he recalled, his voice tapering off into the silence of the room. "The first thing I did was to call the police. Next I called my mother's fiancé, then Leroy, and then you, Nel. I remember mom's fiancé asking me so many questions on the phone about what had happened, how I had found her, and what I could tell him about her death. The police arrived and then Leroy and my mom's fiancé both showed up about the same time. The dude walked in with a beer in his hand. The police asked me what had happened, and then started asking him, too. Before I knew it, they had taken him in for questioning."

"They took him in?" I asked, still a bit confused by what Curt was telling us.

"Yeah. They took him in," Curt reiterated. We were shocked. The man who had been there for Curtis' mom, given Curtis his car, and was about to be his stepfather had been taken in for questioning?! Unbelievable.

"Over the past week," Curtis continued, "My mom's been hanging out with an old friend. I heard Mom and her fiancé arguing about this dude one night, but mom squashed it. I didn't think anything else about it until now. I think her fiancé may have killed her," Curtis stated matter-of-factly.

Steve, Rich, Dion and I looked at Curtis, stunned. We could not comprehend what he had just told us, let alone the fact that we all knew the person who Curt believed had murdered Ms. Williams. I glanced around and broke the silence by asking, "Where do we go from here?" Nobody said a word.

We didn't know what to say to Curt or to each other. We just didn't have the emotional vocabulary for it. Our presence had to be enough because it was all we had to give, and because we knew that the only ones we had to lean on were each other.

---

When boys exhibit behavior that we as adults find troubling – when they stifle their emotions, mumble when we expect them to talk, lash out in anger when we want them to solve problems in healthier ways – we have to remember that there is often a reason behind all of it. And the best way that we can help our boys grow and learn is to first understand.

In "I Don't Want to Talk about It: Overcoming the Secret Legacy of Male Depression," psychotherapist Terrence Real discusses how many boys become increasingly emotionally numb as they grow up. Much of what boys learn from school, society, friends and family creates a model of manhood that has more to do with stoicism and toughness than it does with emotional expressiveness. To take it one step further, Real describes how boys often can't even identify their emotions in the first place, let alone express them. *Alexithymia* is the formal term given to this phenomenon, and Real reports research findings that as many as 80 percent of men in U.S. society might have some form of alexithymia. It's like when you ask a man what he's feeling and he either can't verbalize it at all, or he gives a response that has more to do with his thoughts than his feelings. Many men and boys have a hard time distinguishing between the two.

If we want boys to talk, it might be up to us as adults to provide them with the words to get them started. Unlike with many girls who are more emotionally adept at an earlier age when it comes to verbal communication, boys are more likely to just sit and observe – and then later explode when they don't have the tools to adequately express what they're feeling. As a consequence, boys often end up feeling misunderstood, invisible and ignored, even though they often can't explain exactly why

So often, we just don't develop strong emotional vocabularies on our own as we grow. I remember when I was in high school and a young lady I was dating asked me how I felt about her. I said, while nodding my head up and down, "You are cool. You are straight." When she returned the sentiment, she did so by rattling off an eloquent list of adjectives and similes to describe her feelings toward me. In other words, she had a very strong emotional vocabulary and, as evidenced by my response to her question, I didn't. I remember feeling frustrated then, and often throughout my childhood and young adulthood, that I didn't have the words I needed to express myself.

What I've discovered through my work is that I was in no way an anomaly. That's why it's important to get boys to journal and to guide them through conversations. For example, I teach parents who are raising sons the Rose and Thorn game from the Family Dinner Project. The game is based on the premise that most people love roses, but hate the thorns. In the game, the roses represent the things that are easy to talk about, the good parts of our day, and the thorns are those aspects that are a little more painful to discuss.

We have to let our boys understand that it's okay to talk about the thorns because they're unavoidable. They're real. Here's an example of how the game works:

"Mosiah, what was your thorn today?" I might ask my son.

"I received a 95 percent on my test."

"Well, that sounds like a rose to me. What was your thorn?"

"Well, I got in trouble because my friend Leo got caught cheating off my paper, and the teacher thought I gave him permission to do it."

Bam. There we go. In a few short minutes, I've taken a conversation with my 8-year-old son to a place where he understands that it's okay to verbalize the things that upset him. It often doesn't take long to get to the heart of the matter and to let our boys know that it's healthy to talk about the not-so-beautiful parts of our days, that we don't always have to "man up" and hold it all inside.

In addition to helping guide boys in conversations, there are other techniques we can use to help them feel more comfortable opening up. For example, instead of looking a young man in the eye when we want to engage him in conversation, we can take him on a walk – minimizing both the face-to-face contact and the perceived threat of engaging in a way he might not be equipped to handle. Whereas some teachers, parents, and other change agents might feel that boys' unwillingness to respond to pointed questions or initiate eye contact is disrespectful, there's often more to it than that. Boys do practice communicating in emotional ways outside of the classroom and away from adults – like, for example, by playing the dozens – and our challenge is to help them translate these learned skills into the classroom and similar settings in proactive ways.

To build emotional literacy in boys, we also need to teach and model strong emotional vocabularies ourselves. At a very young age, many girls play with dolls. They talk to their dolls. They dress them up. They engage them in conversation. Boys don't often do the same. Because boys tend to be more impulsive, they're more likely to use their trucks to run over the dolls. That might be okay at age 6, but as kids grow and get further along in school, these gender differences often become more pronounced. The point is that boys often respond to the world differently than girls. Boys and girls can be sitting in the same classroom, listening to the same teacher, reading the same book and doing the same assignment. And yet there's a chance that they're getting two different educations. Because their paradigms are often different to begin with. And recognizing these differences for what they are, without judgment, is important if we want to equip all of our young people with the tools they need to thrive.

If you're reading this as a parent of a son, the best advice I can give is to be sure to listen to him – long, often and well. In her book "The Everything Parent's Guide to Raising Boys," author Cheryl L. Erwin notes that one of the best ways to encourage boys to express themselves is to learn ourselves how to listen without judgment, and then model this non-judgmental listening with our boys. This is often much easier said than done, especially when we as adults never learned how to listen well as children, but it's important to figure out how to do so. Erwin describes how we can do this through showing empathy and not rushing to solutions, but rather giving some time and space for boys to explore their own emotions. For those of us who are "fixers," this can be especially hard. But it's important that, even when we don't agree with what our boys tell us, we give them opportunities to formulate their feelings into words. Being good listeners ourselves is often the first step toward connecting with our boys so that we can then work to solve problems together.

Erwin also notes that allowing young people, and especially boys, the space and freedom to be themselves is important to their emotional vocabulary development. Instead of telling boys what they should or should not be feeling or how they should or should not express their emotions, we need to create safe environments – free of shame, rejection, and unnecessary pressure to conform to societal expectations – where they can discover their own strengths and weaknesses and how they express them to the world. If we want our boys to dream, we have to know when to hold their hands and when to let go, when to step into the ring and when to let them work it out on their own.

The media, our society, and other outside forces are going to provide boys with more than enough exposure to what it means to "man up," "toughen up," and live up to the expectations of masculinity that they'll encounter at most every turn. Maybe the best thing that we can do is to provide an alternative – to nurture our boys, to provide them with compassion and tools for expressing themselves, to let them know that they don't always have to be the tough ones. That it's okay to cry.

And I think we also have to remember that because many boys already have a propensity toward anger and aggression, when we're interacting with them during times of conflict, it's our responsibility to remain calm, respectful and even-keeled. It's okay for us to be upset, of course, but when we react in anger then we're only furthering the cycle that we're working so hard to address.

---

In KAOS, we were boys trying to figure out how to be men without the words to express ourselves. And then we were living in an environment where we were exposed to a lot of violence, discord and chaos that created both stress and trauma in our lives. To compound the ongoing stress we felt, when the first major tragedy in many of our lives, Curt's mom's death, struck, there was nobody there to help us work through it all.

What's so perplexing to me now, looking back on the aftermath of Curt's mom's death, is that no adult in our lives engaged us in much conversation around the trauma. Nobody – not our parents, teachers, school counselors – had any means in place to help us process what we were experiencing. It affected us all because we were as close as family, and yet we were just left on our own to try to figure it out. And we didn't have the skills we needed to do so.

With all the trauma that I saw around me growing up, I don't remember my mother once asking any of us how we felt. And I lived in a household where we talked and engaged with each other, where I was exposed to education and culture and the world. Yet in this particular area, I think there was a great void that was left unfilled.

Even though our parents knew our friends, they weren't really connected to each other. It wasn't like they got together or even talked to each other about what we were going through or how they might strategize to support us. It was *our* connection that bonded us. We comforted ourselves with the few skills that we had. We medicated each other with what we thought we needed at the time, which was above all else just being available to each other. We didn't have any answers, but we were *there* for each other in the best way we knew how.

But even though we had these bonds and supported each other, it wasn't until I began writing this book that my KAOS brothers and I began to share some really intimate things that we had been dealing with both at home and at school while growing up. Even though no topic was off limits back in the day, there were just some things we didn't discuss as kids. I think each of us felt that he was the only one going through what he was going through. Or that we didn't have the language to express what we were feeling anyway, so why bother.

When young people face incredibly stressful events and their sense of security is shattered, the psychological and emotional trauma that results can often leave these young people feeling both vulnerable and helpless in a world that already feels too dangerous. Exposure to trauma can be further complicated by the intersection of gender, race, socio-economic status, and other facets of one's identity and/or circumstances. Even though violence is something that members of our society deal with at least indirectly on a daily basis, many of our youth who live in urban environments face violence of a more acute and direct kind. It's a real struggle. Young people witness their friends and family members being shot, beaten up, killed all around them, and they become understandably angry.

Many of us in KAOS, and especially Curt, were dealing with post-traumatic stress disorder (PTSD) and we didn't even know it. There's much discussion today about how we can treat PTSD in war veterans, and yet there still exists an ominous silence about how to help our young people who go into battle daily on the streets in their own neighborhoods. And because of boys' lack of emotional vocabulary to describe what they're feeling when questioned, this kind of PTSD may be affecting even more young people – and the adults they grow into – than we're aware of. For example, if you were to have asked any of us after Curt's mom died if we were experiencing PTSD, I'm sure we would have told you no. We didn't have the awareness or the understanding of what the full effect of this violence, this trauma was in our lives.

Violence lingers. It's sometimes hard to pinpoint its effects, let alone fix them. And yet we see its manifestations all the time, in boys who are so quick to anger, so quick to throw a punch or hurl a slew of obscenities that seem to erupt out of nowhere. Everything has its origin in something. And every path of destruction leaves a trail.

There's even a growing body of research that links childhood stress and trauma to a higher risk of all sorts of diseases and chronic illness as adults, even if as adults the individuals live relatively low-stress lives. So when we're talking about the effects of stress and trauma on our young people, we might literally be talking about matters of life or death.

There are a lot of theories about the effects of violence on our urban youth, especially in connection with research and conversations about gang culture. And even though theoretical foundations are important, they are only part of the discussion that we need to be having. So often, the conversations focus on blame more than they focus on solutions. Maybe it's because we live in a society where we're a lot better at diagnosing problems than we are at fixing them.

I remember one time not too long ago when I was sitting at a table at Johns Hopkins University with some researchers discussing gang theory. Here I am coming from one of the most notorious gang cities in the country and I'm listening to these researchers theorize about the root causes of why young people join gangs and then go on to inflict such violence on themselves and others. And I couldn't help but ask: "But what can we offer to these young people who are hurting, who are surrounded by the most violent of circumstances day in and day out? How dare we tell these young people not to be in gangs when we're unable to offer them alternate means of connection, support, and protection?"

I'm in no way advocating gangs and gang violence, but I am suggesting we do a better job of providing our boys with a sense of security in the world. We can't tell youth to get *out* of something unless we're willing to work really hard to provide them with something stable and real they can get *into*.

As a teacher, the question often becomes: how do I prepare *myself* for my students who are dying? There's no pedagogy class on this. The irony is that I was doing all of this fighting as a youth and then not too many years later I found myself writing violence prevention manuals. I'm not saying that I was better prepared than anyone else, but I will say that having a personal and human connection to the work we do – whether from our own experiences or from listening to and learning from others' experiences – is important because it gives us some humanity to connect to the theories. Theories alone aren't going to save our children.

We have to be willing to engage in difficult conversations about trauma and loss with our young people even if we're not the ones directly inflicting the pain. And if we know we're unprepared to handle the conversations ourselves, then we need to be humble enough to seek out those who are better equipped. Every time we see or hear another news report of a violent tragedy unfolding, I hope we can recognize that no matter the skin colors of the victims and of those inflicting the violence, we're all in need of some deep healing. Because the mutuality that binds us all means that we're going to have to be able to take better care of each other if we're going to make it in this world.

# CHAPTER 4

# IT TAKES A VILLAGE

*No matter what the name, We're all
the same pieces, In one big chess game.*
- Chuck D.

Back in 1987 when I was still a sophomore at De La Salle, I remember walking home on Green Street after a long night out with Curtis and just wondering where the years had gone. It seemed like we were growing up and changing fast, and as I walked down that familiar street I had to smile to myself. Watching younger kids throw around a football, seeming so carefree, took me back in time for a moment. It seemed like just yesterday that me and my boy Andre had hit the same streets as young kids, playing football with the other neighborhood kids and getting cursed out by the old people for playing ball on their perfectly manicured lawns. We didn't have any fields to play on, so it was either get cursed out or play tackle football on the concrete – as young kids, the most difficult decision we had to make on any given day was whether to endure the cursing or the concrete.

Andre grew up with me on Green Street, and we shared a lot in common. We were very athletic kids and because our builds were so similar, people confused us for each other often, even though we really didn't look anything alike. If I had a dollar for every time people called me Dre and him Nel, I'd be rich. We were also very competitive with each other, and always chose to play on opposing teams just so we could vie against each other. Basketball, football, baseball, racing – it didn't matter *what* we were playing as long as we could go hard and dare each other to win.

Our involvement in sports was a mode of survival for us, even if we were too young to recognize it as such. Although Green Street was relatively safe, we were surrounded by gang territory. In Black Chicago the Disciples gang, also known as the Folks, formed in the South Side in the 1960s and the Stones, also known as the Mos, organized as a Civil Rights organization in the 1950s. Both of these gangs served as Robin Hood for the South Side and fought to protect the community from white and European gangs before they turned on their own. We knew who was affiliated with what gang by the way they wore their hats – Folks had their hats broke to the right and Stones to the left. It didn't matter if you were in the gang or not, whichever gang ruled your neighborhood was the gang you represented. Since Folks ran the Chicago neighborhood that surrounded Green Street, I repped Folks with my hat broke to the right.

Even though we were bounded by gang territory, playing sports gave us a free pass in the Folks territory and most of the kids on our block held that pass like a badge of honor. It wasn't uncommon to see us in Leo High School's empty parking lot playing softball or two-hand touch football or participating in track relays against kids from 79th and Peoria, 80th or 83rd and Green, and Carpenter.

To us, these neighborhood games were serious business. We would come together to practice for our big rivalry matchups and even engaged older kids from the neighborhood to serve as our referees. Two of them, Gerald and David, organized all our competitions because they knew sports like the backs of their hands. They taught us the fundamentals of the games, helped us use rocks to make plays and run drills, and broke up fights when things between us and the other teams got heated.

Dre wore glasses, which didn't go over too well out on the field or court. Those lenses always seemed to either be popping out, fogged up, bent up, or otherwise jacked up. There wasn't a baseball, football or basketball game that went by without him yelling "My lens! My lens!" as he stopped to adjust something on those bootleg glasses of his.

Like me, Dre was raised in a single parent home, except he was raised by his grandmother. His mom wasn't around much, and I don't remember ever meeting his father. He lived with his grandmother, two aunts, and sister Tammy. Dre's grandma was strict and ran a really tight household. Dre was a church kid. He didn't have a choice in the matter. His grandma had him in church all the time. And I mean *all* the time – Sunday service, Sunday school, late service, Vacation Bible School, you name it, Dre was there.

For most of us in the neighborhood, sports served to keep us on track up to a certain point. But as we got older, our neighborhood athletic battles began to be replaced by battles of a different sort. The gangs that surrounded our neighborhood became more and more enticing to some of us, and by the time we reached high school, the streets had begun to pull on Andre. He descended deeper into this other life and it was like his grandmother couldn't save him, his Bible school couldn't save him, the church elders couldn't save him, and his mom – who was struggling with her own demons most of the time – couldn't save him.

Somewhere in between our childhood games and the lure of the streets, though, KAOS entered Andre's life. And even though we couldn't save him, we did give him a place where he felt like he belonged. And he fit in with us – there really wasn't anything hardcore about Andre. He was, like all of us, just a kid looking for a sense of belonging.

Andre became a Junior member of KAOS one day when he saw the crew, about 20 of us in total, hanging out on my porch – joking with one another, laughing, and play fighting.

"Hey Dre!" I called out when I saw him coming down the block bouncing a basketball. "Let me holla at you."

Andre walked up the stairs of my porch and gave me some dap.

"Hey, yo. This is my boy from way back – Dre. He lives across the street and we've known each other since we were kids," I introduced him to KAOS, let everyone know he was cool.

"Wassup," the crew said unanimously, sounding pretty uninterested, as boys often do when meeting someone new.

Dre hung out with us for a while that afternoon, talking and laughing about stuff and that – along with the fact that he was friends with me and Jerry, another KAOS member who lived on my block – was all it took for him to be accepted into the fold.

A few weeks later at a high school dance party, some of the crew noticed that Andre was stepping just like the college fraternities. Someone from KAOS approached him and asked him if he could teach us some moves.

"Yeah, man," Dre replied.

So he offered to teach the crew how to step, and the crew accepted. Those cats spent hours learning the intricate moves Dre taught them, and it paid off. Dre's moves garnered the crew a lot of attention from the ladies. Even Curt, who didn't like to dance, loved to step.

---

But it wasn't all fun and games. I remember one day near the end of my junior year, walking up onto my front porch to my mom standing there waiting for me. I knew immediately that something was wrong. Really wrong.

"LaMarr Darnell Shields! If you don't get your butt in this house..." I would have known that voice anywhere, and I also knew from her tone that my mother was *not* happy. My eyes turned from the hustle and bustle on the block to my mother. And as my eyes met hers, I *knew* that this was a moment I would remember, regretfully, for the rest of my life.

She stood there – stiff, raised eyebrows, characteristically stern look on her face, curly hair pulled back in a tight ponytail – with what appeared to be a letter in her hand. I had a strong inclination that whatever was wrong, I was responsible for it and I was in trouble.

"Ma," I implored cautiously. "What's wrong?"

"*This* is what's wrong," she said as she slapped the piece of paper onto my chest. I grabbed it as she took a step back to watch me read it. I flipped the page over and saw the words "De La Salle Institute" scrolled elegantly across the top. Before I even read the first word, the only thing I could think was *Oh. Shit.*

*To the Parents of LaMarr Darnell Shields, the letter began. We regret to inform you that Mr. Shields has been asked to leave De La Salle Institute. At the beginning of his junior year, he agreed that he would adhere to guidelines and regulations set forth during a meeting with school administration that included amassing no more than 10 infractions. By the end of the year, LaMarr had exceeded this number by one. As a result, he has been asked to leave De La Salle Institute and will not be able to return in the fall.*

I looked at my mother in disbelief. *Exceeded by one infraction. One?! This is bullshit!* I said to myself as I thought back to the first day of junior year when Brother Tim, the school counselor, had brought me to his office and laid down the ground rules for the year.

"For the past two years," he had warned in an unusually stern tone. "Your insubordinate behavior has been a hindrance to your learning here at De La Salle."

*Insubordinate? What does that word mean? Did this white man just call me a racist slur?* I asked myself. I was in his office again, looking at the white Jesus crucifix, mad that it was day one and they were already going in on me, calling me words I hadn't heard of.

"Now, here is how we are going to help you to be focused this year," he instructed as he sat on the edge of his desk, looming over me. "You will have 10 opportunities to make a mistake, and by *mistake* I mean get into a fight, have an altercation with a teacher, or do anything else that would cause you to be sent to my office. Once that tenth infraction occurs, you will be asked to leave De La Salle Institute. Is that understood?"

I looked at him, not knowing how to make full sense of what he was telling me. "Yeah," I mumbled, "I got it."

Ten months later, I stood on my porch looking at this letter outlining my expulsion. I knew that some of my KAOS friends had more infractions than I did and were still at De La Salle. I had to admit, though, that they got their work done and earned better grades than I did. I hoped that had something to do with why they were allowed to stay and I had to go. But I also had Marlon and Larry G., who had paved the way for me out of De La Salle as they had already been asked to leave. I knew, though, that to my mom none of this would matter.

"Ma, I..." I started to plead my case as I followed her inside the house.

"Don't say a word," she instructed. "I just want to know one thing," she implored as she sat down on one of the two newly upholstered couches in our living room. If I had thought she was serious out on the porch, I *knew* Ma meant business now because we were never allowed to sit on those couches. "What are you going to do now?"

I heard in her voice not the disappointment of a single moment, but the disappointment of a lifetime. This disappointment in my mother's voice still rings vividly in my mind today as I speak with single mothers of Black and Brown boys throughout the country – women who, for the most part, are doing the best they can to build bridges between their own struggles and the struggles of their sons.

And the personal disappointment I felt in that moment echoes the disappointment I've seen so often in the young boys I work with. They, I, we – we're disappointed and silenced by our poor emotional vocabularies. We don't have the ability to express in words the depth of our disappointment. We're disappointed in ourselves and in our absent fathers, in our inability to live up to the dreams of our single mothers, in our lack of understanding as to exactly *how* we manage to get ourselves so deep into trouble. And we wonder how to navigate these disappointments without the support mechanisms that we need to help us out, to guide us right, to tell us that somehow, some way, we'll make it out and we'll be okay.

Things shifted in my life when I changed schools. My trek to Leo was not nearly as laborious as my journey to De La Salle had been. There was no stolen bus ride, no trip on the L, no mad dash through the projects. Just a walk across the alley to 7901 S. Sangamon St., the home of Leo Catholic High School.

Leo was founded in 1926 by the Congregation of Christian Brothers of Ireland as an all-male Catholic school named after Pope Leo XIII. By the time I got there, Leo Catholic High School was known primarily for its athletic program, and remains to this day the South Side's athletic hub. As with De La Salle, Leo boasted its own prestigious alumni including Hon. Thomas Fitzgerald, retired Chief Justice of the Illinois Supreme Court, Bishop John Gorman, Auxiliary Bishop of the Archdiocese of Chicago, Corporal John F. Fardy, whose bravery on Okinawa near the end of World War II has been celebrated around the country, and Tim McCarthy, the Orland Park police chief and former Secret Service member who was wounded while saving the life of President Ronald Reagan during his assassination attempt in 1981.

As impressive as all of that was, I still wanted to spend my senior year with my friends at the school I had chosen. And it wasn't only because De La Salle was all I had known, it was also because ever since my freshman year, the Brothers had told us how special we were because our class was the centennial class. Though I had never shared this with my boys, I still wanted to be part of that celebration, to have my photo on the wall as part of that 100th Anniversary class photo. But I no longer had that option because I'd messed up. I would have to settle for spending my last year at Leo, and that was that.

I much later found out that once my mom had made the decision to enroll me in Leo, De La Salle actually called her and said that I could return and graduate with my senior class. But by then my dad was too angry – he responded that De La Salle was too racist and that I was just going to stay at Leo. So at Leo I remained. My father, who wasn't there for so much of my life, seemed to have had the final say on where I'd graduate from high school.

*This school is hot,* I thought to myself as I walked into Leo's foyer. The building was smaller than De La Salle and the floor creaked with every step I took. Everywhere I turned I saw familiar faces from the neighborhood. Although Leo began as a predominately white institution, by the time I arrived there in the late 80s the majority of the student body was African American.

All that was well and good, but I was still nervous. Here I was a senior at a new school feeling like a freshman all over again. Not knowing what else to do, I rebelled. The first week of school this junior cat and I got into it over a girl. We fought in front of the school one afternoon after classes let out. This, of course, didn't bode well for my future at Leo.

The principal immediately pulled me into his office, pacing back and forth in silence for a while before speaking.

"Look, Mr. Shields," he began as he stared me directly in the eyes. "I do not have time for your games. I broke protocol to enroll you in this school in the first place. Now, either you do what you're supposed to do, or you get out!"

He was right. I had already squandered my chance to graduate from De La Salle, and I wasn't going to disappoint my mother, or myself, by getting kicked out of another school. I made a pact with myself in that moment to do better. I had no other choice.

"Okay," I replied. "I hear you."

---

Although by no means De La Salle, Leo began to grow on me. I already had a crew there, as many of my KAOS brothers were Leo students. And the racial climate at Leo was the total opposite of that at De La Salle. From my perspective, now that I was in an environment where I was in the majority, things weren't nearly as volatile as they had been at De La Salle. It seemed that if anything did pop off, it was quickly dealt with and contained. But looking back, I have no way of knowing whether the white kids at Leo felt as I did. For all I know, they could have felt the way I had at De La Salle, as they fought to find their way in an environment where most of their classmates didn't look like them.

I decided not to play sports at Leo. I also realized something very valuable about myself while there, something that I had allowed the climate at De La Salle to keep me from fully acknowledging – I was smart.

Classes at Leo were pretty easy. I didn't know at the time whether that was because some of the curriculum was a repeat of what I had already learned at De La Salle or because the teachers were just more lenient. My GPA, which had been incredibly low at De La Salle, skyrocketed at Leo, as did my ego. Cats thought I was a genius, and I was pleased to become an academic rock star.

My mom, however, was not so easily convinced. She said that the first time my report card came in and she saw all those As, she went right up to the school to see what was going on. It wasn't that she didn't think I was smart, just that the sudden jump in my grades seemed a bit suspect. Sure enough, my mom discovered that much of the senior year curriculum at Leo was the same material that I had already covered my junior year at De La Salle. She was angry, as she tells it, that here she was paying out this money for private school tuition only to have me learn what she had already paid for me to be taught the previous year.

All of my teachers at Leo were white. Mr. Conrad, my English teacher, was the only one who took a real interest in helping me. He was a preppy guy who wore glasses, Dockers and slick button-down shirts. He looked like an Abercrombie & Fitch model. He was a fairly young teacher who believed his mission was to inspire us to do and be better. And he *really* knew his literature.

Mr. Conrad looked like a kid, but I remember he had this really deep voice. And this dude was so smart. I knew nothing about Nelson Mandela's movement prior to entering Mr. Conrad's class. I was coming from English classes at De La Salle where Mr. Duzrak, whom I loved, had had us studying these old dead white men like Chaucer, Blake, Wordsworth, and Shelley. And then here I was at this new school and Mr. Conrad had us reading literature by all these revolutionary Black authors. I admired Mr. Conrad's strong command of his classroom, which was something that Mr. Duzrak just hadn't had over at De La Salle.

One of the things I remember most about Mr. Conrad's class is that it was there that I learned that one of my good friends couldn't read. He was a star athlete and the girls loved him. He was funny and well-respected by his teammates. He and I spent a lot of time together, so it was really painful for me to discover that he had difficulties reading and that I hadn't recognized it before. I was shocked that we were about ready to graduate from high school and my brother couldn't read. Shortly after graduation, I had a conversation with him about it, even though I felt really uncomfortable bringing it up. I wanted him to know that I would do anything to help him, that I had his back both on the streets *and* in the classroom. It wasn't about me judging him, because none of us were perfect, but about letting him know that he didn't have to be ashamed. And I think just being able to have this conversation was important to both of us. Looking back on it now, I'm reminded that it's often during the most uncomfortable exchanges that we gain the most wisdom. I learned in that moment why courageous conversations are so important, especially when we believe that the discussion might give someone the permission to reach out for the help he or she needs, to recognize that none of us are alone in our struggles.

I would later find out, of course, that my friend was not an anomaly. Student-athletes who can't read well, but play in the money-making high school and collegiate sports of football and basketball, are not a new phenomenon. And they certainly weren't only roaming the halls of Leo High School. A CNN investigation uncovered many public universities across the country with students in the basketball and football programs who in college were reading at an eighth-grade level or below. There's also research that indicates that within some of these universities, there's a staggering achievement gap between the collegiate athletes and their non-athletic peers.

In April of 2014, Eric Cooper, the President of the National Urban Alliance for Effective Education, published an article in the Huffington Post entitled "The Real Madness: College Athletes Who Can't Read," which speaks to the implications of reports that college athletes struggle with both reading and coursework. Universities accept the athletes on their athletic merit and then often fail to provide the academic support needed to fill in the gaps. We're cheering these young men on the athletic fields and then letting them fail in the classroom. It's like we care about their success when they've got a ball in their hands, but are unconcerned with what happens when they put down the ball and pick up a book. We have young men playing like adults and reading like fifth graders. As a society, we can and should do better.

So in my friend's honor, I later made it one of my missions to encourage boys to get excited about reading. I created my own movement and called it Boys Read, Too! because I didn't want any of the boys on my watch to end up like my friend. With the assistance of teachers and coaches, my friend did a good job of covering up, but he was the one who had to pay the price. He eventually did get some help, although I'm unclear to this day as to whether he can really read at a proficient level. He's doing well in life now and has made his way in the world as a successful businessman. I'm really proud of him, but I do know that he's still disappointed, looking back, that he was pushed all the way through school and never given the academic help that he so desperately needed.

---

While I managed to be better focused at Leo, I couldn't help but notice that my friend Curtis was falling deeper into street life, even though there were still times that we were inseparable.

After Curtis' mother died and he moved in with his dad, he started to roll around in his dad's pimped out blue Cadillac. That car got us girls and it got us in trouble with the police. One day, we were getting out of the car in front of my house when Chicago's finest surrounded us with their guns drawn. They slammed us on the ground and took our IDs, keys and everything else in our possession that day. I'm not sure what they *thought* we had on us, but all they found were our school books and some Hip-Hop and House cassette tapes. They eventually pulled us up off the curb, demanded to know where we lived – to which I nodded at the house right in front of us – and asked us a host of other questions before letting us go.

Curt and I would go drinking together and fall asleep in the Cadillac, wake up the next morning, wash up in the bathroom at McDonald's, and then hang out all day again. Senior year was slipping away from us and even though we were still tight, I had no true understanding at the time that the slow wedge that was forming between us would soon become a void too large to cross.

One night, our differences became very clear when we talked about going to college.

"Nel, I gotta get out of here," Curt shared. "We're still doing this Morehouse thing, right?"

This was a conversation that I had avoided for quite some time. By Christmas of senior year, I knew that I couldn't go to Morehouse. Though my GPA was a 3.8 at Leo, my sub-par grades at De La Salle meant that my overall GPA was way too low for Morehouse's standards. I had no idea what life after high school graduation held for me, but I did know that college in Atlanta was not an option.

"Yo, man," I said hesitantly. "I can't." As I went on to explain to him my academic reality, I watched his face just sink. He was devastated. Our plan to go to school together was not going to materialize into any sort of actuality. And I think in that moment, it really hit Curtis. Hard.

"Cool," was all he mustered.

One of the things I couldn't wrap my mind around at the time was how quickly Curtis really started to lose his way once he had lost his mom. His mother was his whole world, his compass. Not knowing any better, I thought that he would recover with time, that he would find his way back. But instead I just watched him slip further away from me. And I had no idea how to help him, how to bring him back.

# PART II

MI CASA ES SU CASA

# CHAPTER 5

# IN THE NAVY NOW

*Wisdom is better than silver and gold.*
*I was hopeless, now I'm on hope road.*
- Lauryn Hill

At 18, I knew I had to leave. I had to get out of Chicago and go somewhere. Anywhere. I was determined not to be left behind. The idea of living a life I loved wasn't really in the forefront of my mind. My thoughts were much more along the lines of: *Whatever the hell I do with the next few years of my life, I know I've got to get out of here.* I thought the Navy sounded like a good idea because I knew that I'd need money to pay for college someday. After looking at my grades and my mother's bank account, I knew there was no Morehouse College in my future. But I thought if I had some money saved up, I might have a fighting chance at somehow getting to college somewhere.

I graduated from Leo with Honors. At graduation I could not help but feel a tinge of sadness as I stood in my traditional tuxedo next to my classmates. *I should be graduating with my boys at De La Salle,* I kept thinking. Though I was proud that I had made it, that I had accomplished something great, I still believed it would have been so much greater at De La Salle. I also could not shake the sense of academic failure that had haunted me during my time at De La Salle. It's like no matter how much I had proven to myself at Leo that I was actually smart, that academics were something at which I could excel, it was hard to let go of the damaging words of Señor Hogan, other teachers, and my white classmates – constantly reminding me that I didn't belong, that I wasn't worthy, that I'd never go anywhere or make anything of myself.

This feeling of inadequacy just became more pronounced when I looked around at all my KAOS brothers preparing to go away to college while I, at the time, was going nowhere. I felt like I should have had some clearer direction, but I was so aimless. And in my lack of direction, I felt like I was letting down not only myself and my mother, but all my KAOS brothers as well.

Larry was the first of KAOS to leave for college. Larry and I were both expelled from De La Salle the same year, and that shared experience bonded us even though we ended up going on to graduate from different high schools. He was headed to Xavier in New Orleans. Larry had been the most out of control dude growing up, even though his mom and step-dad were strict. He was the guy I used to cut school with. And yet he was still somehow able to get into a really good college.

The night before Larry left for Xavier, we decided to send him off in a way he'd never forget. We knew we'd be able to dare him to do anything because he was just down like that. So all of us drove over to his house, walked up to the house together, and rang the doorbell.

"Hey boys," Larry's mother greeted us with a smile as she flung open the door. "What are you all doing here so late?"

"Good evening," we chimed in unison.

"You know we couldn't let Larry leave without saying goodbye," Rich added in his best Catholic schoolboy voice.

Larry's mother smiled before turning and calling for her son.

Larry came to the door cautiously. He already knew we were up to something. "Wassup, fellas?" he asked.

"Get out here, boy!" one of us yelled before snatching him out of the doorway and nudging him down the stairs and onto the driveway.

"Close the door!" I yelled to Rich, who promptly complied.

Almost immediately, we started ripping off Larry's undershirt, shorts, boxers and socks – all the while singing our KAOS theme song, "Everywhere we go, we let the people know that KAOS is in the house!" until Larry was stripped completely naked. By the time we were finished with him, his underwear dangled on top of his mother's car antenna like the American flag.

Larry yelled out to his mother, "Ma! Ma! Look at me! They took off all of my clothes!"

When she heard his yelling, she opened the front door, only to see her son, surrounded by KAOS, butt naked in the driveway.

"Boy, get your narrow behind back in this house!" she exploded in typical mom fashion. "And all of you, take your behinds home, too!"

We all gave him some dap and laughed.

"This was cold, man. Just cold," Larry uttered as he bent down to pick up the scraps of his clothes off the ground before trudging back inside his house. He still had a huge grin on his face, though. He knew this was our way of sending him off to the next chapter of his life in true KAOS form, and he knew we all loved him.

We didn't realize it at the time because Larry was the first to go off to school, but with his leaving we started a ritual that we'd carry with us through a lot of goodbyes and transitions. And the soundtrack to these goodbyes was always the New Edition song, "Boys to Men," that reminded us of our crew.

When boys don't have structure or rituals, they create their own. We wanted to be on the other side of drugs and gangs and even though we weren't a gang, we did have a lot of the same characteristics as one – we had our own rituals and we were able to stand in the gap for each other when many of us didn't have men in our lives to fill that role.

---

But no matter how strong our KAOS bonds were, it was time for us to start to forge our own individual paths. No matter how scary that seemed to me at the time, I knew I had to get it together.

I had first gotten the idea to go to the Navy after attending a college fair my senior year at Leo. I was in a different place in my life than the day me and my boys in KAOS had rolled into that first college fair and had our eyes opened to the possibility of attending HBCUs. I was beginning to let go of that dream and figured it was time to be practical and to figure *something* out.

"The Navy is the best place for high school graduates," the recruiter told me. "You get to travel the world, all the while receiving a paycheck."

*Travel? Paycheck?* That was all I needed to hear. I took the ASVAB, a test used to predict "academic and occupational success in the military" and when my test results came back affirming my academic promise, I shared with my boys what I was about to do.

"Nel, are you out of your mind?" they asked, confused. I had known that they would be upset, mainly because I had always talked about going to college after high school. But I felt like the Navy was my only real option. My mother would never allow me to sit around her house, hanging out and eating up all her food with no plan. So, since I couldn't go to Morehouse and needed a way to pay for whatever college I did end up attending, entering the military and then going to school on the GI bill seemed like the next best thing.

"No," I replied. "My mind is made up. I leave on September 25th."

Curtis looked at me. Hard. But he never said a word.

---

The four-hour flight from Chicago to Orlando was the first airplane ride of my life, and I was infinitely more nervous on that day than I was on my first day at Leo, more nervous than all those days running through the projects on my way to school at De La Salle. Sitting on that plane, I just couldn't stop my mind from racing: *What's going to happen once this plane lands? What will the Navy be like? What have I gotten myself into? How soon will I be able to go home?*

It seemed like only seconds after debarking the plane that I was funneled straight into a room where an officer stood waiting to cut my hair.

"I already cut it low so you wouldn't have to," I offered, hoping that would be enough to keep him from shaving my head.

"Sit down and shut up," was his reply.

The next morning, I woke up at a Naval training center in Orlando, Florida. I was startled out of sleep before dawn by the sound of a drill sergeant shouting, "Wake up. Wake up. Wake UP! You have exactly 10 minutes to shit, shower and shave. I would suggest you get your asses out of bed now and get moving!"

I hopped out of bed with the others, ran down the hall to the bathroom, and took the quickest shower of my life. I knew in that moment that the Navy was not the place for me.

We did a lot of marching – from the mess hall, to the barracks, to the training field and back again. And we did a lot of saluting to every ranking officer who walked into any room. I didn't like any of it. At all. Our training also included a lot of endurance testing, including swimming and running. Thank goodness I liked to run and could keep up, because otherwise I would have been in big trouble.

By the end of my first week, I had broken out badly and my skin was burning. I was in desperate need of hydrocortisone cream, but I didn't say a word to the sergeant. I had learned quickly from my observations that anyone who spoke up was verbally assaulted, and I just wasn't up for playing into these officers' mind games. In my own mind, I was already working on a plan to get home. And fast.

During the second week of my Navy stint, I found out that my father was having open-heart surgery. That same week, I was called in for hearing and vision tests that I purposely failed, and I likewise faked some ailments so I could be sent to Medical where I would wait to be released and sent home to Chicago. The next three weeks while I awaited my release were the longest 21 days of my life.

We weren't assigned many responsibilities in Medical, mainly because we were supposed to be sick. While there, I encountered Southern whites for the first time. They were different from the whites I'd known at De La Salle in that they were open and blatant in calling us names like "coon" and "nigger" to our faces.

Reflecting back, one of the paradigms that spending those years at De La Salle instilled in me was a distrust, and sometimes even disdain, of white people. So now here I was in the Navy – in an environment where I was openly being called "nigger" – and the only Black officer I encountered, who I thought should have had my back, just didn't. The officers would tell us that the only color they saw was blue.

While in Medical, I also encountered the Blackside Posse – a group created by the African Americans as a form of protection from the white boys during our time together in Medical. The way that the men in the Blackside Posse interacted with and took care of each other reminded me of KAOS. And they took me in without question.

One day as we sat around Medical doing nothing much, one of the members of the Posse asked me if I'd ever read the "Autobiography of Malcolm X."

"Nope, never read it," I replied.

"Here, young blood," one of them offered as he handed me the book. "It will change your life."

I was no stranger to Malcolm X. Though I'd spent my days in Catholic school, some of my family members were part of the Nation of Islam and often spoke of Malcolm X and his teachings. Growing up, I was more of a follower of Rev. Dr. Martin Luther King, Jr., but reading the "Autobiography of Malcolm X" allowed me not only to see Malcolm X and his philosophy in a new light, but to reconsider Dr. King and his philosophy as well. It made me look intensely at both their lives and their friends and to see why their life experiences were so different in many ways. It made me think about the decisions Malcolm X made that precipitated the way he lived and died.

The timing of reading this influential book couldn't have been better. I began to experience a transformation while reading it during a period in my life when I so desperately needed some change. In the book, Malcolm X recounts telling his teacher that he wanted to be a lawyer and his teacher responding that "niggers don't become lawyers" and that Malcolm X needed to "do something with his hands." From then on, most everything Malcolm X did he did with his hands, including fighting, shooting up, beating women, and committing armed robbery.

This account underscored the fact that we need to be so mindful of the words we use with young people, and it got me thinking about what I could do with my own hands that *didn't* involve fighting. I wanted to write poetry and stories. And later when I started to work with boys of color, I'd always recommend this book to them because I wanted the young men to be exposed to the message that has stuck with me always – a message about transforming your life from the space that you're in and ultimately finding your calling, your purpose in the world.

Getting kicked out of De La Salle and then going into the Navy were probably two of the most transformational times in my young life, even though they were such short seasons and were so difficult for me. But I learned, as I read that Malcolm X had too, that sometimes it is only in going away that we become more clearly ourselves. It wasn't until Malcolm X traveled to Mecca that he saw that he wanted to do something different in his life.

While in Mecca, Malcolm X was exposed to the concept of "universal respect and brotherhood" that changed his entire outlook on life. He began to shift away from the notion that all white people were evil and, with this realization, moved away from preaching Black separatism.

Reading the book helped me to make a decision about what I was going to do once I returned home. I knew that I needed to apply to and enroll in college as soon as possible. I knew that I needed to expand my horizons, that I needed an education. I was hungry for change. Scared, of course, of all the unknown territory ahead, but hungry nevertheless.

I was shipped back to Chicago on October 21$^{st}$, exactly 26 days after I'd first left home. My boys scooped me up from the airport and thought it was funny to see me in my dress whites. Though we were all happy to see each other, I knew my time back home would be short. Soon after my return to Chicago, I applied for late enrollment at Grambling State University in Louisiana. While I waited to find out whether or not Grambling was going to accept me, I sold cemetery plots as a telemarketer, saved money, and prepared to enter the next phase of my life.

Looking back on it now, the song "All My Life" by the Foo Fighters was kind of a theme song to my life up to that point. Being the youngest child in my family, being so sickly growing up, having a late birthday, and then being the first one to go so far away – first to the Navy and then to college – it was like I was "all my life... searching for something. Something never comes, never leads to nothing. Nothing satisfies but I'm getting close. Closer to the prize at the end of the rope."

I was getting close to something big, although I had no way of knowing exactly what that was at the time. My acceptance letter to Grambling came before Christmas and shortly after the New Year I left Chicago and made the long journey south to Louisiana.

# CHAPTER 6

# GRAMBLING: WHERE EVERYBODY IS SOMEBODY

*They're gonna try to tell you no, shatter all your dreams.*
*But you gotta get up and go and think of better things.*

- Mac Miller

My mom delivered me to the Greyhound bus station in downtown Chicago on a frigid January morning. She had planned on driving me down to Grambling State University herself – she would have driven me anywhere – but was scheduled to go in for surgery that week, which left no choice but for me to make the journey on my own. She dropped me off at the bus station with nothing more than a big trunk filled with my stuff, a bus ticket, and some prayers. She hugged me goodbye and told me that this was my opportunity to become a man.

Ready or not, I stepped onto that bus – decked out in my Chicago Bulls hat and coat – and headed south, all alone, to begin my adult life. It took me a full 24 hours to travel from Chicago through all of Illinois, Tennessee, Arkansas and Mississippi before finally arriving in Grambling, Louisiana. During the bus trip I thought about my immediate future – all the new people I'd meet, the new places I'd explore, the new experiences I'd have. I was nervous about showing up alone in this unfamiliar place, sight unseen. But I was excited!

What I did know was that Grambling was a HBCU made famous by its world-renowned marching band and Coach Eddie Robinson, the winningest coach in collegiate football history. I had also done a bit of research to learn more about the college.

Eighty-five years before I arrived at Grambling, a group of African American farmers, part of the North Louisiana Colored Agricultural Relief Association, had decided that they wanted to open and operate a school for Blacks in the region. They reached out to Booker T. Washington, who had founded his own college for

African Americans called Tuskegee Institute in Alabama, and asked him for help getting started. Washington sent a good friend, Charles P. Adams, to assist. Adams subsequently became the first president of the college, which opened up as the Colored Industrial and Agricultural School in 1901. More than two decades after its founding, the school underwent a name change and became the Louisiana Negro Normal and Industrial Institute. At this time, the school began awarding two-year diplomas and professional certificates to graduates. Less than a decade later the school changed its focus to teacher education and in 1944 awarded its first degree in elementary education. It wasn't until 1946 that the school became known as Grambling State University. That most recent name change took place when white patron P.G. Grambling donated the land on which the school had been constructed. Three years later, Grambling was accredited by the Southern Association of Colleges and Schools.

I didn't know until I arrived at Grambling that not only was I going to the South, I was going to the country. And the magnitude of what I was about to do – start a new phase in my life at this strange school where I knew virtually no one – really hit me when I stepped off the Greyhound bus. I took one look around at the sleepy bus station, which looked *nothing* like the bus station back in Chicago, and realized that I really was on my own. *It should never be this hot in January,* I thought to myself.

My first impression of the area was unremarkable. I arrived on a Sunday, and in small Southern towns Sundays mean nothing is open because everyone is either at church or, well, at church. The bus station, which was just a small room where people waited to board Greyhounds traveling in every direction, was vacant except for a lone employee stationed at a solitary desk.

"Excuse me, sir," I began as politely as I could muster. "My trunk is missing." The man looked up from whatever he was reading, but didn't say a word.

"Sir, I said my trunk is missing," I repeated a little more insistently.

"I heard you the first time, young man," the clerk said in his thick Southern drawl before slowly getting up to walk toward the bus outside. I followed him.

Together we searched the storage compartment looking for my belongings, but came up empty.

"Give me your luggage ticket," he instructed as he held out his hand for the little green stub I had placed in my pocket before boarding the bus back in Chicago. I rummaged for it and handed it to him. He turned and walked away from me without another word and – after what seemed like an eternity – he returned and handed me back my ticket. My trunk wasn't anywhere in sight.

"Somehow your luggage traveled to New Orleans without you," he said. "It should be back here tomorrow. You can pick it up then."

*Great.*

I walked out of the small bus terminal, glanced to my right, and was surprised to see a mini-steeple with a sign that read "Grambling State University: Where Everybody is Somebody." *Well, at least I made it to the right place.*

One of my first challenges after locating the main office and checking into my dorm room was to figure out how to register for classes the next day. I woke up that Monday morning, returned to the bus depot to retrieve my trunk – which had thankfully made its way back from New Orleans – and then headed over to registration. I remember that the lines were crazy long, but I didn't even care. I was excited to be at college, a place of higher learning, surrounded by brothers and beautiful women, all of whom looked like me. Everything seemed like a mess, but I didn't want to be anywhere else but in the middle of that mess. It was overwhelming, but awesome.

I was standing on campus one of those first days, with nothing but a book in my hand and a confused look on my face, when a woman's voice caught my attention.

"Boy, where you from?" she inquired.

I looked around to make sure she was talking to me before I replied. She introduced herself as Barbara Lewis and I quickly learned that not only was she a counselor at the University, she was also a Chicago native and somehow knew one of my uncles. She took me under her wing, brought me to her office, and looked up my admissions file. She told me that I was eligible for a scholarship due to a high ACT score that I didn't even know I had earned. She walked me through the steps to applying for the scholarship and facilitated my navigation of the registration process. She even helped me get free textbooks that first semester.

She and my mother later connected and remain good friends to this day. I learned from my interactions with Mrs. Lewis that people will look out for you if you are humble enough to accept help when it's offered. She and I often battled about anything and everything, but I knew she always had my best interests at heart. She became a major ally, taught me how to successfully find my way through the college system, and introduced me to the right people.

It didn't take me long to make friends. I lived in Knott Hall, which was the athletes' dorm. I felt at home there and even had the intention of running collegiate track. But when I arrived in Louisiana I realized it was too hot to run. I was glad, however, to live among athletes. Grambling, like a lot of Southern colleges, was a huge football school. And I loved being in the middle of the action.

Foreign language was mandatory for political science majors at Grambling, and I naturally chose Spanish to meet this requirement. My first Spanish professor was an African American woman, and I sensed from day one that she was not a strong Spanish speaker. On the second day of class, she approached me and let me know that she could tell from the drills we had done in class the day before that I really knew the language. She invited me to take a test that, if I passed, would allow me to advance to the next level of instruction.

I had only taken two years of Spanish at De La Salle, but the language was in my blood. I knew that I had a deeper understanding of Spanish than most of the people in my college classroom, including my professor. But before I could get too far ahead of myself, become too confident in my skills, I felt Señor Hogan's words creep back into the forefront of my mind: "No, I do not encourage you to move on to Spanish III." This time, though, I decided that even though he thought I couldn't do it, I wasn't going to let that man's belief in me, or lack thereof, stop me from going after what I wanted. I knew I could pass that Spanish test! And I was determined to prove Señor Hogan wrong.

"I'm in!" I told my professor. "How soon can I take the test?"

"Meet me in the classroom across the hall tomorrow morning at 10 a.m.," she replied. "You can take it then."

And that's how I found myself, less than one week into my first semester of college, sitting in a classroom in Woodson Hall taking a test to see if I could skip Spanish I.

The exam was so easy that I almost felt insulted. It tested my knowledge of simple vocabulary like colors, days of the week, numbers and basic phrases. I damn near took it with my eyes closed. Word about me passing the test spread, and Eric – my man from Indianapolis who was always looking for a hook-up – came to me and said, "Look Nel, everybody knows you passed that Spanish I test. I don't want to sit up in that class another day. Can you take the test for me?" I laughed at him because I knew that he of all people *really* needed that intro class.

But I also thought, *What the hell? I can take that test again!*

"Sure man," I told Eric. "Let me know when and where she wants you to take the test and I'll do it for you."

"My man," he said before giving me some serious dap. I passed his test, too.

---

This is how I found myself in Dr. Charles Brooks' Spanish II class less than two weeks into my first college term. Dr. Brooks was a brown-skinned intellectual who stood no taller than 5'9". He had a thin black mustache and even though he was not a buff dude, he made up for his lack of physical stature with his impeccable taste in clothing – suits pressed, bowties down, shoes shined. We all considered him the most dapper professor on campus. Dr. Brooks was the foreign language department and only students who he deemed as gifted were granted admission to the upper levels of Spanish, so having a chance to be in this man's class as a freshman was just amazing to me.

Dr. Brooks may have been brilliant, but he wasn't overly nice in the classroom. In fact, sometimes he could be downright rude. He was very sarcastic, which most of us didn't appreciate, and his Spanish pronunciation was not the greatest. He'd do this weird thing when he spoke the language where the words would come out through his teeth – kind of like my mama used to do before she whooped me when I was a kid. Also, like many professors at Grambling, he had a level of arrogance to him. In his case, maybe this was because he had almost single-handedly built the college's entire foreign language department from the ground up.

Despite his poor pronunciation and discourteous demeanor, though, Dr. Brooks did have a strong command of the grammatical structure of the language and a love for and deep knowledge of Latin cultures. He really pushed me in class and from the very beginning of Spanish II he regaled me with all of the advanced courses I'd be eligible to take in the next few years. I was part of a small group of rock star students who he really challenged. He had us reading and translating Spanish literature almost from the start, which amazed me. I finally, for the first time in my academic career, felt like I might be able to master something that had started off as, literally, such a foreign concept.

---

I began to fall into a pretty smooth routine at Grambling, although of course I'd get homesick from time to time. I had a hard time with the fact that Curt and I seemed to be growing further apart, but tried to convince myself that it was probably due to the physical distance between us as much as anything else. Everything was going well. And then I got the call.

It was a Saturday morning in late spring. I was coming off of one of those legendary college nights that I knew I'd remember for years to come when I was jolted from a deep sleep by the loud ring of the phone in my dorm room. I picked up to hear the voice of my cousin, Jerry, on the other end of the line, but it took me a minute to figure out what he was trying to tell me. He was thousands of miles away in Chicago talking about Andre and how he had given him a hug and had sent him off to the prom. All I could think at first was, *Man, Jerry, do you realize what time it is? Why are you calling me so early to tell me about Andre's prom night?* And then I started to comprehend what Jerry was actually saying and I dropped to my knees. *Dre is what? Dre is DEAD?!*

Andre was found dead in an ally very close to his grandma's house, his childhood home, crouched down in the fetal position. He had been shot in the leg. The bullet had hit an artery, which ruptured, and he just bled out.

I listened as Jerry told me this, but I couldn't really comprehend, let alone accept, the words I was hearing. Even then, as mature as I thought I was, as close to death as my KAOS boys and I may have come a few times on the streets of Chicago, I just didn't think that any of us could actually *die*. Like most boys, we thought we were somehow invincible. Untouchable. Like Al Capone.

I hung up the phone with Jerry – what else was there to say? – and wept silently on my knees in my dorm room alone, not wanting to wake my two roommates.

A few short days later, I sat in Curtis' car in front of the Greyhound station in downtown Chicago, preparing to roll with him to Andre's funeral, where I was slated to speak. Curt and I learned on that car ride that when each of us had each gotten the news that Andre was dead, the very first person to come to mind was the other. We agreed that as hard as it was to try to comprehend Andre's death, as much as this hurt, if anything were to happen to one of the two of us we didn't know if we'd be able to survive it.

It was the first time I remember us being so transparent with each other. While driving to the funeral, I also told Curt that I was so nervous to speak and that I wasn't sure how people were going to receive my message. It would be the first time that the cats in KAOS would hear me talk on something so serious. Curt assured me that I would do well, that there was no one more qualified to deliver words of comfort to our crew that day.

What struck me about Andre's death was that even though I didn't think that it should have happened to any kid I knew, it *really* shouldn't have happened to Andre. As I've said before, Andre was a church kid who grew up with his grandmother in a very loving household. He had so much support growing up, so much love surrounding him, so much faith to guide him. And he was a smart cat. By every indication, he should have made it out okay. He should have at *least* been able to survive his childhood. But he didn't.

I don't think we can examine what Andre's death did to those who loved him, though, until we first delve more deeply into his life. Andre literally began his life on the move. His mother, Carolyn, gave birth to him in the car on the way to the hospital.

She described it like this: *It was wonderful. He was born in the car. I didn't have any hard labor with him or anything. He was my first child, my baby boy. I loved him to death. He was a healthy seven pounds at birth. I was 18 years old when I had him and was still living at my mama's house. I was home the day that my water broke and I just kept walking around the house until I finally fell to my knees. And my mama told me I better get up off my knees so we could go to the hospital.*

Carolyn shared that when she first brought home the news that she was pregnant, her mom had been very upset. But despite her mom's disappointment, Carolyn herself was nothing but happy from the very beginning. As she recalled, *I just knew I was going to drop out of school and stay home and take care of my baby. I thought it'd be easy because I was already kind of taking care of my younger siblings.*

When Andre was an infant, Carolyn raised him as a single parent with the help of her mother. Andre's father wasn't around because Carolyn never told him that she was pregnant with his child. When he would ask her about her pregnancy, she would tell him that the baby wasn't his. When asked why she lied to Andre's father, she responded that she was *young and confused, you know. I wanted to be grown and take care of everything on my own.*

Carolyn says that her mama never asked her who Andre's father was. She says that she used to sneak around quite a bit before she got pregnant, so her mom really didn't know who she was with or what she was doing.

Andre never knew who his father was, either. Carolyn says that she doesn't remember Andre ever asking about his dad: *In a way I do regret not telling him and in a way I don't. I was disappointed in the type of person his father became and I didn't want Andre to know about any of that.* Also, Carolyn married another man when Andre was very young, so she believes that maybe Andre thought her husband was his father and that was why he never asked her who his dad was.

Carolyn's bond with her son was a close one: *Andre and I were very, very close. I loved my baby with all my heart. It was hard, but I really didn't get a chance to finish raising him because of his death. It happened so fast, so it all just kind of got cut off. I had my mother and she helped me out so much. She used to say, "Well, you had him, but this is my baby."*

Carolyn said that she and Andre remained close, even though when he was young his grandma, Carolyn's mother, actually gained full custody of him. Carolyn lived elsewhere with her then husband and Andre's younger siblings. Carolyn described it like this: *I was young when I got married. Andre stayed with me for awhile, but then one day there were these bruises on his leg and we went back to Mama's house. She asked me about the bruises and I said I didn't know how he got them, because I didn't, but she thought my husband had done it. So after that I had to go to court and that's how Mama ended up with Andre. I could see him, but I couldn't have him around my husband. I was over at my mother's house a lot, doing what I had to do. Nothing could stop me from being with my child. There was some abuse, I think, with Andre and my husband. Andre never talked about it – he was real little. He probably wouldn't even remember it.*

Carolyn shared that she really regretted getting married: *I shouldn't have put nobody over my son. I was young and I thought it was love, but it wasn't love.* She also confided that she was pretty wild in her younger years: *Yeah, when I am talking to people and telling them about my life – I'll be honest with you, I had fun, but I was young. I didn't know then what I know now. I'm supposed to know better now, but when I was young I had a baby and thought I was grown, but I was far from grown.*

The biggest regret of Carolyn's, life, however, was losing Andre too early. I got the call about Andre's death not long after Carolyn herself found out that her son had died. She recalled the day, in intimate detail: *I was working at a thrift store on 94th and Ashland when my cousin Alice came in and said, "Carolyn, you gotta go! I said, "I gotta go where? I can't go anywhere. I'm on the register." I kept asking Alice what was wrong, but she wouldn't tell me. I remember her going to find my manager and then coming back and saying that it was alright for me to leave, that I needed to come with her.*

*Alice drove me to my mama's house and I remember thinking it was strange that there were all these people on Mama's porch. Alice still wouldn't say anything. We walked into the house and these detectives were there and I remember one of them telling me that he wanted to show me some pictures of my son. Then he* said, "Your son is dead." Just like that. And I said, "No he's not. He's probably over at his girlfriend's house. He's not dead. I just seen him last night." Andre had come over to the house the night before and asked me if I needed anything and I told him yes, I wanted a pack of cigarettes. And so of course he went out and got them for me. I do remember that he was with this guy that night that I had never seen before. I knew all his friends and so I thought it was strange, but I was steady drinking that night and didn't have a chance to ask him about who he was with.

So I'm standing there in my mama's house and the detectives say that I have to look at some more pictures and I say that I don't want to see no more pictures. I had to send some other family members to the morgue to identify his body because I just couldn't go. And they came back and said that he looked so peaceful, like he was just asleep. That's when I passed out. And Mama came home from volunteering at the hospital and then she found out and got really upset.

Less than a week after Carolyn heard the news of her son's death, we were all gathered together for a funeral. It wasn't really the sort of college homecoming and KAOS reunion I had expected, but there we were.

I asked Carolyn what she remembers from the day of the funeral, and she shared the following: *The funeral was bad. I didn't want to accept it. I didn't believe it. My baby son, Marquis, he's the one who helped me through it. Marquis had to be 10 or 11 when Andre died and he coached me through it all. Immediately after the funeral, I was still being Miss Grown. I was fast, running around the streets, trying to block it out of my head. When I started reading the articles in the newspapers and his obituary and the autopsy report, that's when it all started to sink in. I have all those things still. I look through them sometimes.*

*So when Andre died, my baby son Mickey (Marquis) was 10 or 11 and my daughter Tammy was a teenager. Mickey was young, so he really didn't know what was going on. But Tammy knew a lot of stuff about Andre that I didn't know. She was real upset about his death, but I wouldn't talk to them about that. I just left it alone. We didn't talk about grief or anything. I just let it take its course.*

Since the day of Andre's death, Carolyn has never driven by the street where they found her son's body. She'll drive all the way around the block just to avoid having to pass by where he died. And to this day she doesn't know who killed her baby.

When asked about her hopes and dreams for Andre, she said: *I thought he was going to be an athlete because he loved playing football, but he didn't have a chance – he died right when he was getting ready to graduate from high school. I had him when I was 18 and he died when he was 18. I didn't graduate from high school and he didn't have a chance to either.*

When asked what message she had for mothers, she replied: *Well, for one I tell them you have to keep your hands in your face and praise Jesus because He's the only one who can help and get you through. You might want to try to work it out yourself, but it's not up to you. It's up to God. You have to keep praying over your children. You treasure all those moments until your babies get big and you can't hug 'em and rock 'em anymore. Andre wasn't no bad child at all. He always told me he loved me. He never gave my mama no problems. We stayed in church – all of us was raised in church from little on up, so it was either Mama's way or no way. So if Andre did miss out on something, it was for the best. But when he got out there in the world and was around people that I didn't know, I feel I kinda lost him. All children do something behind their parents' back, though. I didn't know what was going on with my son like my mama didn't know what was going on with me. There were rumors that he was in a gang, but I really don't know. I struggle a lot with my memory.*

And for young men, her message is to *be obedient to your parents and stay in church. Like I tell my grandchildren now, you have to be obedient because the Bible doesn't lie. You have to study the Word. They be saying, "Grandma, you too holy." But it pays off. We aren't going to make it out here on our own. You've got to keep your hands in God's hands. He will make you stronger. I don't have no animosity toward whoever killed Andre. And I told my baby son, Mickey, when he lost his son – my grandson – and asked me how I coped, I told him that I just put it in God's hands.*

So I spoke at Andre's funeral. And it was there at the altar that I knew in my heart that whatever I did with my career, speaking and inspiring people was going to be an important part of my path. I knew I wanted to provide hope, support and empowerment to help individuals and families overcome whatever challenges life threw at them. I knew I wanted to help people be and do better. The response that I received at the funeral from the crew, my family, and Dre's family affirmed for me that I had a gift to move a crowd and I knew I needed to use it. Somehow. Some way.

My message that day was "What Makes You So Strong," which was inspired by Rev. Jeremiah Wright's book by the same name and a poem by Sterling Brown called "Strong Men Keep A' Coming." I almost mimicked Rev. Wright's sermon upon which his book was based. I shared his metaphors of strength.

Then I spoke about hope and about being called home. Living on Green Street as children, we neighborhood kids always had to be home at a certain time. There was such a predictability to the hum of the evening routine – some of us had to be in when the street lights came on, some of us had to be in when we were called for dinner, some of us had to be in when our older siblings rounded us up. I used this image of us being called into our homes to paint a metaphorical picture of Andre being called home, at a time that was all his own. I talked about the fact that Andre's death marked a new beginning for all of us – for Andre, for his family, for me and my boys in KAOS who were away at college, for the Junior KAOS members preparing to graduate from high school and enter college or the workforce.

And I talked about change. About how our KAOS crew had spoken a lot about our dreams and futures before that day, but we had never discussed our own deaths. And that from that point forward, we'd no longer be able to say that. I spoke about how Andre's death was about us getting stronger. About how each loss in our lives would bring us closer.

My KAOS brothers and I stood outside the funeral parlor after the service just hugging each other and letting the tears fall. I remember there was a strong police presence on the block that day because there were rumors that Andre's death had been gang-related and the cops were wary of some sort of retaliation.

---

A few days after the funeral, I was back on a Greyhound bus headed south to finish up the final month of my freshman year in college. I returned to Grambling a different person than I had been just a week before. Death changes you.

Back at college, many of my friends expressed their surprise that Andre was the first friend I had lost. Many of them had buried so many friends by then. Grambling had a large population of students from California and it seemed like so many of my West Coast friends especially were kind of numb to death by this point. I remember them telling me, "Yeah, we've lost a lot of homies. We're used to it. You'll get used to it, too."

I didn't want to get used to it. Ever. And I was both saddened and concerned by the numbness that my college friends expressed on the subject. I wondered what this said, not about them as individuals, necessarily, but about the society in which we were living.

I was pretty homesick during the last month of my freshman year. I had only been away at Grambling for a few short months, but I was ready to go home for the summer. I had a girlfriend in Chicago at the time. I missed my mom. I missed my KAOS crew. And I was worried about someone else dying before I arrived back in Chicago. The talk of retaliation for Andre's death that had been swirling around since the funeral made me uncomfortable and anxious. I just felt like I needed to be home.

Summer came before I knew it, though, and I returned to Chicago for what I can only describe as a legendary Chicago summer. During the days I worked with kids at the YMCA and at night KAOS partied. A lot of Chicago kids went away to school at HBCUs, so there were parties all around the city catering to the different colleges. One night it was a Spelman party and the next night it was a Morehouse or Hampton party. And KAOS just made the rounds.

And then there was the Taste of Chicago, the world's largest food festival and an iconic staple of any Chicago summer. This was *the* place to be seen, and all the college kids home for the summer flocked to the festival, sporting their school gear and expanded horizons. Of course KAOS was right up in the mix. The festival was held then, as it still is today, in Grant Park, adjacent to Lake Michigan in downtown Chicago. When we were in high school, KAOS was known for picking up girls and fighting at the Taste. But returning to the scene as college kids, we had let go of the fighting and were just there for the girls. We rarely ate there, though, because the food was so expensive and if we had the money we wanted to save it to spend on other things. Like partying. And girls.

It wasn't all about partying that summer, though. Those of us who were home from college knew that we also had some knowledge to impart to our Junior KAOS members. To that end, we would stage huge KAOS debates about HBCUs versus traditional, predominantly white colleges. We Senior KAOS members would arrive at the debates sporting our college gear and then debate in front of our audience, the Junior KAOS crew, who had just graduated from high school and were anticipating heading off to college themselves in the fall. My cousin Jerry was home from Southern University in Baton Rouge, Lance was representing Iowa State. Derrick G. was repping Louisville. Clarence was home from Morris Brown. Seron talked about his experience at Morehouse. Marlon and George had returned home from the University of Arkansas at Pine Bluff. Des was back from the University of Illinois at Champaign-Urbana and Larry G. was home from Dillard. Kelvin joined us from Northern Illinois University. Steve, Dion and Rod talked about their time at the Illinois State. Bill, Maurice and Mike R. had attended Western Illinois University. Troy was at Chicago State. Curtis and Rich recounted their experiences at the University of Illinois at Chicago. Wood and Aaron (Julio) had attended Southern Illinois University. Mike G. had gone to Daley College. And Marcus was home from Northeast Missouri State (now Truman State University).

It was crazy to think that just a couple of years earlier, we Senior KAOS members had been wandering around that college fair wide-eyed, like the blind leading the blind, and now the Junior KAOS members had all of us as real-life examples of what was possible, what college looked like. It looked like them. It looked like us. It looked like KAOS.

I lived with my mom and my older brother that summer – my sisters were both living on their own by then – and as much as I had longed to be home, once I got there a part of me really missed college life. At Grambling, there was always something popping off in the yard. I had become accustomed to living with all of my friends and had gotten used to a life of constant excitement. The tension I felt between my two different worlds – my college one and my Chicago one – seemed to grow increasingly stronger as the summer wore on.

And all of the time spent rolling with KAOS was juxtaposed against a deep loneliness that I felt that summer. I had difficulty sleeping. At night I dreamed of losing my friends, wondering who would be next. I reflected on all the street fights we had been involved in and how close we *all* may have been to dying at one time or another. We had fought over such petty things, not important causes like those of the people I was beginning to study and learn about in college had fought over. I'd get lost in books – picturing KAOS marching during the Civil Rights Movement and fighting in Soweto alongside Nelson Mandela. I'd picture us protesting with Che Guevara and Fidel Castro in Cuba or Zapata in Mexico, shouting "La Lucha Continua!" The struggle continues.

I began to see that, collectively, KAOS had so much pent-up energy, so much pain. We didn't know how to channel any of it, so we killed our dreams on curbs and at the bottom of Boone's Farm bottles, we let our hopes drown in Lake Michigan, we left behind future plans at our favorite spot, "The Point" on Lake Shore Drive. I started to question whether I was changing too fast or whether my brothers weren't changing fast enough for me. I wondered where I fit in. I was stressed with feeling like I had to choose.

# CHAPTER 7

# BUEN VIAJE

*They got money for war but can't feed the poor.*
*- Tupac*

"Why the hell does this man continue to talk like this?" I whispered one day to a classmate as we sat in Dr. Brooks' Advanced Conversational Spanish class. It was my junior year of college and I still couldn't understand half of what the man said when he taught. His Spanish classes continued to challenge me, though, and I loved them for that reason. Even though Dr. Brooks didn't decorate his classroom with posters and maps of Spanish speaking countries, I still felt like I was beginning to understand Latin American culture through his teachings.

He had us doing more than just answering basic questions in the language. He made us read and translate literature, engage in conversation in Spanish, and immerse ourselves in the culture as much as we could considering we were in a classroom at an HBCU in Louisiana surrounded by an almost exclusively English-speaking world.

My understanding and love of the language broadened, as did my vocabulary. I was nearing fluency in a second language and it felt amazing. I considered it an honor to be in Dr. Brooks' classes and was determined to go as far as the department would allow. I enjoyed the nuances of Spanish and loved hearing myself speak it. I also felt that speaking a foreign language added something unique to my game with the ladies. The sistas couldn't resist a brotha speaking Spanish.

"Mr. Shields, can you repeat yourself? I cannot hear what you are saying," Dr. Brooks demanded that day in class.

"Um. No, Señor. I didn't say anything," I responded.

"I'm not hearing you right. Meet me after class."

*Damn. He heard me.*

Once class was over, I packed my bag and walked over to Dr. Brooks' desk to see how much trouble I was in for whispering to a classmate during class. He wasn't an intimidating man physically, but his presence was still quite imposing. I didn't know how much he had heard and I didn't have an excuse ready if he asked me why I was talking out of turn. If he asked, I was going to tell him the truth. "Yeah, man, you talk funny!"

"Shields, follow me to my office."

"Ok," I responded. That wasn't what I had expected, but I was going to roll with it. When I stepped into the office, I realized this was my first time there, and I was surprised by what I saw. Dr. Brooks had rows and rows of books, all in Spanish, on two bookshelves in the corner of the room. On his walls were framed posters, paintings and photographs of people, landmasses and buildings in Spain, Mexico and Puerto Rico. I took it all in, reading the captions in Spanish easily.

"Like what you see, do you?" Dr. Brooks asked, interrupting my observations.

"Yeah. This is some nice stuff, Dr. Brooks," I responded honestly.

"Shields, I asked you in here because I want to propose something to you," Dr. Brooks began as he sat in the chair behind his desk, setting his books down and motioning for me to sit as well. I took my bag off my shoulder, sat, and placed it between my feet.

"Ok," I responded hesitantly.

"Every year during Christmas vacation, I take my brightest students with me on an immersion trip to Mexico. We travel through the country, staying in a variety of hotels and in the homes of families gracious enough to host us. We eat authentic Mexican food and immerse ourselves in the culture. We walk in their shoes, so to speak, for two weeks. I want you to join our group this year. What do you think?"

The first thought that popped into my head was, *Christmas in Mexico? Hell no!* The last place I wanted to be for Christmas break was away from Chicago, my family, and my boys in KAOS. KAOS had made a pact that no matter what, we'd return home to spend holidays together, partying like we used to in high school. Besides, Christmas to me meant snow, cold weather, riding the L and a Christmas tree, not hot Mexico, beaches, and speaking only Spanish for days on end.

"Dr. Brooks, thank you for considering me, but I'm gonna have to pass. My mother doesn't have the money to send me to Mexico and I just don't think this would be the best thing for me to do right now," I said, collecting my things and preparing to exit the office. "Maybe next year."

Dr. Brooks looked at me and shook his head. "That's unfortunate," he said, "especially since you are my most gifted Spanish student."

*What did this man just say to me?* I asked myself. I almost demanded he repeat himself, just to make sure I hadn't misheard him.

He must have seen the confused look on my face. "Yes, Shields, you are," he continued to speak, diverting his eyes down to his wool pants to remove a small piece of lint. "This trip is what you need to take your Spanish-speaking skills to the next level, to move toward becoming bilingual. You're not too far from that now."

*Me? Bilingual?* I thought to myself, immediately thinking back as I did so often to sitting in Señor Hogan's Spanish classroom at De La Salle, listening to him snicker as he told me – in front of the entire class – that I was not equipped to move to Spanish III.

I pushed Señor Hogan's words to the back of my mind as I realized Dr. Brooks was still standing there anxiously awaiting my reply to his invitation. Deep down, I knew that Dr. Brooks was right. Speaking Spanish was almost second nature to me. In my head, I automatically translated words from Spanish to English and back again, and my comprehension of sentences, phrases, and the nuanced meanings of words came easily. But that was all book Spanish. I wanted to know what it felt like to be surrounded by the culture, to read the street signs, to hear the music, to learn the dialect, to speak the Spanish that the people spoke. But was that really possible for me, a boy from the South Side of Chicago, a boy who had been told by numerous teachers through the years that he wasn't worthy, that he didn't belong?

"Think about it," Dr. Brooks said, interrupting my musings, "and let me know if you change your mind."

"Thanks," I muttered before walking out of his office with thoughts of Mexico on my mind.

He had seen something in me that Señor Hogan had either overlooked or hadn't even dared to believe I had the potential for. One of the major things that separated Dr. Brooks from Señor Hogan was that Dr. Brooks would always tell us that he was hard on us because he believed in us. And he showed us the potential that existed out in the world. He would tell us that he wanted us to know that we were valuable and that we could do anything that anyone from anywhere else could do.

Not long after the meeting in Dr. Brooks' office, I sat in the front seat of the official GSU bus headed toward Nuevo Laredo, Texas. I had called my mom after my conversation with Dr. Brooks and even though I had tried to convince her that I wasn't interested in going to Mexico, I know she heard the longing in my voice. She gathered the family together and scrounged up the funds to make the trip a reality. Though my boys in KAOS were disappointed I wouldn't be coming home for Christmas, they supported my desire to take the trip. Besides, whatever one of us experienced only extended KAOS' reach and influence. We'd taken over the South Side while in high school, Louisiana, Georgia, New York, and other states when we went to college, and now we would extend our reach to Mexico. Chicago had been everything to me, but my horizons were expanding and I was ready to step out of my box in a big way.

After I had agreed to go on the trip, some of the students who had traveled with Dr. Brooks to Mexico in prior years started prepping me and some of the other newbies on what to expect from the trip.

"He's different in Mexico," they told us. "He's mellow, not so stiff." I took in all of their observations and then let them go. I didn't want anyone else's experiences to color my own and I wanted to be open and accept whatever the experience brought my way. If I was honest with myself, I also wasn't interested in how Dr. Brooks would react to being on foreign soil. I was more concerned with how I would fare in Mexico and whether I would be able to hold my own. I'd be lying if I said that I wasn't at least a little bit nervous.

Once our bus arrived in Nuevo Laredo, we boarded another that took us across the border to Mexico. Along the way, I watched the scenery continue to change – from the lush green of Louisiana to the dry lands of Texas and then to the even dustier landscape of Mexico. We arrived in Monterey, Mexico and then headed by yet another bus to the small town of Saltillo, the first of three major destinations on our three-week adventure. In Saltillo I stayed in a home with a family and four other students. When our *padres*, our parents for the duration of our week-long stay, came to pick us up from the bus stop, I became the translator between the other students and the Mexican families. I didn't realize until that moment how close to fluency I had come.

This was around the time in my life when I was converting to a vegetarian diet and I remember that at mealtime I'd say *"Sin carne, por favor."* My *madre* supported my vegetarian ways by frequently making me fresh-squeezed juice, but she also joked with me by opening up the freezer to show me the dead goat hanging there, just waiting to be turned into dinner.

While in Saltillo, we'd take a cab each morning to La Universidad where we attended classes. And then in the evening Dr. Brooks would make rounds to visit all of us and our host families. The circuit reminded me of a Southern minister's rounds through his community. What I remember finding interesting was that our madre didn't really seem to care for Dr. Brooks. I'd overhear her and other members of the family talking about how poor his Spanish was, which was funny to us because he was usually the one correcting our pronunciation. And yet year after year she continued to work with Dr. Brooks and to host college students from his program.

Lunch in Saltillo was the biggest meal of the day and after eating the whole town would shut down for the afternoon while we all took our *siestas*. What was interesting about being in Saltillo was that so much of what I thought I knew about Mexico prior to my trip was challenged there. One of the most shocking things to me was that my host family had a housekeeper who was only 14 years old. She would work at the house all day, and I remember asking her why she wasn't in school. She told me that she couldn't go to school because she had to work for her family. My mind started racing: *What about child labor laws? What about education creating an avenue of hope for you and your family's future?* I didn't quite know where to take the conversation from there, but I do remember telling her that she was probably okay with it only because she didn't know anything else. And in that moment I also realized how much I still had to learn about this country, this culture, and the world.

Another surprise was that people in the town looked much more European to me than Latino. Likewise, I think the townspeople found us unusual looking. They stared at us and seemed either shocked or intrigued, or maybe both, by all these Black American college students walking around their tiny town. My friend Danielle had beautiful dark skin and long braids and I remember that people would look at her especially long and hard. I'd like to think it was because she was so beautiful, but it was more likely because people in the town probably never saw people who looked like us unless one of Dr. Brooks' groups was visiting.

Our last day in Saltillo we went to church with our families and then said our goodbyes before jumping on the train and heading to Mexico City. This was the first time I had ever been on a train aside from the L and it was a great way to travel the country. In Mexico City, one of the most populated cities in the world, we stayed downtown in the Hyatt. The Hyatt stood right next door to the Mexican embassy building and I remember that there were homeless people sleeping just outside of both the hotel and the embassy. So much poverty and destitution juxtaposed against so much wealth. One day, my friend Java had a pizza slice in her hand and was about to eat it when this little kid came up, snatched it from her grip, and just stood there and ate it right in front of us. I also remember guards patrolling the embassy armed with large machine guns, which was a new sight for me.

We took the train all over Mexico City. Once we debarked at each destination, Dr. Brooks would walk so quickly that we had to keep pace with him if we didn't want to be left behind. Many of the kids from the South weren't used to the train and all the people getting on and off, so sometimes we'd exit at a stop only to realize that half of the group hadn't debarked with us. We'd then have to wait until the rest of the group were able to ride to the next stop, jump off, and then get right back on the train heading in the opposite direction to join us.

The third week of our trip, which was designed to be our week to chill and relax, we traveled to Acapulco. We stayed in another awesome hotel, except this time we were right at the beach. We ate meals on the beach during the day and went to the discotheques at night. It was amazing to walk along the breathtaking beaches, surrounded by all of this beauty. It was a strange sight, though, for me to see so many people just vacationing and relaxing. Although my family did take vacations, I didn't grow up witnessing a whole lot of vacationing on the South Side of Chicago and had never taken a trip to a place where the only expectation was to chill all day. At the time, Acapulco was one of the premier vacation destinations in the world and here we were, in the midst of it all.

While many of my fellow travelers were settling into vacation and party mode, my mind was elsewhere. I really struggled with the level of poverty that I saw all around me. I felt a deep connection to the people in the community. I remember that at one point Dr. Brooks, who had been observing me for the better part of three weeks by then, told me that I was just *different* from a lot of my peers.

Many of the students were there just to drink and hang out, whereas I was very enthused by the cultural aspects of the experience. I was fascinated by the African history in Mexico and wanted to soak it all in. Having the opportunity to visit all these cultural and historical museums and to climb *los piramides* in Teotihuacan just blew me away. I was experiencing in person all the amazing locations that I had previously only explored among the pages of books. I remember one museum visit where I was so taken by a display of unique and beautiful masks that I couldn't stop staring at them. I saw the African influence in these masks, like in so much of Mexico's culture, and was enamored by it all.

Dr. Brooks and I would argue on the trip, which usually began with me observing him doing or saying something that just didn't sit right with me. At times, I felt like he was taking advantage of some of the people with whom we worked and interacted. It was hard for me to hear him talk to some of the service people with such disrespect. I couldn't understand how this man, who I really did admire in an academic sense, could be so rude to people who had welcomed us into their homeland. I remember one night we were on our way to dinner at Denny's of all places and I protested and said that we couldn't eat there. At the time, Denny's in the United States had been under fire for discrimination against African Americans and Latinos and so I couldn't condone giving them our business, especially when there were so many local Mexican establishments from which we could have chosen. Dr. Brooks responded that even though he respected me and my values, the group was going to Denny's because that was what was on the itinerary. I said fine, sent them all on their way, and sought out another place to eat.

---

Looking back on it now, this first trip abroad really began to instill in me a lot of the foundations for my future Ubuntu teaching. I witnessed struggles and inequities in Mexico that somehow challenged me to recognize the universal promise of education to liberate and give hope to disenfranchised and marginalized people. I also became more aware of poverty on an international scale, and I began to discern that no matter where I went, the darker people always seemed to face the most discrimination, the most poverty, the most hopelessness. It blew my mind.

The darker the people, the darker the issues. What I began to notice in Mexico opened my eyes to what I would later notice in my travels all over the world – more often than not, the people with darker skin in any place are discriminated against by the lighter-skinned people in power. Often referred to as colorism, this discrimination based on skin-color, even within races, has been linked in the research to disparities in income, lower marriage rates, longer prison terms, and fewer job prospects for darker-skinned people.

---

Many of us miss out on the great opportunities for growth that travel can afford either because we lack the funds or because we're caught up in the four-block radius in which we live. When we are able to remove ourselves from our immediate environments, we can begin to open our eyes to the universality of what makes us human. We can also recognize the characteristics in ourselves, our families and our communities that make us unique and diverse.

I have to credit Dr. Brooks with helping me to broaden my horizons and constantly pushing me to see my own greatness when it came to mastering a second language. He often reminded us – way back in the 90s before it was a popular refrain – of the value of becoming bilingual. I remember the time he shared that even though I was a political science major, I had a real gift for learning languages that I needed to put to use somehow.

I had no way of knowing, as I sat on the long bus ride back to Louisiana as a college undergrad, that it wouldn't be long before I'd be back in Mexico with my very own group of students from Baltimore City College High School. And I couldn't have predicted that one day I'd go on to write my first book, in Spanish and co-authored with my own students, and that writing the book would give me an opportunity to acknowledge in the dedication both Dr. Brooks and Señor Hogan – Dr. Brooks for broadening my horizons and Señor Hogan for giving me an opportunity to observe the type of teacher I would *never* become.

There's a paradox, though, that makes this whole expanding our horizons thing easier said than done. Because the reality is that no matter how far we travel, no matter how far we come in our own lives, it's too easy to be pulled back into the environments that have shaped us. And we're quickly judged by people who have no interest in how we've grown or where we're going. No matter how hard we work to change how the world views us, sometimes we're just knocked right back down. This is how it happened to me.

Even as I was getting ready to graduate from college, the majority of my interactions with law enforcement had been negative. None of these altercations resulted from any serious infractions, rather the confrontations usually occurred when I was either mouthing off or trying to evade some traffic law or other. I never paid my traffic tickets and I guess I thought I was untouchable. Don't ask me why I didn't know better, but I didn't.

One day during my senior year my friend LaShawn and I were in her car making the long drive from Grambling back to Chicago. I had to get home to take care of an unpaid traffic ticket because I was tired of having to dodge the police, and she had to go home to handle some family business, as I remember it. So I decided to hitch a ride home with her. We were somewhere near Champaign, Illinois heading north when we saw the flashing lights in the rearview mirror.

*Shit!* I thought. *Here we go.*

Up to this point, all my experiences in Southern Illinois had led me to conclude that it was a very racist place, not the ideal setting for two young Black college kids to get pulled over. LaShawn was driving that day, and as the cop approached the window to take her driver's license, for some reason my spirit told me that this was the same cop who had written me the traffic ticket that I was heading home to deal with. What were the chances?

After a few minutes of checking her license and registration back in his car, the officer returned with LaShawn's ticket and proceeded to ask me my name. And of course I questioned why he needed my name when I wasn't the one driving. I behaved true to form – running my mouth when I probably should have just complied and answered his questions. I gave him my license and he asked me to step out of the car. Of course, I was nervous because we were in a rural area. He informed me that there was a warrant out for my arrest and I was quick to reply, "Damn, dude. I know. That's why I'm *coming* home to pay this ticket!"

Of course no explanation I could have given him would have mattered in that moment. He told me that he was going to have to take me in. So he put me in his backseat, handcuffed me, and told LaShawn that I was going to jail. I left in the cop car with the officer and LaShawn followed us to the station. Upon our arrival, the cop quickly whisked me away, leaving LaShawn to wonder what the hell was going on and where he had taken me. When she asked if she could see me, an officer brought her over to the visitors' area so we could talk. I was on the other side of the glass and I asked her to put her hand up to the glass. I mirrored her hand with mine on the other side, like I had been locked away for ages instead of just hours. I thought it was funny, but she didn't. She just sat there and cried.

I didn't realize the seriousness then of what could have happened to me behind bars. So many of our young men get taken in and don't make it out for a long time. They get trapped in the system. They run their mouths to the police and instigate arguments. And I was no different. I did my share of arguing with law enforcement and was just lucky, I guess, that nothing worse happened to me. In the wake of a number of males being killed by police officers, I now warn young men that – when stopped – they need to remain both quiet and calm. I tell them not to do any of the things that I used to do – argue, run my mouth, put up a fight, ask a bunch of questions. I tell them that their very lives may depend on it.

LaShawn sat on the other side of the glass divider and asked what we were going to do. I told her, of course, to call my mom. She did and my mother must have somehow sent the money up for my release. They let me go, but made it clear that I would have to return to court to deal with the ticket. When I returned for my court date, I remember my father was the one who drove me to Champaign. And I remember he flashed his Chicago PD badge and was told that his badge meant nothing down there. Again, we were in the country, and even though it wasn't surprising that these small town cops cared nothing about a big city officer or his son, it was still a slap in the face to him, I think. I don't remember the details of what happened that day in court, but I do remember that I paid a fine and they dropped the warrant. I remember explaining to the judge that I was in college and the reason I was even on the road that day was because I was trying to come home to pay the ticket. But it seemed that none of that mattered to anyone. I was just another young man of color, sitting in front of a judge, trying to plead my case to deaf ears.

# CHAPTER 8

# THE MAKING OF A LEADER

*Remind yourself, Nobody's built like you. You design yourself.*

\- Jay Z

"Did you hear that the Ques just beat up some dude from New Orleans at the Renaissance Night Club?"

One night during the fall of my junior year at Grambling, my boys and I were leaving a party and heading over to get a bite to eat from the Tiger House when I overheard the buzz about the latest fight. *This shit needs to stop, I mused to myself. I thought I left all this bullshit behind me in Chicago. We're here at COLLEGE and this is what we're talking about? This is where we're focusing our energy? THIS is the kind of brotherhood we're promoting?* It was like my college peers had just traded gang colors for frat colors. I was one to know, having grown up in a city where you could get beat up, shot at, or killed for wearing too much red or blue in certain hoods or barrios.

Now don't get me wrong, I learned later in life that Omega men are an amazing group of fraternity brothers, but at the time I could not help but think that they were acting like a bunch of thugs. I knew their history, just like I knew the history of the Kappas, Alphas and Sigmas, and nowhere in my research had I encountered anything that decreed that "Thou shall kick that ass."

I had been approached by a few different fraternities on campus to pledge when I first arrived at Grambling, but I remember looking around and seeing all of the unrest and just wanting something different for myself. To be perfectly honest, I had an issue with African Americans choosing to call themselves Greek, especially after reading great books like James' "Stolen Legacy" and Sertima's "They Came Before Columbus." It just didn't make sense to me. Also, as much good as the fraternities were doing on campus – from holding forums on a variety of subjects to running food drives – I also heard about lot of stuff I didn't like: fraternity guys raping women (back then it was called "running a train"), excessive partying, and a lot of of fighting. So much violence and disunity.

I guess being there at college, so far away from home, I was missing the type of bond that we had had with KAOS. Even though I saw Grambling's student government working toward some positive change on campus – advocating for better tasting food in the cafeteria, working to improve the financial aid system, and focusing on school safety – they weren't hitting on exactly what I was after. I wanted to create an organization that would unite us as strong African American men, not divide us.

I envisioned a different way to lead and serve, and felt strongly that I was going to be the one to organize the charge. I was further prompted to form the organization that we'd name United African American Men (UAAM) after my good friend, Tarlesha, approached me with her thoughts and concerns about the lack of male student leadership on campus. As the founder of the Distinguished Black Women (DBW) organization at Grambling, people often asked her why there wasn't a male counterpart to DBW. So she came to me and asked if I might want to get something started. Her invitation was the final push that I needed to act on an idea that had already been brewing in my mind.

My brother Henry, one of the founding members of UAAM, described the way in which it all came together as follows: *Darnell came to me and six other guys with the idea. He said that we all had different influences and came from different organizations and backgrounds, but collectively we had what it would take to pull together as a group of strong Black men and do something amazing.*

When I brought the group of us together, I did it very intentionally. UAAM's founding members weren't super tight when we joined to begin the organization. Some of the brothers I knew from class, others from the yard. I didn't choose my best friends; I chose the guys I thought could most effectively push my vision and our collective mission forward.

We got off to a bit of a rocky start in some ways, which only further proved to me how badly our work was needed. I remember that one day shortly after our founding, the college radio station, WKGRM, invited UAAM to join a few fraternity brothers on the air for an interview about some recent fights on campus and what we could do collectively as brothers to control the violence and work towards unity. Well, the interview never happened because during the production meeting, before we even made it to the airwaves, we ended up having some words with the fraternity brothers.

One of my UAAM co-founders and brothers, Kevin Higgins, recalled the day like this: *It was us and the Ques and even though I can't remember specifically how it*

*started, as best I can remember the bottom line was that there was a little bit of*
*jealousy between UAAM and the Ques. They thought that because they were a big*
*fraternity at Grambling, they should be the authority to speak on male unity on*
*campus. But we were saying that they weren't really handling their business in*
*terms of what service truly meant. That led to some heated discussion, so we never*
*even got to do the segment.*

Our first membership meeting, however, did draw over 100 brothers, which showed us that people on campus were hungry for change. Many of the guys who showed up that day were also fraternity members. We didn't mind, because the last time we had checked, before a policeman slammed a brother to the ground, he didn't ask about his Greek status or lack thereof. We were all brothers and I wanted us to work together to create positive change. Kevin described how the environment on campus at the time was ripe for some new leadership: *There were a lot of different cliques on campus at the G. You had this Black consciousness movement starting to emerge and all these brothers and sisters really interested in enlightenment. But you also had a lot of partying going on and it was easy to be distracted. And a lot of fraternities were being put on moratorium because of hazing. They were getting a little off-track and I think with UAAM we filled a leadership void on campus.*

Those of us who were UAAM founders really played off of one another's strengths to get the organization off the ground successfully and to build something solid. For example, I was a strong speaker and Kevin Higgins was a talented writer. So I would go into schools and pitch the idea for our mentorship program and then Kevin would follow up with a letter to the school administration – I'd sell the program and he'd close the deal. For the most part the schools were very receptive to a young group of men who came in well-dressed in ties and suspenders, well-spoken, and ready to help. We developed a strong track record to the point where we were even able to secure a sizable grant for our work. And we had a great advisor on campus, Dr. Durrant. He was from Barbados, had a thick Caribbean accent, and was so well-liked at Grambling that he was the perfect fit for the work we were doing.

One of the major accomplishments of UAAM was the inception of our Becoming a Man program. We went into local middle and high schools and even one of the jails in Monroe, a city about 30 minutes from Grambling's campus. We started mentoring the boys there, who greeted us with such excitement when we walked into the building. We weren't that much older than them and I think they thought we were cool, strolling into their schools looking really slick, carrying with us powerful messages of hope, through our own lives, of what was possible for them and their futures.

Kevin described the focus of our work in this way: *What we were really trying to accomplish was to get young Black men to envision their futures beyond their daily realities. We wanted to show them that there was a reason they needed to get focused on their education and that staying focused would open doors. One of my favorite movies "A Bronx Tale" has a line that says that the saddest thing in life is wasted talent and I think that's really the message we wanted to give to these boys. We wanted to make sure that they understood the talent they had. You know, it's really hard to focus when you've got a lot of stuff going on, and we wanted to show them that if they were acting up in class and getting kicked out, then they weren't ever going to get the opportunities they deserved in terms of moving on to college.*

Henry went on to explain our work as follows: *We took this message of solidarity into the school system and were like, "Hey, we want to give back to generations after us. We want to share our journeys with them!" We really wanted to show young people what they could expect in college. We bridged the gap between where these boys were and where they could be. I remember working at Grambling High, which was right next to the University. We'd go in and give these hour-long talks and then just really engage with the boys in conversation. We received very positive reviews from the teachers, principals, and coaches, as well as the young men themselves.*

We poured a lot of ourselves into these boys because we believed that we could really make a difference in their lives. And in doing so, I think we both learned and shared about what it means to care without condition. One time right after UAAM started working in the schools, we took a group of kids to the movies and out for pizza. As the evening was wrapping up, I realized that my money was missing. I had an idea of which young man had taken it, so I purposely drove him home last. I hit him with that *long* drive home and after an extended bout of silence, I started asking him some questions. I asked him if he had enjoyed the movie and if he appreciated having been taken out for pizza. And then I shared that it was so unfortunate that here I had paid for this great evening for him and the other boys, only to have my money come up missing at the end of the night. He got really quiet and even though he never confessed to me that he had been the one to take my money, I could feel his energy shifting in the car. As we pulled up to his house and he prepared to leave, I told him that I still loved him and that I understood. I told him that I didn't appreciate that my money was gone, but that I would see him again soon. We never revisited the incident, but I hope that he and the other boys we worked with were able to see that we were there for them unconditionally, even when they messed up.

We went into our mentoring work with no formal training, but I think that my UAAM brothers and I understood implicitly what the boys needed – we just gave them what we wished we had had from mentors in our lives at that age and then took it from there.

One of the things that UAAM taught me was that people can be very receptive to a group of young people presenting fresh ideas, especially when the group is committed to helping to change the trajectory of underserved, at-risk youth. I knew that I had something to give back and that all the challenges I'd endured in my own education could be used to help boys and to put them on a different path than they might otherwise have traveled. Stepping into the role of a mentor was new to me, to all of us I think, but it was so powerful. And seamless. And fun. It didn't seem like work at all. The boys thought we were the coolest of the cool, which stroked our egos as young men and kept us going back to those schools again and again.

While I was doing all this work through UAAM, I also had the opportunity to become a part of the Longevity Project through an invitation from one of my professors, Dr. Staten. The Project, which was connected to the Social Research Club on campus, gave me a chance to interview pre-centenarians and centenarians throughout the South about the factors they believed had contributed to their longevity and the longevity of some of their families. Simple answers to questions like "What contributed to your life?" or "Why do you think you've lived so long?" provided me with so much perspective on everything from spiritual practices to family traditions and parental influences of some of the longest-living people in the South. What was amazing about this work was that it provided a juxtaposition to the work I was doing mentoring boys and really gave me an opportunity to reflect on the whole of life's journey.

I was still trying to find my own way, but my work through both UAAM and the Longevity Project helped me to chart my own path in a powerful direction. I was able to take everything I had learned in KAOS about the importance of brotherhood and everything I *wished* I had learned from a mentor but never had, and I was able to channel my findings into something meaningful that made a positive impact in the lives of boys who looked like me. At the same time, I was getting an opportunity to gain wisdom from elders who had seen more change in their lifetimes than I could even imagine. And it was amazing. It was Ubuntu.

---

UAAM celebrated its 20th anniversary just last year, and I echo Henry's thoughts when he shared *that it's good to see something that we started so long ago still going on. The program is still around, and I'm very proud of that.* The organization is now on five different college campuses throughout the South and continues to serve hundreds of boys a year.

I had an opportunity to meet many of the organization's current members when I returned to Grambling in 2008 to speak at a convocation. Being invited to address this event was a dream come true for me, although I have to admit that when I first got the invitation I was skeptical. I didn't think that there was enough that was honorable about me and my time at Grambling, and even thought that the invitation was just an elaborate ruse to get me to campus to discuss my outstanding student loans. At any rate, I was so honored. The realization of my dream of returning to my alma mater was a high of the best kind.

My talk that day was about following your destiny, realizing your dreams, and walking in your purpose. I stood up on stage and shared how many years before I had sat out in that very same audience between two young ladies and how I had told them that one day I was going to be up on the stage speaking to students. I recounted that both of the young ladies had told me that nobody was ever going to listen to me talk about anything. And then I spoke about how we have to be careful about who we let into our space when we're sharing our dreams.

I discussed some of the challenges I had faced at Grambling – being a long way from my Chicago home, navigating the University as a first-generation college student, carrying with me all of the emotional baggage from a high school experience that had reminded me time and time again of all I couldn't do. I stood up on that stage and told all those college freshmen that regardless of how they had ended up at Grambling, regardless of the paths they had traveled to get there, they needed to stay forward focused on where they wanted to go from that moment on.

I connected with the audience through some humor, of course. I told them that when we were students the dorms had looked like the projects while 20 years later they looked like condos. But I shared that even in those project-like dorms, I had been so grateful to be walking into my purpose, to be away from home with the time and space to figure out where my future was headed.

I also shared how grateful I was to have had the opportunity to attend an HBCU with such a rich history, and that I had really flourished in an environment where I had finally been able to connect with teachers who looked like me, who shared my struggles. I told the students that they needed to recognize that they were lucky to be in a college that was going to be able to nurture their growth, give them the care and attention they needed, and treat them like family.

I confessed how many times I hadn't known how I was going to make it out, how I was ever going to graduate. And I shared with the audience that one of my greatest accomplishments had been being asked to return to my alma mater to give the very speech that I was delivering. But that there I was, doing it. And that it was so amazing. I also confessed that there had been many moments immediately leading up to the speech when my fears and feelings of inadequacy had almost gotten the best of me. Like when I arrived at the airport and had to wait for four hours because the driver had forgotten to pick me up. The whole time I just questioned whether anyone even wanted me to speak on that Grambling stage, whether I was good enough. And how the following day the driver had forgotten to pick me up again to bring me from the hotel to campus. And how Barbara Lewis had called me to ask where I was. And how I had questioned, up until the moment I stepped onstage and started speaking, whether it was even going to happen.

Yet there I was, able to share everything I had learned about not giving up hope, everything I had learned from my time at Grambling about how to listen to the stories of those around me and understand that so many people had come from humbler beginnings than I had and how we could all gain strength from each other if we were quiet enough to listen.

Toward the end of my speech I spoke about UAAM and said that I was honored to see the organization still going strong. A huge roar of excitement erupted from the crowd, as the current UAAM members expressed their excitement that one of the UAAM founders was on the stage. In that moment I felt so grateful all over again – for the cyclical nature of life, for another opportunity to share a message of hope with a group of young people who, though unique in their own right, were traveling a path that I too had walked, to show them what was possible if they just kept going. To impart that, to paraphrase the words of Walt Disney, if we remain curious, we can continue to move forward and open new doors.

*Figure 1: The Green Street crew existed way before the KAOS crew (Andre is the one in glasses).*

*Figure 2: The KAOS crew always hung out in my basement.*

Figure 3: Curtis and me horseback riding in Indiana.

Figure 4: Curtis and Marlon at our annual Memorial Day cookout.

Figure 5: One of our legendary cookouts.

Figure 6: Dr. Brooks and the president of la Universidad de Coahuila pose with us on the first day of class.

Figure 7: Learning how to play the guitar in Costa Rica.

Figure 8: Working in Costa Rica or making a mess in Costa Rica with Andrew and the crew.

Figure 9: Building a playground in Puerto Rico for autistic kids.

Figure 10: I was participating in a march in Adjuntas, Puerto Rico for farmers' rights.

Figure 11: My first year as a teacher, I traveled to Mexico with several of my students from Baltimore City College High School.

Figure 12: We made history at Baltimore City College High School when we published a children's book in Spanish, El Primer Dia de la Escuela.

Figure 13: David Miller and me with former Baltimore Ravens Ray Lewis, Steve McNair, Mark Clayton, and Wade Brown (not a Raven) at Ray Lewis' annual Thanksgiving event.

Figure 14: Receiving nothing but love from a group of students on the Tohono O'odham Rez in Arizona.

Figure 15: Picture Day at Johns Hopkins University with the PRAISE Scholars.

Figure 16: Marina and me leading our first Spark Retreat in Joshua Tree, California.

# PART III

## BORN TO LEAVE

# CHAPTER 9

# WHY I DON'T TEACH FOR AMERICA

*The mind is a terrible thing to waste.*
*I show love cause it's a terrible thing to hate.*
- GURU

In the summer of 1994, just a few short months after having graduated from Grambling with my bachelor's degree in Spanish and political science, I boarded a plane in Chicago for Houston, Texas. It was only my second time on an airplane. I had experienced my first flight when I had joined the Navy and had traveled to Florida for basic training. My heart had been set on heading west to California this time around, as I had been scheduled to attend the summer-long Teach for America (TFA) Institute at UCLA, but at the last minute TFA had changed the site of the Institute and had told us that instead of California, we were headed to the University of Houston. As excited as I was about beginning my teaching career, I was less than thrilled to be headed to Texas. I had spent time there before and, well, LA just seemed so much more intriguing. But Houston it was, so to Houston I went.

The day I arrived at the University of Houston, the campus was abuzz with news of the brutal murder of a young African American boy that had taken place only miles away from where we gathered. *What a telling start,* I thought, *to my introduction to the world of teaching.* I also couldn't help but judge all of the Ivy League kids who were joining me for the TFA Institute. I was sure that few of them were accustomed to brutal murders taking place around the corner from where they lay their heads down to sleep at night.

As I wandered around the University campus, I had another of my life's *How did I get HERE?* moments. Just months before, I had been a college student at an HBCU with dreams of becoming a lawyer, and here I was, surrounded by white people who were excitedly welcoming me to Teach for America. It all felt a little disorienting, but as with so many other times in my life, I could easily trace the dots looking back.

This was how it happened. Upon my graduation from Grambling State University, my friend Rodney Thomas had mentioned TFA. He was a business major and had seen a flyer about TFA and thought it might be a good fit for me. At first I wasn't at all interested, as I had my sights set on law school. I was a political science major and had developed a fascination with the notion of being paid to argue. I had also always admired lawyers – the way they looked and sounded, the causes for which and people for whom they fought.

Every year at Grambling there was a convocation speaker whose sole mission was to pump the student body up for the year. One year, I think it was when I was a sophomore, the speaker was an attorney for Grambling who lived in Chicago. I remember watching how animated he was, how engaging his stories were, how captivatingly his deep baritone voice commanded the audience. His name was Thomas "TNT" Todd and after hearing him speak that day – coupled with the response I had received after speaking at my KAOS brother Andre's funeral – I thought I knew what I wanted to do with my career.

Attorney Todd was actually a graduate of Grambling's rival school, Southern University in Baton Rouge, and had made history in 1968 when he had tried the first criminal case against a Chicago policeman for depriving an individual of his civil rights. I didn't think it was a coincidence that Attorney Todd's voice provided the vocal sample that opened up my all-time favorite Public Enemy song, "Fight the Power." At the beginning of the song, the listener can hear Attorney Todd's voice ringing out loud and clear – "Yet our best trained, best educated, best equipped, best prepared troops refuse to fight. Matter of fact, it's safe to say that they would rather switch than fight." The song "Fight the Power," along with the movie "Do the Right Thing," had influenced KAOS in many ways. The song had been the soundtrack to our lives. It touched on racial tensions, relationships, and everything that had been in the forefronts of our minds as we graduated from high school and wondered how we were going to make our mark on the world. As a Public Enemy fan, I felt that the group's unique message really began my personal journey into activism and black consciousness. While NWA had me challenging the police, artists such as Public Enemy and KRS-1 caused me to look at the injustices minorities like my Black and Latino friends were dealing with and to see that they were real.

So even though I had my sights set on becoming a lawyer, much of the mentoring work I had participated in through UAAM, coupled with my studies in African and Latin culture and the Spanish language, were actually laying the foundations for my future career as a high school Spanish teacher. I had had strong models throughout my own education of the type of teacher I did (and did *not*) want to become, so when Rodney presented me with the TFA flyer, I thought why not give it a shot.

Among the TFA materials, one of the unique elements of the program model that jumped out at me right away was the fact that the organization only recruited college graduates who had *not* majored in education. I fit the bill in this regard, so at least I knew that I was likely to pass the initial applicant screening process. At that point, I didn't know anyone who was involved with TFA, so I had no real concept of what I was applying for. I knew I wanted a job, I had learned that there was a shortage of teachers and, in particular, African American teachers, and so I thought my odds had to be pretty good of getting into the program and then landing a teaching position.

I applied to TFA during my last semester in college and then moved to Memphis with my college roommate Kevin for a few months after graduation to teach pre-K while I anticipated my TFA acceptance letter. I remember my excitement on the day that I got the mailing informing me that I had passed the first screening round and inviting me for an interview. I'm sure the program back then was competitive, but I don't think that it was as highly selective as it has since become. For me, though, a gate to the path of teaching had swung open and I was more than ready to walk on through.

Before the interview, I had to fill out a bunch of paperwork and write several essays about my teaching style and experiences. Although I hadn't had any formal teaching experience, my work on those essays confirmed for me that I truly *had* had quite a bit of practice working with young people, from my summer job at the YMCA to the work I did in college through UAAM and my most recent stint as a pre-K teacher.

Prior to coming in, the TFA materials instructed me to prepare a sample lesson to teach in front of a panel that would judge me on the lesson's quality and my teaching aptitude. I prepared and presented a middle school history lesson because I had initially applied for a social studies teaching position and had my sights set on teaching middle school or junior high. I had loved my seventh and eighth grade years at school, before the challenges of high school hit, and so it seemed natural for me to teach at this level.

In my lesson, I compared the Civil Rights Movement to the social movements surrounding race and equity in the mid-1990s. I wanted to make the lesson both clear and relevant and I think I nailed it that day. I remember that after teaching it, I had to field some questions from the other five TFA candidates in the room that day – another African American guy, an Asian lady, and two white people, one male and one female. I was able to answer all of their questions with ease, and it felt so natural for me to be standing up in front of a group teaching on a topic about which I was passionate.

After we had presented our lessons, we were made to participate in a round table discussion where the TFA interviewers presented a scenario for us to discuss. As I remember it, the hypothetical scenario went something like this: "You are a middle school teacher who has been chosen to be the director of a play about Rosa Parks. There are two students who are vying for the lead part in the play; one is African American and one is Caucasian. Which student do you choose for the part of Rosa Parks and why?" We had about five minutes to gather our thoughts before we engaged in an open debate on the scenario in front of the interview panel.

My mind began to race as I started to question whether the primarily white TFA representatives, who were holding the key to my first teaching job in their hands, expected me to be honest and tell them what I really thought or merely wanted me to recite what I thought to be the politically correct answer. What should have been such a simple moment of speaking my truth was anything but easy for me. As I sat there, I was haunted by the long-familiar feeling of inadequacy that I often felt around white people. The notion that had haunted me since my days at De La Salle. Once again, the words of Señor Hogan, telling me that I didn't belong, that I wasn't worthy, rang loud and clear in my head. I was seeing in this moment the effects of having been a victim of white supremacy throughout my formative years of education – how it manifested itself in feelings of self-doubt at the most inopportune of times. I knew which answer I wanted to give in response to the question posed in the scenario, but I questioned my decision because in the moment I began to care more about what the people observing me thought than I did about what I thought.

Part of me thought that I should just recite the "safe" answer, which I believed to be: "I choose the white girl to play Rosa Parks because Dr. King stood for diversity and taught that we should judge a person not by the color of her skin, but by the content of her character. So if the white girl did the best audition, then she should get the part." But another part of me longed to stand on my own conviction and choose the African American girl because Rosa Parks was an African American woman. I understood the power of images and if both of the young ladies were equally qualified when it came to their acting ability and articulation, or even if the white girl's audition was a little stronger, I felt that when it came to the image of Rosa Parks and her movement and how she should be depicted on stage, the African American girl would be the better choice. In my mind, the image of Rosa Parks was that she was Black first, a woman second, and an activist third.

I continued to mull it over: *Do I choose the African American girl, or do I choose the white girl because I'm sitting in a room with mostly white people and I think that's a safer answer to give?* I wanted the teaching job and wondered whether by answering honestly I might squander the opportunity right in front of me.

I remember that the other TFA candidates in my own group seemed to whitewash their decisions, and said that since Rosa Parks was standing up for the rights of all people, someone with white skin could play her role and it would be just as effective because the message was about equality and not Blackness. But I was like, *Yeah, I don't think so.* I wound up standing my ground, choosing the African American for the reasons previously stated, and walking out of the interview already on the defensive – already angry at the job I thought I hadn't gotten because I was honest and spoke my truth. For me, the interview hadn't been about making a decision and sticking with it. It had gone deeper than that. It had been about standing my ground in a situation where it would have been so easy not to. Because sometimes all of this standing alone gets exhausting. And in my early 20s I was already feeling tired.

Before you start to think I'm crazy or that I was making a huge deal over something that wasn't so serious, let me take you back a bit in history to the 1980s in New York City, where five Black and Latino boys – who became known as the "Central Park Five" – got caught up in a case of justice gone horribly wrong. What happened was that these boys were picked up one night and held for questioning regarding the brutal rape of a white woman in Central Park. Under a situation of extreme stress, fear and coercion, the young men gave individual written and video confessions, made up of fabricated stories fed to them by detectives, to implicate each other in a crime that they hadn't committed.

It was an instance of a justice department hell bent on solving a heinous crime swiftly and with ease during a time in New York City's history where racial tensions were already running extremely high. The crux of the tragedy as it related to the boys was that all five young men were tried and convicted of crimes they hadn't committed, due in large part to their own false confessions. All five served jail sentences of seven to 13 years. Eventually, the serial rapist responsible for the horribly brutal attack confessed, but only after all five boys had served their time.

It's a complicated story that could be the subject of a book of its own, but the question raised is what causes people, and in particular Black and Latino boys and young men, to give in under pressure instead of standing tall in their truths? One answer, although by no means complete, is that we grow tired of fighting a system in which we are viewed as criminals more often than not.

On a much smaller scale, I see a version of the "Central Park Five" phenomenon often with boys in school. Black and Brown boys are called out of class, walk into a room to see me and maybe a few other adults sitting around a table, and their very first questions are usually "What did I do? Am I in trouble?" It doesn't matter if they know that they didn't do anything out of line that day, that week, or that month. They have been conditioned to think that in certain environments, facing people in positions of power, they're guilty until proven innocent. And these are *children* we're talking about. They look around the room, feel inadequate, and become convinced that they've done something wrong even though they know on another level that they have not.

I nearly walked down a very similar path during my TFA interview. I *almost* went against my convictions because of the pressure I felt to give in to what I thought was expected of me. This is the effect of white supremacy. These are the realities that follow me through my life.

Maybe I overthought what was going on in the room that day with the TFA scenario, but I really don't feel that I did. Because I believe that if you were to gather a group of TFA teachers together today, the majority of them would tell you that in the same scenario they had chosen the white girl to play Rosa Parks – even if they had known that didn't make the most sense, even if they had *wanted* to choose the Black girl. And I think some TFA teachers would share that, like me, they once sat in a room as the lone dissenter among a group of educated people who all went with the flow in explaining how a little white girl would be the more appropriate choice to play a Black Civil Rights figure.

I was told by some recent TFA teachers that Teach for America still uses the Rosa Parks scenario in their candidate interviews. And I wonder how many teachers, who start off their teaching careers sitting in a room and saying what they believe is expected of them, choosing the white girl because they think it's the safer choice, then go on to teach curricula they don't believe in. Administer tests they know aren't measuring the brilliance of their students. Follow school, district, state and national educational policies that are imprudent at best and harmful at worst. And I wonder, in a system that is still so predominately white, how their decisions to go with the flow have had an added adverse effect on teachers of color.

It's interesting to look back on my TFA experience through the current lens of my work centered around issues of equity and access. I teach a workshop called "Becoming a Global Educator" where we talk about teaching across landscapes and working with culturally, socially and economically diverse populations both within the U.S. and internationally. It's one of the more popular workshops I lead around issues of diversity, beliefs and racism. So now here I am pushing people to have difficult conversations and to be comfortable in their own skin, when I know firsthand how challenging it can be to do so in certain environments.

Not too long ago when conducting a workshop, I asked the audience about times in their lives when they had been marginalized. I asked each of them to recall in as much detail as possible what they were wearing at the time of the incident, how old they were when it happened, how it made them feel at the time, and how it made them feel in the moment of recollection. One audience member, a Latino man who looked to be in his 60s, stood to share his experience of being called a "stupid spic." He began to tear up during his recollection, even though the incident had occurred over half a century in the past. Half a century. This is the depth of the pain.

Sometimes in my workshop I ask participants to specifically consider the first time they realized that racism existed. It's interesting that when I inquire about marginalization more generally, nearly everyone can recall a time in his or her own life when he or she was a victim of marginalization. In this way, a difficult and painful topic is sometimes mitigated by the shared nature of the experience. But when I ask about racism specifically, the issue can tend to divide a room fairly quickly. Maybe it's easier to talk about topics that are more universal, such as gender issues and ableism, than it is to talk about racism – a subject that many of us have been avoiding discussing our whole lives, especially in mixed company.

Discussions of race are often so uncomfortable because it's difficult to hold them in a way that doesn't set up some dichotomy between those who look like me and those who don't. But because issues of race are so deep, so filled with pain, it's important to name them for what they are so that we can begin to work through them together. Even when the conversations become uncomfortable and when people disagree with our deep belief that we still have a long road to travel.

In my own life and work, I've found that when we can work to establish safe spaces for such conversations to take place, they often are a lot more honest. This is where Parker Palmer's work of touchstones has become so important to me. The touchstones are a simple list of principles that can be used to guide how we work and interact with each other. One touchstone says that we should "speak our truth in ways that respect other people's truth," whereas another one instructs us to "attend to our own inner teacher" and yet another calls us to "trust and learn from the silence." I use them in my work, but I also use them in my personal life. They keep me humble, they keep me grounded, and they help me navigate through the pain. My life and work also often reference the second of Miguel Ruiz's four agreements, which reminds us to "not take everything personally." So often it's hard not to feel like we are carrying the weight of an entire culture on our own backs. Whatever the burden, it's usually not ours to bear on our own. When I speak I have to remind the audience, and myself, that I don't represent every man of color and the only story I can really tell with complete truth is my own.

I often share with the audience at the beginning of a talk or training my belief that we're all just little boys and girls dressed in grown folks' clothing. And I think that's been true for me often in my own life. I'm 24 years old sitting in an interview room and wondering whether or not to speak honestly in light of the company I'm in, but in the same moment I'm also the 16-year-old kid walking into Giordano's Pizza with my KAOS crew, upset that we're being treated so poorly by the wait staff, convinced that it's because of the color of our skin. Was it just us thinking that way? Was it the cloak of white supremacy that somehow colored our perspective and prevented us from differentiating between the effects of our own actions and the racism that we were so used to encountering in certain contexts?

When I work with young men of color today, I often hear some variation of the sentiment, "Man, Dr. Shields, Ms. So-and-so doesn't like me because I'm Latino. She's racist!" I never tell them right away that they're wrong, but I also challenge them to qualify their statements and to think a little bit deeper about what they're saying and how they're feeling. I might ask a young man some questions based on the specifics of his circumstances as they've been told to me, sometimes by the teacher herself: "Have you thought about the fact that you came into class high yesterday? Or that you've called this teacher a bitch nearly every other day for the entire school year? Or that this teacher is married to an African American man and raising two Black boys herself?" I ask questions like these to get the young men to think about their situations in a little more detail before they throw out the "She's racist!" line. Because sometimes it's racism and sometimes it's not. Sometimes it's complicated and sometimes it's simple. Sometimes it's systemic and sometimes it's personal. But whatever it is, we have to get to a place where we can begin to engage in some more honest dialogue about the intersection between white supremacy, systemic racism, and personal responsibility.

---

Three weeks after I walked out of my interview wondering if I had just destroyed my chance of becoming a teacher, I received a letter in the mail notifying me of my acceptance into the Teach for America 94 corps. The letter said that I'd be receiving more information shortly about the summer training program, which would serve as my brief induction into the world of teaching. I quit my pre-K job and traveled home to Chicago to pack up a few things and head south to Houston. I knew next to nothing about the TFA organization and since the Internet looked like a bit different then than it does today, I had no choice but to go forth with little to no knowledge of what I was getting myself into.

I showed up for my first day at the TFA Institute, and while those around me were in shock about the nearby murder of a young child, what was even more foreign to me than news of violence was the prospect of so many overly excited white people who looked to be my fellow teaching corps members. I was coming out of four years at an HBCU where almost everyone looked like me. Most of us were of similar socio-economic statuses, so whether we were from big cities or small Southern towns, we appeared to have more in common than not. Arriving in Houston – the fourth largest Black city in the country – to find myself surrounded by so many white people was really a shock to me.

It was a steep learning curve for me at first because I had never been around so many white folks in my life in such an intimate setting. I began to notice differences right away in how they talked, dressed and ate. Even though De La Salle had been predominantly white, there I had only experienced sitting in a classroom surrounded by white kids. I had never thought I'd be *living* with them in such close quarters.

The first morning at breakfast I scanned the dining hall, located the table where all the Black corps members were sitting, and joined them. It didn't take me long to realize, however, that most of those Black folks ran in slightly different circles than I did. Sitting at the table were graduates of Ivy League schools – Harvard, Yale, Tufts, Brown. I was blown away because I had not yet met African Americans who had attended such prestigious schools. I wasn't intimidated, though. I was proud to be sitting among them as a graduate of Grambling State University. Even though they had graduated from such prominent institutions, they still knew and respected the history of HBCUs and I was representing that history. I soon found out that I would have to explain to my white counterparts in the coming weeks what it meant to be a graduate of an HBCU, but the African Americans, even if they hadn't attended HBCUs themselves, seemed to get it. They knew the history of Grambling's band, the reputation of our winning football team, and the fame of the great Coach Eddie Robinson, the winningest coach in college football.

I also discovered that the Ivy League African American TFA corps members were so *angry* about their college experiences. It surprised me. They were irate about issues of race, gender gaps, and poverty. I found all this hostility strange because coming from an HBCU my hot button issues had been somewhat different. At Grambling we had had difficulties registering for classes, getting healthy food in the cafeteria, and dealing with the constant fights and arguments that broke out over roommate issues and what cities we were repping. We had had problems like girls not showing up to class when it rained because they couldn't get their hair messed up, but we didn't have the deep issues of racial conflict that I was hearing about from my Ivy League counterparts. My challenges at Grambling seemed to have arisen on a more level playing field because of all the issues we had faced there, white supremacy really wasn't one of them. I guess I had assumed that for students attending the great institutions, somehow the question of what it meant to be Black in America would have faded into the background. And yet there they were telling me that, even though they had done everything to prove they were worthy enough to gain their colleges' acceptance, they had still caught a lot of hell in the classrooms once there.

---

TFA divided us into groups based on the geographic regions in which we were hoping to teach. I was placed in the New Jersey group. The application had asked us to list our top three choices and I chose New Jersey, Washington, D.C., and Baltimore. Jersey was my top choice because I knew that teachers in Jersey were highly paid and it was close to New York. I had never been to New York, but I was aware that it was super expensive and so I thought Jersey would be a good, practical alternative. D.C. and Baltimore were my second and third choices because I knew both of the cities had strong Black communities.

The New Jersey group was comprised of about half a dozen African Americans and a bunch of white folks. A guy named Brick was our director. When we had any issues, he was the one we would reach out to. He helped us frame our teaching pedagogy, taught us how to design curriculum, and gave us our marching orders. Ironically, he had only had a couple of years of classroom teaching experience. I was a bit skeptical in the beginning of what this man with so little experience was going to be able to offer me. But I was also excited to be there and eager to learn all I could.

After we had met our group members and learned more about how we'd be moving through the Institute, we were assigned roommates. My roommate was a Jewish guy named Mark, and we had an unbelievable connection from the moment we met. I had never shared living space with a white guy before and had never even really *known* a Jewish guy before Mark as best as I can remember. Mark's girlfriend was an Egyptian woman, and so I guess that gave us an instant point of connection. His girlfriend was African; I was African American. He loved music; I loved music. He was funny as hell; and I thought myself to be quite the comedian too. We would stay up all night talking about the types of teachers we would become, the kind of lives we wanted to live.

What was interesting was that even though we had this strong connection as roommates, more often than not when we entered the cafeteria he would go off and eat with his folks and I would seek out mine. Outside of the teaching groups to which we were assigned, that was sort of how we traveled. We segregated ourselves based on race, culture and class. I found this interesting because here we were going to be teachers in diverse settings, but we still self-separated ourselves just like back when we were in high school. And even within the small group of Black brothers and sisters, there was some division between those of us who had graduated from HBCUs and those of us who were Ivy League grads.

Every day after breakfast we would be shipped off to local schools throughout the city where we'd teach and receive feedback on our lessons. My fellow middle school teachers and I were assigned to Jack Yates High School to teach middle school students who had been placed there in a summer program. Jack Yates was a wild house in the 3rd Ward, a community that was home to both Texas Southern University and the University of Houston. The 3rd Ward was filled with stately old mansions, rundown historic commercial buildings, and crime statistics that ranked it consistently among the most dangerous neighborhoods in the country.

After teaching all morning, we would return to the University campus and spend the afternoon playing goofy games – throw your shoe in the middle of the aisle, sit on someone's lap, etc. I couldn't stand those games and felt strange because in the African American community we hadn't played games like those. I knew the activities were about socialization and trust, but I remember feeling so uncomfortable – sitting on someone's lap, embracing someone I didn't have a connection with. Someone who didn't look like me or sound like me, someone with whom I thought at the time I had nothing in common.

It felt as though I was being forced to immerse myself in this multicultural experience at the Institute, only to be taught by white folks how to go back out into the world to teach Black and Latino kids, many of whom were growing up in situations that resembled those of my own childhood. TFA was shipping teachers out to underserved communities filled with minority, high-poverty populations, and I found the whole situation so ironic, from the low numbers of minority corps members that were coming into TFA, to the TFA staff that was almost exclusively white, to the lack of true culturally diverse pedagogy in the instruction we were receiving.

I wondered, if we were going to be trained to go out into underserved communities and if TFA was supposed to have a great model of recruiting a highly qualified and competitive teacher pool, then why weren't there more people who looked like me sitting beside me? Part of the answer to that question was that there weren't a large number of minority college graduates turning to the teaching profession. Also, if my memory serves me correctly, a lot of minority teachers were having a hard time passing the now-obsolete National Teacher Examination (NTE). And yet I couldn't help but feel like TFA was missing the boat somewhere.

I felt like I needed to *do* something to help us process what we were witnessing. So under a tree on the college grounds, with the heat beating into our backs, I convened a meeting with my fellow African American and Latino male TFA corps members. We were midway through our time with the TFA Institute, and I wanted to check in with them to see if I was the only one feeling the way I did.

I began the meeting by asking my brothers if they had ever been on trip that didn't turn out the way they had planned. I was assuming that if they were anything like me, their answers would all be affirmative. Almost anyone who has taken a major trip knows how many things can go wrong along the way. You plan all year, but the planning means next to nothing until you actually begin the journey. Maybe you're relieved that you get to leave your daily grind for a week or so. Maybe you're anxious about all the unknowns that lie ahead. But however you feel at the trip's outset, you're bound to come across roadblocks and speed bumps that either slow you down or lead you off course altogether. And since usually none of these detours can be avoided, hopefully you will have the stamina to keep going, make the best of what's thrown your way, and try to enjoy the beauty of the journey anyway.

Then I asked my fellow TFA teachers how they were handling *this* ride. And boy, did I get a lot of answers that confirmed my own feelings about the experience up to that point. And some say men don't talk! Maybe the oppressive Southern heat inspired the outpouring of opinions – maybe they thought that the quicker they responded, the sooner I would conclude the meeting and we could all get up out of that heat. After all, it was the middle of the summer, we were in Texas, and by now they all knew how much I liked to talk.

At any rate, they shared how they felt, and then I ended the meeting with a bit of inspiration. "Despite the obvious disorganization that we are noticing around us," I told them, "we must keep moving forward. We must make the best of these detours and interruptions. We must turn adversity into advantage, as I've heard John C. Maxwell say time and time again. Because many of the urban youth we teach will live on the same streets that we tried to escape when we were younger.

Avoidance isn't the answer. What we are going through this summer is all a *big* test. I'm sure TFA didn't intentionally set it up as such, but that's the way it is. It's a test to see how we will handle the journey. Be very clear, we have a unique responsibility and it's up to us to answer the call. Many of the districts we will be going into have children who look like us. We might be a minority here, but we are a *majority* in many of the areas where TFA sends its teachers, and it's up to us to take the responsibility of this, all of this, seriously."

Sitting under the tree that day in the hot Texas sun, I realized that many of the fellow Black men I had assembled were quickly losing their fire for an opportunity that most of us – in the beginning – had been *so* excited about. And I was no exception. I had to find a way to get my fire back, and quickly. Calling this meeting and inspiring my fellow teachers was the first step for me. The next was to stay intently focused on my teaching career ahead and not to get caught up in the minutia I observed around me. And let me tell you, there was a lot of minutia. It felt like the closer the time got to when we were actually going to be sent off to teach in our own classrooms, the more focus seemed to be placed on making sure we had all our photocopies together and our daily lessons planned and organized. I didn't know at the time what preparation I really needed to be able to enter the classroom as a teacher with confidence, but I did have an inkling that all this incessant photocopying wasn't it.

According to its website, the mission of TFA is to "enlist, develop, and mobilize as many as possible of our nation's most promising future leaders to grow and strengthen the movement for educational equity and excellence." TFA founder Wendy Kopp started the organization in 1989 after writing her senior thesis at Princeton University about the educational achievement gap between students in high- and low-income areas. The original focus of TFA was to build a teaching force to help close that gap, and I think that whether we knew it at the time or not, much of our dissent had to do with the disconnect we felt between this mission and the preparation we were receiving.

It's worth noting that it wasn't just me and my fellow minority teachers who questioned some of our TFA preparation that summer. Many of our white colleagues also verbalized their dissatisfaction and distrust with the process. In Kopp's book, she even mentions us – the 94 corps – because of the general unrest that many of us had vocalized about the direction of the relatively new program. And yet none of the TFA staff that summer ever asked *any* of us how we were feeling.

As the summer unfolded, I continued to feel my spirit pushing back against the direction things were heading with the preparation program. I wanted to learn from master teachers, those who had been on the ground – who had history and some battle scars from spending time in the trenches, who had trained other teachers, and who had done some unbelievable things in their careers. It was hard for me to take direction from teachers who only had a couple years of teaching experience behind them, who seemed so green. I also wanted some teachers who looked like me and to whom I could relate.

---

And yet – ready or not – the end of the summer arrived and it was time for me to receive my teaching assignment. I thought that I was headed to New Jersey, but at the last minute that job fell through and I found out that I was being sent to Baltimore. *Cool*, I thought. I knew almost nothing of the city, even though I had placed it as the third choice on my list of places I wanted to teach.

The only Baltimore school I was familiar with was Dunbar High School because some of the great athletes came out of Dunbar and went on to play in Chicago, including Sam Cassell, Muggsy Bogues, Reggie Lewis, Kurk Lee, Reggie Williams, David Wingate and Skip Wise. The Baltimore TFA director asked me if I had heard of City College and I said no. They told me that it was a city-wide high school, but that meant nothing to me until I learned that in Baltimore city-wide schools are magnet schools. I was excited to find out that I was going to be the first TFA corps member to be assigned to teach at such a school. There was a bit of jealousy among the 12 TFA Baltimore corps members, because not only had I not even been part of the Baltimore corps at the Institute, but here I was getting an unbelievable opportunity to teach at this old, historic school on the hill. This school had birthed tons of leaders and had a reputation that preceded it, so I didn't pay too much mind to the jealousy. I was too busy being excited! I was going to be a teacher!

As the school year got underway, the jealousy and unrest slowly mounted as many of my fellow Baltimore TFA teachers faced major challenges at their schools – daily fights in the hallways, lots of disrespect from students, threats on their lives – that I just couldn't relate to. Several TFA corps members actually walked off the job that year, and yet there I was in an environment where I was not only surviving, but thriving. City was a great place to start my career and, for the most part, I was having a really positive experience.

Not that I didn't encounter some problems. As grateful as I was for my job and all the opportunities it afforded me, I battled constantly with the Baltimore TFA director. The TFA supervisor who oversaw my teaching would report back to the director about how well I was doing and the director consistently retorted that nobody taught that well their first year. He'd give me mediocre reviews, with the explanation that I couldn't really be doing the things that my supervisor reported to him in only my first year of teaching. I was upset because I already felt like many of the white TFA teachers were receiving more support than my fellow African American corps members and I were receiving. And the lack of support only added to the litany of our complaints against and distrust of the TFA establishment. We heard reports of housing support, financial resources, and other benefits that some TFA members were offered but that we weren't being given access to.

I didn't have much time or energy, though, to try to figure out why some corps members were receiving support that we weren't. I was grateful for the bonds I had formed with my roommate, Cheria Dial, and some of the other TFA Baltimore corps members with whom I could easily relate. We had each other to lean on and did the best we could to remain focused on our new teaching careers. As long as I concentrated on the positive, I was able to keep things moving forward.

---

When I've traveled throughout the country to speak, I've noticed through the years that when TFA is mentioned as part of my introductory bio, I often get a very mixed reaction from the audience to the fact that I came into the teaching profession by way of TFA. From district superintendents to school site administrators to teachers, I've noticed that the reactions tend to be polarized – folks either love TFA, or they hold strongly negative opinions about the organization.

So even though I was aware when writing this chapter that the only experience I could speak to fully was my own, I didn't want my voice to stand alone in the conversation. I reached out and spoke with a number of TFA graduates in my circle, both those who were with me in Houston that summer and others who had gone through the program at a different time. We spoke about what had brought us to TFA, how well we felt TFA prepared us to teach, and how we felt that TFA fit within the larger context of our work. The other viewpoints I encountered were, not surprisingly, a bit mixed, which only reinforced for me that the conversation was far from over and there was much work left to be done.

A TFA colleague of mine, Ruth, said that the most helpful thing to her about the entire TFA experience was that she had a female African American advisor who could really relate to what she was experiencing as a new teacher. Ruth said that in a program overflowing with theory, her advisor really focused on the practical aspects of the lives of the students she'd be teaching and the environment in which she'd be working.

Yolanda, another TFA friend, shared that as a senior in college she had been a bit directionless. She had been considering becoming a counselor or clinical psychologist when she had come across a TFA advertisement in a career magazine one day. She had decided to check it out, figuring that the corps would give her some experience working with children while she decided which career path she wanted to pursue. What Yolanda remembered most about the TFA Institute was a time when two TFA teachers had approached her shortly after her arrival on campus and had started questioning whether or not she was qualified to be there. As she described it, *that was kind of my introduction to TFA and probably one of the reasons why I'm not an incredible supporter of the whole organization. I finished my two-year teaching commitment in Baltimore and then moved on from the classroom. I never really developed this huge fascination with TFA, even though I have since come back to work with TFA as a teacher advisor.*

My TFA roommate Cheria said that she had joined TFA because *I really had no idea what I wanted to do with my life after graduation. I came across an ad for TFA in the newspaper and was like, "Oh well, if I don't know what I want to do, teaching underprivileged kids is probably a good thing to invest my time in while I figure it out." I remember going to workshops during the Summer Institute and feeling like a lot of what we were learning was common sense to me. Folks seemed to be really worried about having discipline problems. And I thought, "Yeah, I don't think I'll have those issues." I think some people thought I was just naïve for thinking that, but as it turned out I didn't really struggle with classroom management when I started teaching. I believed if I was genuine and cared about my students, they'd sense that and would behave differently than if they just thought I was there to collect a paycheck.*

Another TFA Baltimore corps teacher shared with me that he had joined TFA because *I was feeling this strong desire to give back to kids in urban areas. I had founded a tutoring program when I was in college and it was very successful, so I was searching for something to do with youth after graduation. I applied to TFA and was accepted, although my memories of that whole summer in Houston are really vague. I know that the Houston experience was supposed to prepare us for what we would experience in the classroom, but it really didn't do that for me. I felt unprepared walking into that first school to teach, where I ended up staying for seven years. And most of the support I did get once I started teaching came from outside of TFA. I really got very disconnected from TFA. I didn't want anything to do with them. It's pretty much the same now. I share that I was in TFA, but I don't really wear it like a badge of honor like I know some people do.*

Ruth also shared that *as far as TFA as a whole, I'm not going to say they really prepared me to be the teacher I am today. I think great teachers are great because* that's what they're supposed to be doing. I will say that TFA was mostly about white folks teaching other white folks how to teach Black kids. That's pretty much the gist of it in a nutshell – what more can I say about it? You have mostly white folks going in to these areas to teach Black kids, and I have to question why we don't have more minority master teachers preparing these new TFA teachers how to teach the students they'll be teaching.

Another corps member echoed Ruth's sentiments when she shared that *basically, I agree with Ruth that you can't teach what you really don't know. Especially in the early years. People want to talk to me about their more recent TFA experiences and I tell them that you can't really compare them to what we went through because now TFA has all these resources and assessments they've developed over the years. We didn't have any of that in the early days. I do remember that they'd always tell us to "Carpe Diem!" and "Be flexible."*

Another one of my friends from TFA talked about the ways in which his experiences at a small, predominately white private college in Virginia had prepared him for the environment he found at the TFA Summer Institute: *I came to TFA from a college with these white kids who drove BMWs and Mercedes as freshmen. So I brought a level of frustration with me into my TFA experience because I was still carrying this baggage from college. Then I walked into TFA and found this same mindset of "Here we are to prepare you guys to do this because we know best." It just didn't sit well with me spiritually. I don't really remember much else except feeling disconnected from these folks and understanding that what they couldn't do for me I'd learn how to do for myself. I knew I had to make it happen either way. I do remember the meeting under the tree – everyone talking about their issues, thinking that this experience was going to be so much more valuable than it was.*

Cheria shared that she, too, had come to TFA from a predominantly white, upper class environment so she was prepared in some ways for what she experienced at the TFA Institute that summer in Houston. Little of it was surprising to her.

Sharheka, another Baltimore corps teacher, revealed that *TFA was an unusual choice for me because I was a very shy student in class, so teaching is not what I thought I'd end up doing at 21 years old. I considered myself to be a pretty new immigrant at the time, having arrived to New York from India at the age of 14. I was finishing up my college career at the University of Michigan when I found out about TFA. At the end of what I thought was a fabulous college education, TFA seemed like a good way to find my way to the heart of a nation that I was beginning to call my home. In terms of what had been given to me and in terms of the opportunity I'd been afforded, I felt like teaching would be an ideal way to both give back and challenge myself because it involved me stepping out of my* comfort zone and being a leader. And teaching not only challenged me to speak up and lead, but also to then turn around and inspire my students to learn and lead. For me, as a woman of color, it also felt politically like the right thing to do. Because I had a desire to teach in schools that were primarily filled with children of color, I felt like TFA was a great avenue to that. I guess if you're not interested in making huge amounts of money at 21 years old and you're keen on change, then teaching feels like the right thing to do.

Sharheka also shared her appreciation of the fact that TFA was different from a conventional teacher preparation program. She said that the TFA Institute worked well for me because even though the preparation felt abbreviated, I had a wonderful mentor in our little group, Eric Greene. He was just amazing and I was very inspired by him. One of the things he said, right before I was going to enter the classroom clearly panicked was, "Just remember this is a show." And I thought that was fabulous, because he said, "Teaching involves performing, and the show must go on." So this helped me put on my "show woman hat" and I did my thing. Then I was able to step down and be my own person. Eric also picked me and another teacher to go to Baltimore, which is a very special city to me. Sarah Hellbran was one of the founding members of TFA and she was in Baltimore City. She was a white female teacher who just truly inspired me and ended up becoming my dear friend. So I felt like I really got lucky. The training was intense, but the intensity prepared me to be a teacher. And so I'm thankful that TFA introduced me to these people who transformed my life. Like my mentor and colleague Dr. Shields and my circle of friends around Dr. Shields.

With all said and done, I am grateful that TFA chose me. Without TFA, I have no idea how my teaching career would have unfolded and I don't know if I ever would have discovered a home in the great city of Baltimore. That being said, I think I'd be irresponsible in talking about my TFA experience without representing – as best as I can – much of the unrest that some of my fellow corps members and I experienced.

Two years ago, in the summer of 2013, I spoke at a TFA-sponsored event in Chicago for people of color. The event was held at IIT, just minutes away from De La Salle. And I listened as these future teachers discussed the disingenuous ways in which TFA was addressing topics of race in their trainings. I listened to the teachers – nearly two decades after I went through the TFA Summer Institute in Houston – talk about the forced, scripted conversations about race, the disorganization of the Institute's structure, the focus on the minutia. TFA had given them a forum to discuss these issues that we had never had, but that didn't seem to do much to minimize their pain. In a single moment I was taken back to the feeling of roaming around that campus in Houston, barely out of college myself, trying to figure out what my role was going to be in addressing the educational ills of the world, so deeply seeking some sort of guidance, some sort of mentorship, some sort of map. And I had been seeking it from an environment that just wasn't equipped, at the time, to provide me with what I needed.

Only recently, I was discussing this book chapter with a buddy of mine, a Morehouse alumnus and TFA graduate who is now a school principal. And he shared that one of the challenges he faces as a school leader is that he gets a lot of TFA teachers who just do their time and then leave his school, and the teaching profession, for other pursuits – law school, business school, other careers. Teaching seems to be a mere stepping stone for them. And even though some of them are great teachers, he knows they're probably not going to stick around. He shared that it's hard to build a team and a school culture when your school feels like it has a revolving door. Of course, this isn't only a problem with TFA teachers. Dr. Monique Henderson's recent article in the Hechinger Report notes that many high poverty, high minority schools are having a hard time recruiting and then retaining a quality teaching force.

TFA is a complex organization working in a complex educational system that operates as part of a complex society. Discussing the role that TFA has played in my own life hasn't been easy, nor has it been simple for me to contextualize TFA in its broader context. At minimum, my hope is that in discussing my own experience, I've been able to contribute to the larger narrative of how we're preparing our teaching force in general and how TFA is preparing future teachers in particular. I also hope I've been able to contribute in some small way to the role that race plays in the matter, because to ignore the racial implications would be to silence my own experience, the experiences of so many of my fellow TFA corps members, and the experiences of all those students who TFA graduates go on to serve.

# CHAPTER 10

# THE CASTLE ON THE HILL

*Teach the youth and speak the truth. Show 'em what peace can do when they'll reach for you.*

\- Rakim

City is the type of school that teachers retired from. It was a dream job. Officially known as Baltimore City College High School, the school was founded on October 20, 1839 when Nathan C. Brooks and 46 students convened in a rented building on Courtland Street to study either a Classical course, focusing on Greek and Latin, or an English and Mathematics course. The school is the third oldest public high school in the United States and today describes itself as a "citywide college preparatory institution with selective admissions and an emphasis on the liberal arts and sciences." It focuses on "academic programs that incorporate communication, intercultural awareness, and inquiry-based learning and… aspires for [its] students to demonstrate excellence and to succeed in the best colleges."

I learned early on that facing teenagers every day keeps you humble. First thing in the morning, they don't care how you feel – they don't care if you're hung over from the night before, or if your student loans are late, or if you're worried about the principal just dropping by your class unannounced to see if you actually have a lesson plan. Every day as a high school teacher you face 170 or more angry, horny, high, drunk, sarcastic, intelligent, anxious, energetic, self-absorbed, challenging and lovable students all vying for your attention. And there is no escape. No one is interested in the fact that you couldn't sleep the night before, that you then overslept and your car was towed from the parking lot across the street because you didn't get it out in time. They are asking for test scores that you promised to get back to them two weeks ago, questioning when the next big project is going to be due, challenging the relevance of the lesson you're presenting that day.

But you keep going back because you hope that you can make a difference. You hope that just by showing up and trying to figure it out along the way, you are making some sort of impact.

I talk a lot these days about the importance of authenticity, and – according to one of my former students – this was ingrained in me even in my earlier days of teaching: *Mr. Shields taught me how to be my authentic self. Everyone would say that he taught Spanish a different way and I have to agree. I had only had white Spanish teachers before Mr. Shields. So to have a young, Black Spanish teacher who was very proud of his heritage and was able to incorporate so much of who he was into his teaching just inspired me so much. He was authentic and that is why we would walk into the classroom and see a Malcolm X or Fidel Castro poster, why we'd learn about our African culture as it related to being Black in America. He was not trying to duplicate anyone else – he merged what he knew well with who he was and that's probably why he really started to excel as a teacher at City. And I learned from that example that the best person that I can be is myself, that the best story that I can tell is my own.*

I grew into my own as a teacher at City. Every single day I walked into my classroom and learned something new – about teaching, about my students, about myself. Although I honed my craft, like most beginning teachers those first years were a time of growth. And I made a lot of mistakes.

As one of my former students reflected, *I feel like we grew with Señor Shields because in those early years of teaching he was just trying to figure it all out. He was pretty disorganized and I remember feeling like he was just really trying to find his way. But I do hear how he did mature a bit later on. He did inspire me to apply to Teach for America and become a teacher. Looking back, it makes me feel a bit better about myself for struggling a bit too in my early years of teaching.*

What was interesting – but not unique – about my students was that they always tried to find a way to get me to talk about something that had nothing to do with Spanish class, especially on test days.

"Señor Shields," someone would yell from the back of the room, "do you think O.J. Simpson is going to prison?"

They knew me so well. They knew what topics would get me talking. I would tell them that the more time I spent talking, the less time they'd have to finish their test.

"Ah, Señor Shields! You're trippin'," they would say in unison.

I loved discussing current events with my students, though, because I really wanted them to have a perspective on the world – that was why I loved teaching a world language. I remember our discussion of the O.J. case being a pivotal point in my teaching career. We were told not to talk about it in class. When someone tells me I can't do something, however, I'll be the first to rebel. And I think that's why so many students gravitated toward me – they liked my rebellious spirit and found it intriguing.

The day the O.J. Simpson verdict came down, the news was unfolding during my last period class. I turned on the TV so my students and I could watch. But I told them to be *muy tranquilo* because Mr. Wilson, our school principal, had prohibited the televisions from being on during class. We knew silence was the only way we would be able to get away with watching the verdict.

We watched the trial and discussed what was happening at the same time. Everyone was so well behaved. They had *never* been this quiet during a regular class session. The students were on the edge of their seats, listening to the closing arguments and hoping to hear the verdict before the bell rang. Like the Trayvon Martin and Michael Brown cases, this trial was like one generation's emancipation. It wasn't about whether or not O.J. was even guilty. He probably was. But the feeling among many African Americans was that all Black males were on trial in that courtroom, and the verdict would have a symbolic meaning that went behind the specifics of the case. Two minutes before the bell rang, the verdict came in. Not guilty.

My students rushed into the halls screaming, "He's not going to jail! O.J.'s not going to jail!" It was like Abraham Lincoln had freed all of them from slavery as they ran out of that classroom. I couldn't believe it. It was a conversation that many teachers shied away from, but not me. I let my students talk about it, while I remained neutral on the subject so that they could form their own opinions. I knew that my job wasn't to sway them, just to ask some tough questions. They'd listen to all my questions and then ask, "Whose side are you on, Señor?" But I wouldn't respond.

I must admit, there were some days I could have walked out of the building and never returned – not because of the students, but because of some of the difficult teachers and administrators I had to work with, some of the policies we were made to follow. Then there were days when I wished the superintendent would walk into my classroom and see how much joy I felt teaching, see how much joy my students felt learning. I loved teaching and believed that I was called to do it. Sometimes I think I could have stayed at City forever.

The funny thing was, as I've mentioned before, City was not even where I was supposed to begin my teaching career. My Teach for America assignment had had me heading to New Jersey. Then, at the last moment, I had gotten a call and found out that I was headed to Baltimore instead. I knew nothing about the school, nothing about the Baltimore school system, and nothing about the city itself, really.

The first day of my teaching career, I remember standing in the assistant principal's office, leaning against the wall, when a very official-looking woman walked in. She was dressed in a sharp suit with her hair pulled back, eyes beading in on me through the type of eyeglasses that somehow demanded attention. She took one look at me and told me to take my hat off. I looked around to see who she was talking to, but since I was the only one in the room I figured I must have been the object of her curt request. I informed her that I wasn't wearing a hat, I was wearing a kufi. I let her know in no uncertain terms that where I came from, a hat by definition was something with a brim. Then I asked her whether she would have asked me to remove my yamaka if that had been what I was wearing instead.

Following this exchange, I shook her hand and introduced myself as the school's new Spanish teacher. Looking pretty embarrassed, she apologized profusely. But I was thinking, *Why did it matter that I was a teacher? What if I had been a student? Was she only embarrassed because she now knew I was her colleague, or because how I had responded to her had made it clear how I had felt about her unreasonable request?*

I think this was one of the first times I realized that whatever my role was as a teacher had to translate into how *I* responded to conflict, whether inside or outside the classroom. Personally, I had much more experience acting a fool and instigating conflict than I did with deescalating it. De La Salle had provided a ripe environment for me to go off the handle frequently. But as a teacher, I was going to have to deescalate situations with students all day long; it was part of my job description. So it was important to me to walk the walk, even in settings where I felt defensive and could have easily exploded. I couldn't ask something of my students that I was unwilling to live out myself.

The incident also got me thinking about how often we judge others, and especially our students, based on what they're wearing. And that this judgment says as much about our own fears and perceptions as it does about our students and their wardrobe choices. Chuck D., lead singer of Public Enemy, said in his song "Welcome to the Terror Dome," "Gear I wear got 'em going in fear," and I wondered if there had been something about my kufi that day that had made the assistant principal afraid.

The interesting thing about becoming a teacher is that, for many of us, we start our careers when we still have so much growing up to do ourselves. We are young and trying to figure our own stuff out at the same time that we're responsible for shaping future generations. It's complex.

When my roommate Cheria and I landed in Baltimore after the TFA Summer Institute, we had papers indicating that we had teaching contracts, but little else. We didn't have any money, we didn't have a place to live, and we certainly didn't have much of a clue as to how we were going to manage being responsible for so many teenagers all day, every day.

Cheria described the time as follows: *We figured out we were both going to Baltimore so we decided to room together since we were in a pretty similar situation as in neither of us really had any money. I'm not even sure how we ended up in an apartment. I think LaMarr was the one who convinced the apartment complex manager to rent to us, even though all we had was an appointment letter for our teaching. So neither of us had money for a down payment or any furniture. We just had the stuff we had taken with us to training in Houston. But since LaMarr has always been a pretty good talker, it worked out and they let us move in and even gave us some furniture to borrow. LaMarr even arranged it with them so that we didn't have to make our first rent payment until we got our first paychecks.*

It wasn't all hard work and struggle, though. We had a lot of fun. Our apartment was one of the places where people liked to congregate. We had friends over a lot and would celebrate holidays together. We started a Kwanzaa celebration and there was always a lot of music.

Cheria described her memories of the time: *He had this really big speaker system. So we would blast music a lot. I can picture LaMarr – he would always sleep in a t-shirt and pajama pants – running through the apartment to turn up the music. I remember this one Phil Collins song, "In the Air Tonight," that he would just blast. Like blast it, blast it. If you know the song, you know there's a part of it where it's really quiet and then the bass and drums come in really loudly. I think that was his favorite part of the song. The memory is so vivid. There was just a lot of laughter because he liked to joke so much. And because he was a vegetarian, he was always introducing me to new vegetarian foods. I would say, "I don't think I'm gonna like this," and he would just tell me to try it, that it was so good. So I still eat veggie sausage patties because of him. Twenty years later and I'm still eating them.*

Cheria became pregnant with her oldest son while we were living together, I was there at the hospital when he was born, and for awhile afterwards we remained roommates. Cheria shared that *my son calls him Uncle Darnell. He's always been very instrumental in my son's life.*

And because we were living together and both teaching Spanish, Cheria and I were able to plan a lot together. As Cheria remembered it, *When we first started out, LaMarr could be a little last minute with his lesson planning. It was easy to share things since we were teaching similar classes. He'd ask me, "What do you have planned?" And I would say, "I've got this, this and this." "Oh can I just do that?" he'd always ask. And I'd be like, "Really? Really?" But it was funny and it was fine. Because he was teaching at City College, which was a magnet school, and I was teaching at Southwestern, which was one of the lower performing schools, our shared lessons ended up being a great motivator for my students. I'd tell them, "Hey, kids who are City College are learning the same things in Spanish that you all are learning because their Spanish teacher is my roommate." They'd be like "Oh, okay." Sometimes students at low performing schools can feel like they are not getting access to many opportunities. So I think it helps for them to know that some of their peers at schools with more resources are learning the same things.*

---

I discovered early on in my teaching that the physical design of my classroom was important to me. Ubuntu teaching is focused on community, and my classroom environment became the foundation of the community we were creating.

More than a decade after they had learned within those walls, some of my former students could still describe in detail the physical setup of my classroom. *His classroom was shaped as a U,* a former student shared. *The U made it more intimate, more personal, than a lot of our other classes. You'd see everyone's faces when they spoke. It became more of a family-type classroom.*

Another former student recalled that *Señor Shields was a performer, so his classroom was bright. You walked into his classroom and it was like you were walking onstage. There were a bunch of pictures of Spanish-speaking countries – billboards and pictures and things to take you to other countries. They transported you. And there was one big ol' sombrero. And a giant picture of Malcolm X above his desk.*

My students recognized that an early part of my Ubuntu teaching meant bringing who I was into the classroom: *His corner where his desk sat was like his home – it was very Afrocentric and was definitely a reflection of him. I spent a lot of time looking at this corner for inspiration.*

I think they also recognized that the chaos in my classroom did have a purpose to it: *When we walked in, English stopped at the door. It was almost like organized chaos because other teachers would walk in and be like, "Wow – where am I?" It was like a whole new world. But we loved it. It drew us in and kept us captivated. To this day, if anyone were to ask me who my favorite teacher was, Señor Shields is the first person I think of. He was just ultimately the best.*

And I guess that somewhere along the way I found that spark that I had been seeking during my summer at the TFA Institute, because another former student shared that: *He truly ignited this fire that words really can't explain. Sometimes you just know when a person "has it" and he just had it – he just had that spark where it was like, "Wow, this is where you should be. This is it."*

---

My students sure did challenge me, though! Especially the class of 1998. I started teaching when they were freshmen and was assigned the privilege and, I'd soon find out, challenge of being their class advisor. They were so smart academically, but they were crazy. They wreaked a lot of chaos and were routinely getting me into hot water. No other teachers even wanted to help advise this class because they had become so notoriously disruptive. I remember one time they wrote a letter to the school administration explaining why the school needed to essentially fire my co-advisor because they wanted me to be their only advisor. I remember the assistant principal calling me up to the office over this letter, asking if I had helped the students with its crafting because it was so well written. I hadn't, of course. It was *all* them.

And yet, I felt like advising the class was a divine assignment for me because they reminded me so much of *myself* as a student – intelligent, but mischievous and devious as hell. For the first time in my life, I was really given an opportunity to reflect on how I had been as a teenager, why I had caused so many of my teachers – and my mother, of course – such grief, and how I could help these kids channel their energy into more positive avenues. I understood them deeply and, in doing so, came to more fully understand myself. And this kind of understanding is one of the greatest joys of teaching and of life – being able to see yourself reflected in the journey of another.

---

I realized early on that one of my strengths as a teacher was the ability to connect with my students and meet them where they were. This Ubuntu quality of the reciprocity of relationships was something that I took very seriously.

One of the most powerful examples of this concept can be found in a relationship that I developed with a young man by the name of Henry Brim. I've told the story in many different incarnations during workshops and trainings through the years, but here I'm going to let Henry tell the story, in his own voice:

*Señor Shields and I literally ran into each other one day,* Henry recalled. *I was walking up the front steps to the school and, being totally blind, I just kind of collided with him. We bonded right away and our relationship grew from him just being someone I looked up to to really being a mentor in my life. Some fellow students and I wanted to start our own organization on campus and Señor Shields ended up being our advisor for that. He really encouraged us to read books outside of school about and by African Americans so we could be prouder of who we were and where we came from.*

Henry shared that our bond became increasingly important to him after the death of his own father: *When my father passed away, Señor Shields really stepped in and supported me through my grief. He helped bridge a huge gap in my life. My father passed away on a Sunday and I remember that following Monday listening to my mother make all these phone calls and tell the story of my father's death over and over again. I just went up to my room and cried uncontrollably. I don't think my mom knew what to do with me, so she called Shields and he came over immediately after school.*

*He hugged me and said to me, I'll never forget his words, "Who is there to make the clown laugh when the clown is upset?" See, I was always the funny guy at City, the supporter for everyone else, the one who – despite all my own personal challenges – always uplifted others. And Shields' words to me that day, that I remember word for word even though it was over twenty years ago, stuck with me and made me realize that it was okay to ask for help, that it was okay to be supported through my own grief.*

*And then when I came back to school, he really helped me channel all my pain in a positive direction – through community work, giving back to others and supporting those who needed it. It's like he helped me take my own energy plus the energy my father had had plus the energy LaMarr had and put them all together. And I just ran with this energy. I went rampant! I became such an advocate for those who could not help themselves.*

The ironic thing is that Henry was never actually a student in my class. And yet we had such a strong connection. Henry said it was because: *He was compassionate and he knew how to connect and relate to the students. I don't know if it was the fact that he was an African American man – we didn't have that many Black male teachers – or that he was young, or both. But he was really just able to relate to us as individuals. I've seen him angry, but I've never seen him raise his voice. He's always been very calm, compassionate, energetic and passionate. Once he became involved in something, he would go in all guns blazing. He was so focused, so as a student I knew he was someone I could trust.*

Students moved from my Spanish class to the classroom of the teacher next door, who taught the higher-level courses. But for some reason even when students left my class to move onto the next level, they would keep coming back – before school, after school, during class. I couldn't get them to leave. As Henry described it: *the biggest difference and I'll be blunt and honest was a cultural difference. At this time, the other Spanish teacher and a lot of the other teachers at City were Jewish. Not to say they were racist, but the connection that Brother Shields had with a lot of us they just didn't have.*

One time, I brought in some guest speakers from the Nation of Islam and some teachers on campus made a big deal about it. They accused me of being anti-Semitic and, as Henry described it, he and some of the other students felt that *it was a form of racism toward us. These teachers just couldn't accept that Brother Shields had a connection with us that they didn't have. He was demanding a level of respect and rapport that they just struggled with. Like a captain on a ship – Brother Shields was able to guide us through the storms a lot more calmly than they ever could. And after school we'd all hang out in his classroom, so I think some of the other teachers were jealous of this connection. We'd go to him for extra assistance. This other Spanish teacher had a stronger command of the actual language, but we'd still go to Señor Shields for help.*

I stayed in touch with Henry after he graduated. Henry became a father before I did, and even though I didn't have any parenting experience myself yet, he said that I helped him transition into fatherhood. As he described it: *being able to ask Brother Shields for advice was important to me. Yes, I had a father, but he had died, so becoming a father without being able to call my father was a tough transition for me. I only knew how to be a son, not a father. Brother Shields didn't have kids himself at the time, but just to have a man to be able to share my feelings with was important.*

I even helped Henry plan his wedding. Henry related how *Brother Shields not only picked out the music, but also coordinated with all these people he knew to help with the venue and food and everything. He helped us have a really nice, but affordable wedding. He even read a poem during the ceremony.* Later, when Henry started doing some motivational speaking and training, I brought him on board with my team to speak and train beside me.

Ubuntu teaching means bringing things full circle, meeting students where they are, filling in the gaps, and recognizing that so often one of the greatest joys of teaching is learning how much our students have to teach *us.*

# CHAPTER 11

## BROADER HORIZONS

*Life is your professor. You know that Bitch is gon' test ya.*

- J. Cole

I picked up the flyer because the questions plastered across it caught my eye – *Do you believe in changing the world? Do you believe in investing in young people?* Of course, I thought! Of all the difficult questions I asked myself on a daily basis, these weren't among them. The flyer was advertising some sort of summer cultural language immersion program and I was intrigued. So I picked up the phone and called the number printed at the bottom of the paper. A gentleman answered with a voice that betrayed his age – it was so deep and soothing that I knew he had to be an older man. After a few minutes of conversation, he and I had arranged for him to come meet me at City to discuss an opportunity for me to travel with him to Puerto Rico. I knew nothing about this man except that his name was Biff and he lived in Pennsylvania.

I would soon come to find out that his full name was James "Biff" Holden and he was a Quaker who ran an organization called Global Works. As promised, he showed up in my classroom at City one day during my planning period to talk about the work he and his organization were doing across the country and abroad. I remember Biff saying that he really liked the energy in my classroom, even though he visited me at a time when there weren't any students present. He liked the international posters that plastered the walls and the music I was playing, and I think he just got a sense being in my space that I might be a good fit for his organization.

I made a deal with Biff that day that if I was going to work and travel with him, I wanted to be able to take at least one of my African American students with me on the trip. And then I told him about a student named Brandon. Prior to Biff's visit, I had talked to all of my students about the possibility of traveling abroad. It was Brandon who had seemed most interested, and like the best fit. I had a good relationship with his parents, I thought he'd be easy to travel with, and – almost as importantly – I thought that his parents might say yes to the opportunity.

So I went down the hall to see if I could pull Brandon out of class to meet Biff. I remember distinctly his teacher saying, "Go ahead. Take Brandon out of my class. He's failing anyway." So I did. And he met Biff. I knew then that I was going to be able to open up Brandon's eyes, and my own, to the world in a whole new way that summer.

---

Prior to officially hiring me, Biff invited me to his ranch in Huntington, Pennsylvania for a weekend staff retreat. He called it solidarity work. The farm was beautiful, but also much more rural and rustic than I was used to. I loved everything about the place!

I can't tell you how strange it was to be whisked into this community of liberal white folks who wanted to change the world. I mean, in a way my experience with TFA should have prepared me, but this felt different somehow. I saw Amish people for the very first time. And I fell in love with listening to Biff talk about his Quaker beliefs. He shared with me the role Quakers had played in the abolition of slavery, women's rights, and peaceful movements throughout history.

I remember sitting in Biff's living room one night that weekend, surrounded by a room full of white people, watching Chris Rock's HBO show "Bigger and Blacker." In the show, which was airing live from Washington, D.C., Rock – in his typical comedic way of really pushing the envelope around issues of race – talked about the difference between "Black folks and niggers." And I remember being the only person of color in the room, feeling so uncomfortable and thinking, *Which one do they think I am?* I sat there in my awkward silence, but couldn't work up the nerve to either say anything or leave the room. While we laughed and some of the bits were funny, the moment couldn't help but raise a whole host of questions in my mind. I don't know if anyone else in the room felt as uncomfortable as I did because I never asked them. Reflecting back on it, I started to question what lesson I *should* have learned in that moment and how I *should* have reacted. Should I have begun a conversation about race? Should I have turned the program off and made a statement about how, in that context, it made me uncomfortable?

I remember years later hearing about an incident involving Maya Angelou that reminded me of my own experience, although her reaction was the polar opposite of mine. As the story was told to me, one evening Dr. Angelou was hosting a dinner party at her house when a guest used the n word. Dr. Angelou stopped the dinner party right then and there and kicked the guest out of her home.

Looking back on my own experience now, I think I might have handled the situation differently – that I might have said something or at least left the room. But I didn't. I just sat there in silence. I was learning lessons and still growing into myself and my place in the world. I was trying to figure out what I was made of, what I should do when I found myself the sole person of color in a room and I began to feel like I was carrying the weight of a whole group of people on my back, and what messages I would take back to people in my own community about these experiences.

There was a lot about that weekend, however, that I absolutely *loved*. I've always felt so at home in nature, so close to the Creator, and here I was in the middle of the woods, sleeping on a bunk bed in a cabin, doing the work that was going to prepare me to teach on a more global scale and to travel to and work in countries with large populations of people who looked like me.

I realized that I was experiencing a subtle but important shift in my life that was preparing me, in some powerful ways, for the work ahead.

***

Traveling to Puerto Rico to work was completely new territory for me. I chaperoned some of the wealthiest white young people in the country. From the son of a Disney VP to heirs to the Baskin Robbins fortune to children of Warner Brothers executives, these children were just *different* than the kids I taught at City. Some of them were quite vested in the experience, but others just saw it as a stopping point to the Cayman Islands, Cabo or Europe. Their parents had sent them to Puerto Rico as a precursor to family vacations in more exotic locations. And here I was, on the biggest trip of my lifetime.

In the beginning, I was honestly more focused on myself and how I was going to be viewed as a young man of color than on what the young people were going through. But what I quickly discovered was that many of these kids had some deep-rooted self-esteem issues and pain. Many of their experiences were really foreign to me, but I somehow became like a counselor to them. I found myself spending more time helping them sort through their personal problems than I did teaching them about the community-building we were supposed to be doing in the country. My belief that you can't give what you don't have really rang true with some of these kids, and I realized that there was a lot that they needed to work through about themselves and their place of privilege in the world before they could give back to the communities that we were serving.

Working with this group of kids really challenged many of my own assumptions about the wealthy. I began to see that I had just as much to learn from them as they did from me. Ubuntu teaching is about recognizing the inherent humanity in *all* of us and that dignity, respect, acceptance and trust are rights to which everyone is entitled. And that summer I really had to work to overcome my own prejudices about so many wealthy white kids who, in the beginning, I honestly just didn't understand.

I remember one day when we were walking down the street and a Greek kid blurted out, "LaMarr, my grandfather would never approve of me hanging out with a Black man." See, these three girls on the trip had made up a song the day before with a hook that went something like, "One day a Black, a Jew, and a Quaker were walking down the street." And I think the song must have made this kid think about some things, because it wasn't moments after the girls walked by singing it that he blurted out his epiphany to me. He went on to say that even though he really liked and respected me, he knew that his grandfather would never approve of our friendship. And he was so clear and transparent about it. He wasn't saying it to be malicious. I think he was honestly trying to figure out in his mind what the big deal was and why his grandfather harbored such racist ideologies.

I also remember the day I discovered that one of the kids had stolen a t-shirt from Wal-Mart. He was very wealthy, but he struggled with fitting in. He ended up being sent home because of the theft and it really opened my eyes to the fact that the struggle for acceptance and validation crosses all barriers. I learned that even if young people have huge trust funds, they still have a need to be heard, seen and accepted. Looking back, I don't think I would have learned this lesson so early, so poignantly, in my traditional teaching role. And I realized that as I was emerging as an Ubuntu teacher, I was coming to see that my teaching wasn't only for young people who looked like me. I learned that I could affect young people of all walks of life, all over the world.

Brent, a student who I met during one of my summers in Puerto Rico, shared his perspective on the program as follows: *During the summer after my junior year of high school, my parents enrolled me in a program called Global Works. It provided a platform for American teenagers to serve those in poorer communities throughout the Caribbean. I decided upon Puerto Rico. The idea was to immerse us in an unfamiliar world with the hope that we would glean a better understanding of the broader world as well as experience selfless service to those less fortunate.*

Brent recalled how we first met: *I first met LaMarr on a Puerto Rican beach. After landing, our disparate group of American teens was corralled together into two rickety old vans. After being dropped off at the beach, we met the rest of the group and the cohort of counselors. I remember feeling very awkward* and shy. There was a contingent of Boston kids who were cliquey, a Californian with dyed blond hair, some very rich Manhattan kids, a few others, and yours truly. I attempted to connect through small talk, but didn't get very far. The social teenage awkwardness took over and I found myself just standing there alone. I then distinctly remember LaMarr introducing himself to me and a few others who seemed disconnected from the larger group. It was the first time conversation flowed. There was no judgment from him, only open curiosity as to who we were. He was calm and cool, but had a strong sense of loyalty that shone in his eyes and his overall spirit. He provided a safety net for me from the very first moment we met.

Brent recalled how one of the kids, Mike from New York City, suffered severe harassment at the hands of some Boston kids throughout the trip. Mike ended up living with a family in the village where we were staying, Villa Sin Miedo, to separate him from his tormenters. Brent said that it was clear that Mike looked up to me and that I had his back throughout the trip. Brent said he saw me as a protector, one of the most selfless roles one can play in this life. Brent was accurate in surmising that I had helped solve Mike's debacle by asking the local family to temporarily house him.

I knew that I had a strong connection with the students, but it wasn't until I heard recently about how Brent had described my departure that I realized how important this connection was for some of the kids. My surprise brings to mind that old adage in teaching – that we often don't know the impact we've made until years after the fact.

As Brent described it: *We traveled to Adjuntas towards the end of our trip. This was a very lush area located in the central, western portion of the island. This was also LaMarr's departure point. The memory of LaMarr leaving is very distinct to me. I remember tears flowing after he left. He was a big brother to me during this Puerto Rican adventure and I had not experienced this level of separation anxiety since first grade when I refused to let go of my mother's hand and get on the school bus. It speaks to a connection and how, if we have an open heart, others can enrich our lives in ways we may not fully understand.*

My early experience in Puerto Rico is one of the reasons I remain passionate today about challenging both teachers and students to teach and learn outside of their comfort zones. I think it's important to get out of the boxes that society has created for us. For five consecutive summers, I traveled between Puerto Rico and Costa Rica leading these Global Works trips. I was proud of the work we were doing to give some amazing cultural experiences to young people.

There was another teacher named Malcolm who was on staff at Global Works and who I really looked up to as both a teacher and mentor. Together, we decided that we wanted to attract kids of color and create our own travel abroad experiences. We wanted to find the kids who could never have afforded to attend a Global Works trip and to provide them with a comparable experience at a much lower cost. Even though we did a lot of good work through Global Works, we had a vision of engaging youth at an even deeper level of service learning.

Malcolm was from Puerto Rico. He was named after Malcolm X and came from a revolutionary family. His mother had actually been one of Malcolm X's nurses. We had an instant connection, a historical connection, a connection of purpose. And he was one of the few other teachers of color who worked with me through Global Works.

It was five years later that our dream of leading a different kind of trip actually came to fruition. And I'll never forget the look on Malcolm's face the day I arrived in Puerto Rico with a group of students to begin a trip that, for so many years, we had only envisioned in our minds. As we disembarked from the plane and he greeted us on his home soil, his face broke into a smile that lit up the whole place. He looked over at me and at all the anxious young people who looked like us and exclaimed, "We did it! We did it! We did it!" And then he smiled again.

On the first phase of our trip we stayed at Finca de Noel, a gated farm tucked away in a fairly remote mountain region of Puerto Rico surrounded by beautiful mango and banana trees. And although there was both a pool and a pool table on the property, it also had a very rustic feel to it.

We'd get up every morning before dawn, letting the sun chase us as we traveled the short distance to the farm where we volunteered. The farm, a co-op run by a tiny woman named Ruth, raised food that went directly to battered women. We learned from Ruth that Puerto Rico has a widespread domestic violence problem among its people and she shared her pride in her ability to be of service through the food she raised on her farmland. Ruth was so grateful for our service and was excited that the kids who came with us that year looked like her and her daughters. She also liked that we had a few young women in our group because Ruth's work directly benefited women in need. I wondered how this woman with two daughters, one of whom had special needs, could maintain a farm of this size all by herself. Despite her small frame, Ruth had a heart that was just as big as her magnetic smile, and I guess that these qualities, combined with a sweeping vision, allowed her to achieve what might otherwise have seemed impossible.

We'd work for about four hours on the farm until the oppressive heat became too much to bear. We'd then break for mango eating and ocean swimming before switching gears in the afternoon. After lunch, we would help build homes. In Puerto Rico, many houses sat unfinished due to homeowners running out of funding, people abandoning them mid-construction to move back to the U.S., and hurricane destruction interrupting or delaying building progress.

Malcolm, who came from a long line of not only revolutionaries, but also skilled tradesmen, was masterful with his carpentry skills. He taught the kids a lot about how to build a foundation and frame a house with skill. There's a saying that claims "Puerto Ricans know how to do two things, throw cement and use a machete." And even though we weren't about to let any of our students swing around machetes, they did get a lot experience with laying cement foundations for homes. The project was called El Proyecto de Ayuda Mutual, Project Mutual Aid or Help, and the way it worked was that one day we'd work on a home with the help of all the neighbors. Then the next day, we'd return the favor by helping the neighbors work on their homes. I loved the concept because of the practicality and generosity it embodied. I wished I could have just wrapped it up and exported it to the U.S. and then gifted it to many of the schools and agencies I worked with back home. I also loved that the kids got to see a different side of the Puerto Rican culture than just the poverty and destitution that struck us all at first glance.

The second phase of our trip brought us to the homestays. They were amazing, although in the beginning the kids were a bit nervous. The families were all screened ahead of time, but for the first time during the trip the youth were separated from each other and from the leaders each night. I myself hadn't anticipated how hard it would be to let them all go that first night – dropping one kid off at one home and the next off at another felt like letting my own children go. And it wasn't easy.

But they learned so much during these homestays that it was well worth our initial trepidation and fear of separation. The kids picked up some colloquial language and learned first-hand about traditions and customs of the Puerto Rican culture. They really became immersed in the community and learned to be mindful of the gifts they were given. I loved witnessing it all, because this was my second home. My roots were in Puerto Rico. *Mi gente*, my people, were here. We taught our students to eat the food they were served no matter what, because the only way that many of the host families could express their hospitality and gratitude for our volunteer service was with food and smiles.

At the end of this phase of the trip, the entire small village threw us a big party. The food, the dancing, and the celebration were just amazing. And I'll never forget the way Malcolm looked at me across the sea of people that night and gave me another one of those bright, glowing smiles. *We are REALLY doing what we said we were going to do!* his eyes communicated without a word.

From the village, we went to work with a family on an old farm that had incredibly antiquated tools. What we learned, thought, was that even though the farm lacked modern machinery, it was way ahead of the times when it came to sustainability, using renewable resources, and green farming techniques. The farmers relied on solar power and had built these amazing greenhouses. Although the family had two children, they didn't have enough farmhands, and we were happy to lend our service to their cause during our brief stay.

Every time I reflect back on this part of the journey, an image comes to my mind, as clear as day. We were out in the fields on our last day of work when the sky started to darken and rumble. We knew that the rain was coming. And I remember one of the little girls who lived on the farm stretched her hands up to the sky, looked upward, and said, "Let the rain come! Let the rain come!" And the sky just opened up. The rainstorm was torrential. But we all kept working. We didn't run for cover. We just worked and laughed and danced in the rain.

To see these African American girls from the city not worrying about the rain messing up their hair or the frogs hopping on their feet or the mud covering their clothes was just the most beautiful sight. Everyone was loving the work and didn't want to stop. We had made a connection with this family at a very basic, but deep level. And we knew we were being of service and giving back through our efforts. We wanted to soak up every minute of time in those beautiful fields with those beautiful people, and the rain only seemed to enhance the experience that day. The skies eventually cleared, but I knew right then that we had just experienced something magical that I'd be able to look back on fondly for the rest of my days.

Our time on the farm concluded the work phase of the trip, and from there we headed to the rainforest to soak up some nature and relax a bit before flying home. We stayed in a villa less than 100 yards from the ocean, and being able to wake up in the morning and walk a few short steps to the beach just blew the kids away. They loved it!

One of our last days on the island, I told the kids to get into their bathing suits and hiking shoes. I didn't tell them where we were going, and of course they complained for a solid hour into the hike as teenagers do. But then we got to this spot where the trees opened up to a huge waterfall and a swimming hole with water as clear as glass. I loved watching the kids jump into the water and splash around with abandon. It was an amazing sight in a breathtaking spot and I couldn't help but to think how grateful I was in that moment to be witnessing a dream of mine fulfilled. To see all these young people who came from neighborhoods that required them to grow up far too quickly just being kids and enjoying life in this magical place brought a smile to my face that I couldn't shake.

These were not the same kids who had nervously boarded a plane with me in Baltimore, passports in hand, just a couple of short weeks before. On the plane ride down to Puerto Rico, I had surveyed them to see what they thought about where we were headed. And even though we had spent quite a bit of time back in Baltimore preparing for the trip, learning about the history and the culture of the people whose home we were going to visit, most of their expectations had been negative ones. Many of the parents had been hesitant to send their children out of the country because they had never traveled themselves and were nervous, and I know this trepidation showed up in the kids' perceptions of what Puerto Rico would be like. I don't even know how, given the circumstances, I was able to recruit kids who looked like me when so few of the children of color I met in Baltimore even traveled outside of their city blocks on a regular basis. But somehow I managed to get enough kids together that first year to make the trip happen.

On the plane ride back home, I surveyed the young people again about their perceptions. And of course their entire outlooks had changed. When I asked the boys what they were going to miss the most, they unanimously said the girls and the food, in that order. The girls, on the other hand, said that they were going to miss the beautiful beaches and the fresh mangos more than anything. For the next three years, Malcolm and I led similar trips to Puerto Rico each summer. And I do believe that every trip changed the lives of all of those involved.

Two summers ago we switched the location of our trips to Haiti and the Dominican Republic. We saw a great need in Haiti after the earthquake and also wanted to include a business piece that was possible there. We partnered with Taharka Brothers, a Baltimore-based ice cream company that touts itself as "a small batch socially sourced and partisanal producer of ice cream and sorbets made from radical recipes." Taharka Brothers was sourcing its chocolate, salt and coffee from Haiti, so we used our trip as a way to not only give back, but also to strengthen the relationship between the Haitian farmers and the Taharka Brothers' business. The President of Haiti, Michael Martelly, was excited to learn that a group of African American youth were interested in serving his country and even mentioned us in a speech before the NAACP, which was his first U.S. address to a Civil Rights organization.

I knew my first year in Haiti that the next summer was going to be special. I was going to be able to bring my oldest daughter, Hadiya, with me. The inspiration for traveling with my own children one day came before Hadiya was even born. When I had first met Biff, he had shared with me that he had passed his love of travel on to his kids. When each of them had graduated from high school, he had given them a single gift – a plane ticket to anywhere in the world for a 10-day trip of their choosing. I had also watched Rule, who worked with us through Global Works, bring his two daughters on our trips each year and teach them so much through the process.

One of my beliefs as a parent is that my kids shouldn't just hear me talk about what I do or watch me teach others – they should be right there beside me, whenever possible, learning and leading and seeing me do the same. Being able to bring Hadiya with me represented the epitome of *why* I do this work. I want to pass my values of service on to my children, but I also want them to be able to *experience* these values in action.

To witness my own daughter in Haiti the summer of 2014 when she was 12 years old was an amazing experience for me as a parent and teacher. I loved watching her engage with kids her age, work in a Haitian school, bring medical supplies to those in need and then process the whole experience artistically through playing music and painting. I remember telling Hadiya before the trip that our motto that summer was "Haiti ain't for no chumps" and that she was going to have to get ready. I told her that she was going to have to get her hair braided, that she was going to have to prepare to be in places with no electricity and no running water. Not only had she prepared, she soaked up every minute of the experience once there.

When we returned home after the trip, we put together an art exhibit entitled The Five Senses of Haiti. Hadiya and the other young people who had traveled with us organized and executed this amazing art show that chronicled their experiences and their reflections on what they had learned while away. They shared their writing, photography and paintings and then spoke in turn about how the journey had impacted each of them personally. It was a powerful way to wrap up my first international trip with one of my children, and reinforced to me the importance of sharing my journey with my kids not just through my words, but through my actions as well.

---

Looking back, I feel lucky to have found my calling to travel and serve internationally at such an early age. Good teachers see good things in good people, and when Dr. Brooks asked me all those years ago, "Do you think you can do this?" he believed the answer to be "yes" long before I believed it myself. And that's part of our role as teachers and leaders – to believe in others before they believe in themselves. That's Ubuntu.

# CHAPTER 12

# CHASING CURTIS

*We get high on all types of drugs, when all you really need is love.*
- Talib Kweli

I reach into my nightstand drawer sometimes when I'm having trouble falling asleep, when my mind just can't calm itself, when I'm missing my childhood, when I'm wondering if the work I did that day made a difference, when I'm wishing I could just pick up the phone and call him.

I know that the voice I want to hear on the other end of the line won't be there, so I reach into my drawer and pull out his letter to me and read it for the hundredth, the thousandth time. Sometimes the words make me so angry and sometimes they make me laugh and sometimes they catch my tears.

*About your letter. You called me your best friend. I never told you this, but I love you. You are also my best friend. Don't be too over-excited. When you and Dion started hanging out a lot I was kind of jealous. I thought he was trying to take your friendship away from me. Now I know I was wrong. And I did cry when you left. I just didn't want nobody to see me. I cried a lot. Well, that's all for now.*

*-- Curtis*

*P.S. Write longer letters. I'm saving them so we can trip out on them when we get older.*

We all have that one thing that we've been chasing, that we'll always be chasing, our whole lives. Maybe it's a dream, maybe it's an unrequited love, maybe it's a friend we left behind. As for me, for the rest of my life, I'll always be chasing Curtis. I'm talking, of course, about Curtis my best friend, Curtis who shared my dream of attending Morehouse, Curtis who I left behind when I went away to Grambling, Curtis who couldn't win the battle against the pull of the Chicago streets and all the accompanying chaos. I'm talking about the Curtis whose face I see when I look out into an auditorium of Black and Brown boys staring back at me expectantly and a little uneasily, wondering if I'll have anything to say that matters.

But when I talk about chasing Curtis I'm also talking about a theory. A way of seeing the world that I'll never be able to un-see. A way of approaching my Ubuntu teaching practice that colors everything I do. The thing about life is that we can't be chasing something unless we're also running from something else. Maybe what we're chasing and running from are two sides of the same coin, maybe they're opposite ideals, maybe they represent the best and worst of who we are.

Chicago is home to one of the tallest buildings in the U.S., the Sears Tower. The name has since been changed to the Willis Tower, but most Chicagoans still call it by its original name. At one time Chicago was also home to the tallest housing projects in the world, which were eventually torn down. If you've ever witnessed the demolition of a high-rise building, then you know what a spectacular sight it is to watch the structure implode, to see it collapse upon itself and then disappear in a matter of seconds. It's amazing to see a building that stood so strong for years be reduced to a pile of rubble before your eyes.

People implode too. Lives that once stood tall come crashing down. For Curtis, that was what happened, and much of my adult life has been spent trying to figure out exactly why. But whatever the cause of the collapse, the result is usually the same – destruction that extends far beyond the site of demolition. If you've ever faced a collapse in your own life, you know what I'm talking about – maybe the breakdown of a marriage, the loss of a job, the death of someone close to you, the failure of a business. Maybe you never thought that it would happen to you, and yet there you are, surrounded by a field of debris, trying to figure out how in the hell you're going to pick yourself up and move forward past the mess.

Even if your implosion was a moderately small one, it's still a job to clean up the debris. And if you're reading this thinking that nothing in your life – or my life – has really crashed down yet, that things seem to have been pretty smooth sailing, relatively speaking, then I say to you, "Praise God and keep reading!" Because the reality is that all of us face the potential for collapse or chaos at some point in our lives.

---

Curtis was my paradox. It felt like the more I evolved and became more completely myself, the further apart we grew. I had an increasingly difficult time coexisting in my two different spheres – my home in Chicago and the world that unfolded for me as I went away to college and then beyond. I would return home to Chicago sometimes and feel like a square peg trying to fit into a round hole. Nothing quite matched up anymore, and nowhere was this disconnect more apparent than in the context of my friendship with Curtis.

The more I tried to coax Curtis into sociable conversation, the more he put up walls. I was talking books and he was talking broads, and I felt a mixture of embarrassment and resentment toward him. We had grown up together, but were now growing miles apart – in our thinking, our styles, our experiences. I didn't want it to be like this, but I had no idea what to do about it. It seemed he was drifting out to sea without a compass and all I could do was stand there helpless on the shore. Or maybe I was the one drifting.

What did I not see happening, while I was running around speaking Spanish, traveling to other countries, meeting new people? What role did I play in alienating my best friend? Was my pro-Black image getting too *big*? Was my vegan diet too much for him? Was I becoming bourgeois?

I knew the road that Curt was going down because it was the same road I saw for some of the young men I was beginning to come into contact with through my work as a teacher. It's like I was charged with saving these boys, and yet I'd look into their eyes and just see Curt's face. And that made me question so much about what I was doing with my own life and career – *What did any of this work matter if I couldn't even save my best friend?*

---

It was six years after Curtis wrote me that letter that I got the call. My roommate Cheria and I were both in our first year of teaching high school Spanish, my days were beginning to take on a predictable rhythm, and life seemed to be moving forward with relative ease. I don't even remember who made the phone call – but I'll never forget how I felt the moment I heard the news. *Curtis is dead.* Three little words that changed my life forever.

I hung up the phone, got on my bike, and rode down to the Harbor and just sat by the water for hours. My body was numb, but my heart was breaking. And I couldn't stop the tears from falling.

Marlon and Leroy, Curtis' cousins, were the ones who found Curtis' body. According to Marlon, Leroy and Marlon were just kicking it when Leroy's phone rang. Leroy picked up the phone to a hysterical voice on the other end of the line. It was Huston, who worked with Curt, barely unable to get out a clear sentence.

Once Huston calmed down, he was able to articulate the source of his hysteria.

It happened like this, according to Huston. Huston had been sick with the flu that day, so Curt had been out working without him. Huston was beginning to feel a bit better when Curt had called him, but Huston knew right away that something wasn't right by the sound of Curt's voice on the phone. Curt said that he was coming to pick Huston up and spoke in the code they had adopted to let Huston know that he needed to bring something. Huston grabbed a nine-millimeter and headed to the door. But when Huston walked outside and saw Curt's car roll up, he knew that something was *really* wrong by the way the car parked. It pulled up straight to the curb, which let Huston know right away that Curt couldn't be behind the wheel. Curt was notorious for double-parking and never parked straight like that.

*What the hell is going on?* Huston questioned himself as he slowly approached the car. The passenger door swung open and, sure enough, Curtis wasn't driving. He was sitting in the middle of the front seat, sandwiched between two guys Huston had never seen before. The guys told Huston to get in, but Curtis just shook his head – indicating to Huston not to get in the car. Huston, seeing the look on Curt's face and the fear in his eyes, turned and ran. As he fled, he heard shots ring out and realized that the car was chasing him, that the bullets were coming in his direction. Huston was able to dip into an ally, lose the car, and get back into his house through the back door. As soon as he caught his breath, Huston called Leroy to recount to him, as best he could, what had just happened. Even though he didn't know what the hell was going on, he *did* know that Curt was in some kind of big trouble.

Leroy and Marlon drove around for three hours, anxiously looking for Curt. Earlier that day, another guy connected to Curtis, who supposedly worked for him, had been killed walking down the street just blocks away from where Huston had dodged those bullets. The dude was shot six times in the back. Huston didn't have any recollection of this other shooting, but Marlon was able to retell the incident with a lot of clarity.

Marlon and Leroy finally did find Curt's car parked, of all places, just a few blocks from Curt's dad's house. They rolled up to the car, but the windows were tinted so dark they couldn't see anything right away. Marlon said that he grabbed the sleeve of his jacket and opened the driver's side door. There was no sign of anyone in the front seat, but then he glanced back and was struck speechless when he saw the scene there. There was Curtis, slumped over and unresponsive. Marlon and Leroy shook Curtis, trying to get a reaction from him, any sign of life. They got nothing. And they knew in that instant that he was already gone.

Marlon dropped to his knees right there on the pavement and began to wail. Leroy joined him. Crying. Screaming. Telling Curt that he wasn't alone, that they were both right there by his side. That it was going to be okay, even though they already knew that nothing was going to be okay.

After a couple more minutes, Marlon and Leroy sprinted the short distance to Curt's dad's house, to the very place that – all those years before – Curt had to go after his own mother's death. They explained to Curt's dad where the car was and what they had found at the scene, then called the police and waited for the officers to show up and file a report.

All of the guys who were around that day, including Marlon, Leroy and Huston, had to go down to the police station to be questioned – because at that point everyone was seen as a potential suspect. Lots of potential suspects, but here I am writing this all these years later knowing that the guys who killed Curtis were never found, never arrested for the crime, never tried for murder. Nothing.

Huston disappeared for a long time afterwards and really never gave any context to what had happened the day Curtis was killed, until just last month when I was able to get him on the phone as we were finishing up the manuscript for this book. As he described his life after Curt's death, he struggled a lot. He had recurring nightmares for a long time and to this day doesn't sleep well at night. He said that he had gotten out of the game right after Curt's death and found work through some temporary agencies, but that he wasn't ever right. He shared that his relationships were a mess because he couldn't trust anybody. He also shared that immediately after Curt's death he had been scared of retaliation because the guys who had been in Curt's car with him that day had known that Huston had seen their faces. So he had had to move around quite a bit for awhile, never sleeping in the same place more than one night in a row. He had been on the run. But no matter how far or how fast he ran, he couldn't run from himself or from all that haunted his spirit.

Huston went on to share that since Curt's death and its aftermath, he has had a whole different perspective on life. He reflected: *I'm not a risk taker no more. I value life more because it can be taken so quickly. Man, Curtis and I had some good times, but I can't do none of that stuff anymore. Life is too short and with the things you do, the quick way is not always the best way.*

When I asked Huston what message he'd like to send to young men reading this book, he shared that they needed to *value true friendship, true brotherhood, those friendships that will never be broken whether you have a dollar or a dime. And when you lose someone close to you, it's really hurtful, really painful. Nothing's* promised to you. You can have a lot of associates, but friends are hard to come by and if you lose them, it's so hard to trust again. It's so hard to start over because you kind of shut the door on being able to go through the steps of building new friendships. You don't want any new friends.

All I know, from what I've seen myself and what I've heard through the years, is that Huston hasn't ever been the same since that day. The stellar high school athlete who was so popular with the girls is nearly unrecognizable all these years later. Sometimes, life is less than kind to those who fall the hardest.

---

Being asked to give a eulogy at Curtis' funeral was a great honor, but it was also daunting. Finding the right words to mark the passing of my best friend's life was difficult when emotions ran high. And I had been running on fumes anyway since finding out how Curt had died. But I managed to rise to the occasion. And this is part of what I shared that day:

*My name is Darnell, and Curtis and I have been best friends since high school. We were both member of KAOS, and we spent part of nearly every day together as teens. When you saw him, you saw me. But as we got older, we started to drift apart.*

*When I think of Curtis as a teen, I remember how much he loved to have fun. Driving fast and talking trash were two activities he loved the most.*

*Even though Curtis was a compassionate and generous soul who would give you the shirt off his back, he was also a risk-taker, so it's not difficult to understand why he got involved in such a dark lifestyle. All he hoped for, and what his mother dreamt for her only child, died in the back seat of his Jeep Cherokee with him. It may comfort us all a bit to realize that Curtis is now reunited with his mother, Lucy Williams, although the ways they both died are anything but comforting.*

*The light has gone out in our lives because our greed for material items has caused someone to kill our brother. As we sit here wanting revenge, we must be mindful of the death we are selling on the streets, daily. We might not be shooting one another, but we are causing a slow death of a community that's already on life support. The killing must stop. Don't you know our children are watching?*

This was only the second time that my KAOS brothers had ever heard me speak publically – the first time had been at Andre's funeral – and I just stood there after I delivered Curt's eulogy trying to make sense of the tragedy of it all.

In hindsight, I really do believe that these losses kept me tied in some powerful way to my roots. I went away to college – Andre was killed. I moved to Baltimore and started teaching – Curtis was killed. It was like I couldn't travel too far from home, I couldn't get too far ahead of myself. I had to remember where I had come from. And who I had left behind.

Curtis and I had such a strong bond, but even that couldn't hold up against the outside forces that in the end we couldn't control. We were fighting the battles in our own lives the best way we knew how and somehow we forgot to protect each other along the way.

I can only guess what Curtis was always chasing in his own life. He was the kid who, when we were younger, seemed to have it all. His mom did well and loved him so much. He never longed for anything. But then when his mom, his everything, was taken away from him, he didn't know what to do with life. And life, in turn, took him for one hell of a bad drive.

---

Have you ever wondered what happened to that one student you let get away, who taught you a lesson greater than any you learned in your teaching pedagogy classes? Who lived in a world that made you question how he was going to survive? That kid who did the right thing in class most of the time, who might have had some hiccups along the way, but who – for the most part – made you laugh, toed the line, didn't raise too many red flags? Except you knew enough about the world he entered when he left school each day to make you question how he'd be able to continue to navigate this life as he got older. You knew the statistics about young Black men in volatile environments. And you worried, even though you couldn't exactly pinpoint why.

What haunts me is that there are so many Curtises out there – who when they lose their everything also lose, well, everything. It was like Curtis felt he had something to prove, and when he turned to the streets he got this false sense that he was big, that he was powerful, that he was invincible.

What also haunts me is that many current teacher education programs don't really prepare us to help the Curtises of the world. Academically, Curtis had all the strengths of a scholar. And yet when his mom died and he was dropped into a new family environment, having everything materialistic he could ask for didn't even begin to fill the void left by his mom's death. He was lost with nobody to help him find his way back. KAOS started to disperse as we all went to college and I guess maybe he was seeking to fill that void too. One detail that I just learned as

I was finishing up this book is that shortly before Curtis' death, he had received a letter in the mail. The letter had informed Curt that his mother's fiancé, who had been tried and convicted for killing his mom, was being released only eight years into his sentence because of prison overcrowding. Eight years.

Henry David Thoreau said that it's not until we are lost that we begin to find ourselves. As a teacher, so many times I've felt lost in the aftermath of Curt's death. I've tried to find myself by looking outward, by continuing to chase after Curtis again and again, but through it all I have really been trying to find myself. The more I've looked outward, the more frustrated I've become. And my frustration has led to some difficult moments in my teaching, where I have tried everything to engage these boys and nothing has seemed to work. Times where I haven't connected with my students because I have somehow lost a connection with myself. My life was on autopilot for awhile and I didn't realize until some time later that I wasn't even asking the right question. I was so focused on what I was chasing that I failed to stop to ask myself what I was running from.

Running, in the end, didn't save me from hurt and pain anyway. Within a few years of Curtis' death, I lost another one of my KAOS brothers, Kerroy, when he was shot and killed on the streets of Chicago. And then almost a decade after that, another KAOS brother, Derrick, drowned in a swimming pool. He and his roommate had been competing to see who could hold their breath underwater the longest. The doctors said that the drowning had something to do with complications from a heart condition, an affliction that none of us even knew that Derrick, a former star athlete, had.

---

Who are *you* chasing and why? What do you expect to happen once you catch that person? What are you running from? Who's chasing you? And how are you going to navigate it all? Sometimes as teachers we almost have this educational arrogance – it's as if once we catch that one student, we think we'll be able to save him. We think we'll be the one to make everything alright. But once you catch that person, *if* you can catch him, there will be another one to follow. That's the nature of the job.

If you're reading this as a young person, I hope that you understand that your *value* is so much more than the sum of all the material things we place in such high esteem as a society. Curtis had it all – the big house, the fancy car – and yet it wasn't near enough to fill the emptiness in his life. We've got to learn how to reach out for help when we need it. There are people who will help us if we're willing to ask. Also, if you know that you're the one who is being chased by an adult in your life, then maybe it's time to stop running. At some point, maybe it's time to surrender. Surrender isn't about giving up or being weak, but it is about being humble enough to ask for help. To pause and question what you're running from and what it's going to take for you to stop, take a deep breath, and say yes to the help and maybe, in so doing, to say yes to your life.

---

There's a hope inherent in running the marathon and traveling the journey, not just in finishing the race, when you realize you are a part of the *process* and not just the end result. In chasing and trying to save that one student, your Curtis, it can sometimes feel as though nothing matters until you find what you're seeking. In this respect, maybe it's good that we can't always catch our Curtis, because if we did, maybe somehow we'd think that our job was complete. And I don't think our job will ever be complete.

It's also about prevention. We can't just wait for the tragedies to unfold and then try to put the pieces together after it's too late. We have to consider the risk factors and then invest as much time, energy and resources as we can pouring into our young people and providing them with *alternatives* to the risk factors. Schools and communities need to identify a range of approaches and specific activities in order to achieve local prevention goals. Research and experience in communities show that it's possible.

All of this also begs the question of not only how we *talk* about helping young people navigate tragedy, but also how we *live* it in our daily practice. Not too long ago, I was working with a group of new teachers. And one of them raised the question of how we deal with some of the larger educational and societal ills on days when it all just feels so overwhelming. From my experience, the best way to deal with the wide scale issues in our society is to do what we can on an individual level. We have to be able to sit with each other in a room and talk honestly, openly and transparently about what *our* role is in chasing Curtis. How are we planning our instruction inclusively? How are we looking beyond academic deficits to recognize when our young people are in crisis? How can we help them navigate their way back when we see them veering so off track? If we can begin with a different mindset, then we can slowly remove the walls that the system has created. We can start from the bottom up. It is possible.

At the same time, we must learn that sometimes the only thing we can do is release and let go. The truth is, in the end, even if I could have seen the writing on the wall, even if I could have known that the path that Curtis was traveling on wasn't going to end well, he wasn't mine to save.

# PART IV

## CHANGE IS IN THE AIR

# CHAPTER 13

# ON LEAVING

*Never looking back or too far in front of me.*
*The present is a gift, and I just wanna BE.*

- Common

By my sixth year teaching at City College High School, I was really beginning to come into my own as an Ubuntu teacher. And yet, I knew that I had to leave at the end of the year. Of course somehow my students got wind of the news before I had a chance to tell them. One day that spring, one of my seniors asked right out if the rumors were true, if I was leaving. Well, actually the student asked if I was *retiring*, and I had to laugh because clearly this student either didn't understand what retirement was *or* had grossly overestimated my age. While I'd love for teaching to be such a lucrative career that I could retire before age 30, I of course wasn't retiring. But I was leaving.

Many of my fellow teachers were confused by, if not downright incredulous of, my decision to leave the classroom. They said that City just wasn't the type of school that one ever *left*. As far as teaching jobs went, City was pretty much a dream. I remember telling some of the skeptical teachers that the God I served said that the world was my classroom and that I knew City wasn't even the best of the best. My students were amazing, but the school had its fair share of problems. And to be honest, prestige didn't mean a whole lot to me. I mean, I grew up in a city with some of the best private and public schools in the country – Kenwood and Whitney Young were always on top of their games – and so I wasn't really impressed by reputation.

By that time, I was married to my wife Meshelle, and when our first daughter was born in 2001 I realized in a new way that my decisions no longer affected only me. Many other people in my life questioned my decision to leave such a stable job, too. I wanted to be a teacher, right? And I had landed my dream teaching job, hadn't I? And I was *good* at it, was I not? All I can really say about that time in my life is that I had begun to feel restless. I felt like there was a larger world beyond the walls of my classroom that I needed to explore. I felt that my teaching needed a different context.

Plus, I had done so much in so little time. I had taken kids to learn and serve abroad. I had created UMOJA, a study group focused on the accomplishments on African American and Latino people. I had been nominated as New Teacher of the Year and had been honored as a Golden Apple Award recipient. My students and I had made history by writing and publishing a bilingual children's book entitled "El Primer Dia De la Escuela," which marked the first time in the history of the Baltimore City school system that a teacher and students had co-authored and published a book.

Some of my students and I had created a teen talk show, "What About Us?" where I in essence took my classroom to the airwaves. We'd had a successful run on cable TV and even had a shot to pitch the show to ABC. A producer, Pete K., pitched the network show idea to me because he had seen my cable TV show, had known I had won a few media awards, and had met me when ABC had come out to City to do a story on me for a segment called "Hometown Heroes." I was excited at the opportunity to put up a show we created on a major network, and so were my students. Unfortunately, our show was still in its pre-production phase with ABC when Pete was laid off due to budget cuts, and without his support and vision the show never aired.

However, I still learned so much from the experience. Pete taught me about production and how to use media as a teaching tool. He also really cared about kids, and he showed me that TV could be a great avenue to share my joy and love for teaching with a broader audience. He called me a natural in front of the camera, and I internalized this praise and encouragement as a sign that I was on the right path, because what I know about Ubuntu teachers is that we can teach in any context. We can cross boundaries. And some days, we are little more than actors on a stage. The class is our audience, the intercom and the disruptive students are the commercial breaks. The scripts are the lesson plans we've stayed up all night preparing.

Pete visited my classroom a number of times and said he loved watching me interact with my students. From talking with puppets on my hands and dancing and singing to teaching vocabulary through my actions and not just my words, I used what I called the whole body method to teach. If I said "abrazo," I would hug a student. If I said "Yo tengo hambre," I would rub my stomach. If I said "Yo estoy leyendo el libro," I would pick up a book and start reading it. It was fun and the students responded well. My methods made them move and kept them on their toes. When they took tests, I'd look out into the classroom and see them using their bodies as instruments to jog their memories.

What I know now about boys' learning styles is that many of them prefer movement in the classroom, not just for themselves but in the teachers' instruction as well. So through my teaching style I was meeting the needs of many of my students without even fully realizing what I was doing. You see, I didn't believe in labeling my kids. So all I did was to turn my focus and put the label on myself. Instead of looking at my students and trying to figure out their shortcomings, I tried instead to figure out my own. I asked myself: *Where do I fall short with engaging my kids? Do I have a teaching disability? A listening disability? A lack-of-empathy disability? Am I the one who needs an IEP?* I knew I had to do whatever it took to get them to learn. Even if it meant making a fool out of myself, over and over again. That was Ubuntu teaching to me. And it was cool to have someone like Pete, who wasn't in the educational field himself, see the value in the way I was teaching and how it might translate to a classroom outside of the walls at City.

I had found my passion for teaching and was feeling pretty good about all I had done. Finding your passion is one thing, but pursuing it is another. I loved my career, but over the years I encountered challenges and setbacks like any other professional. I found myself in work settings that just didn't fit. I worked on projects that were outside of my scope of interest. I lost students. I received angry memos from my school principal for my class being too noisy. I was hated on by some fellow teachers because of my age and my "different" approach to classroom teaching. I had students and parents share intimate stories with me that left me in tears. I dealt with salary cuts. And each time, I made it through with effort, support and the belief that I was in the right place doing the right work.

But once I started to feel a strong pull away from the classroom and toward something else, I knew that it was my time to go. In a way that's hard to articulate, I felt like the walls were closing in on me. I knew I was living out the statistic that says half of all teachers leave the profession around their fifth year of teaching, but I also believed that my reasons for leaving were strong ones. Just as there are so many diverse kinds of teachers, so there are a plethora of reasons why teachers choose to leave the classroom. There are many teacher stories of "Why I'm Leaving" that circulate on social media, featuring overworked, unsupported and under-appreciated teachers who make the painful decision to leave the profession altogether. That's not where I was. Even with standards, testing, new evaluations and unsupportive public policy, I still loved teaching.

And I had tried to live up to the ideal that a teacher could lead without having to leave the classroom. But the longer I taught, the more I felt myself struggling to exist in a hybrid role of being half in and half out. This idea of hybrid teaching and leading has gained traction with the concept of "Teacherpreneurs," which the Center for Teaching Quality defines as "expert teachers whose work weeks are divided between teaching students and designing system-level solutions for public education." I believe it's a great concept and that we *should* afford teachers the opportunity to continue to lead their own classrooms while also being agents of change on a broader scale in their schools, districts and communities, but my reality was that I needed a larger classroom.

I really tried to make the hybrid role work for me, but once I became honest with myself, I realized it was too tough, too confining. My attention was divided and I began to go weeks on end without feeling like I was doing adequate service to either my teaching or my projects outside the classroom. Trudging forward and never feeling successful at anything is not a great way to live from day to day, so I decided that I needed to choose to either fully recommit myself to my job at City or to leave and pursue my teaching and leadership interests outside of the classroom.

I had days in the classroom during that last year that made me question whether leaving really was the right thing to do. I sat there one day and watched as my seniors, who for all intents and purposes were *long since done* with this school business, gave each other feedback on their speech drafts for their culminating Senior Projects. I heard in their statements lessons I had taught them – little things, probably not all that meaningful to most, but still reflective of what I had taught them to do. It's hard to explain that feeling if you've never felt it, but it's an amazing one.

Then after 30 minutes of sustained focus, the class started to get a little rambunctious and I, only half-jokingly, threatened to slam their 18-year-old selves into a seating chart if they didn't get their over-sized-kindergartener behavior under control.

We laughed, the bell rang, they left.

I knew I was definitely going to miss that place. What I didn't realize at the time, of course, was the impact that my leaving City was going to have on my students. Here is some of what they revealed, in their own words, about how my decision to leave City shaped them.

One former student shared: *When Mr. Shields left City, everyone was distraught, but I can honestly say that he followed his heart. He had a passion for teaching, but he wanted to follow his purpose. I just think if you follow your passion it will lead you to your purpose – T.D. Jakes said that. But Mr. Shields' leaving gave me inspiration to follow my dreams. I know he was concerned about his students and that he wanted to stay, but that there were so many greater things for him. We still keep in contact, so in a way it was like he never really left. He was the inspiration for me actually following my own purpose.*

Another former student echoed with a similar sentiment: *Where I am currently isn't where I plan on ending up. It's just a start. I do desire to go further. And what I learned from Mr. Shields is that where you are now isn't where you have to stay. I learned from him how not to give up on myself. Just the fact that he left City and ventured off to do such amazing things shows me that with faith and diligence, I can achieve, I can get over all obstacles no matter how large those obstacles may be. He always said, "You don't have to worry about that. Stop letting your current situation blind you from the big picture. There is something bigger in front of you, so even though you might not always be exactly where you want to be in life, don't feel as if you're stuck. There's always another door open and if you keep that strong faith, you can get there. You know you have to believe in yourself." Mr. Shields was definitely a motivator, a mentor, an awesome Black man, and I was a person who didn't necessarily have many Black men as role models. I had maybe enough to count on one hand –my father wasn't there, so the fact that I can actually include Mr. Shields in that few is just amazing. He opened my eyes to so much.*

It seems that my leaving impacted my students in more ways that I could have realized at the time. I remember the very last day of school with my seniors. Saying goodbye was hard. We cried. We hugged. We laughed. We cried some more. They were leaving City, the Castle on the Hill, and so was I. We were *all* moving on to bigger and better things for ourselves. Even though I knew that my assignment at City was up, it still took a lot of faith to just jump into the unknown and believe that I was going to somehow land on my feet.

What I hope my leaving demonstrates above all else is that we have to follow our hearts. So many of us in the teaching profession just get stuck. We get comfortable. We convince ourselves that because we're really good at teaching in the traditional sense, there's no other way for us to make an impact. I wanted to be more than a teacher to my students. I wanted them to see that in leaving I was following my heart – in spite of the fear, in spite of the loss of the comfortable predictability of a job that I was really good at, in spite of how much I believed in the work I was doing.

If you're feeling stuck in your career and dream of pursuing something more satisfying, you *must* follow your passion. Don't die with your music still in you. We all have moments when we think things just aren't happening like we want them to, or that our careers aren't progressing well. Sometimes it seems everyone around us is experiencing amazing results in their career and moving right along with life, while we're just stuck. Dwelling on the unfairness of it all can lead to anger, frustration, and a lack of clarity. These negative thoughts diminish our ability to focus on what we need to do to move forward. Because it can be during those moments when we feel most frustrated that creativity can kick in. Some of the best solutions emerge from a deep desire to change and improve. You don't have to deny your feelings of disappointment, but this dissatisfaction has to be viewed as a temporary state if you're to get back on track.

As difficult as it was to leave the traditional classroom, I had to tell myself over and over again, *Que le vaya bien*. I had to give myself permission to leave.

---

The first big move I made that summer was to accept a job at Volunteer Central to serve as a coordinator for the America's Promise Alliance. America's Promise Alliance, which was founded in 1997, is devoted to "helping to create conditions of success for all young people, including the millions currently being left behind." Their work is powered by the belief that "all children are capable of learning and thriving, and that every individual, institution, and sector of society shares the responsibility to help young people succeed."

America's Promise was a perfect fit for me as an educator, because I believed in the five tenets that the program espoused – the importance of a caring adult, safe places, a healthy start, an effective education, and opportunities to help others. And working for Colin Powell, the founder of America's Promise, was like a dream come true. I liked the man a lot more than I liked his politics. He was the first African American appointed as the U.S. Secretary of State, and was the first – and so far has been the only – African American to serve on the Joint Chiefs of Staff. I also liked his grassroots story, that he was the son of Jamaican immigrants and that he was raised in the South Bronx.

My role as a Promise Fellow was to develop programs and partnerships throughout Baltimore City that embodied the organization's mission and vision, and I loved the work. It was during my time at Volunteer Central that I co-created Youth Explosion alongside David Miller, who would later become my business partner, and Darlene Mungin of the Historic East Baltimore Community Action Coalition. For the next five years, David, Darlene and I worked collaboratively with other youth leaders in Baltimore to create the largest non-faith-based youth conference on the East Coast.

Surpassing even the magnitude of the conference were the amazing examples of young leadership that rose up from this event. I, along with 10 transformational young people, quickly became the face of youthful leadership in the city. In designing the event, we worked hard to have youth and adults working side-by-side in every stage of conference planning and implementation.

My friend Christina, who I met in Baltimore when I was doing community organizing and who worked closely with me on Youth Explosion, shared the following as to how the conference came to be: *It took a little while before we figured out what we needed to do, but I remember this particular meeting when it all came together for us. We asked ourselves how we could collaborate, because here we were all doing amazing things in our own programs, all doing our own work with young people, which was fantastic, but we knew we needed to do more. There were problems yet to solve and we felt like we had the passions and the energy to solve them together. We had the idea to do a conference, and once we solidified the idea we really got to work. We worked on it daily. We really all worked together well to make the conference happen that first year.*

Our goal, which I think we achieved successfully, was to reach the youth where they were – to speak to their experiences and life out on the streets and then to show them some avenues of hope. We brought in keynote speakers and then divided the youth into workshops for the day. Workshop topics ranged from how to overcome fear to how to prepare for college and how to start your own business, and they had really clever titles like "The Truth about Cops and Hip-Hop," "Young, Gifted and Gay," and "I'm Not My Hair," just to name a few. We were focused on engaging the youth and speaking to what *they* wanted to talk about, not what we *thought* they should want to talk about. We had to hook them to get them in the door, so we made sure that we wove in some fun activities with all the learning.

The conference concluded each year with a march to City Hall to protest the lack of support that Baltimore was giving its young people at the time. Long before the protests over Freddie Gray and Trayvon Martin, we took to the streets – but not before equipping the youth with the necessary tools to protest in peace. Over five years of hosting the conference, we were able to galvanize over 5,000 young people throughout the city to protest school closings, youth violence, and the building of a juvenile correctional facility.

We also grew the conference every year because we really listened to the participant feedback we received. If the young people made a suggestion about what we needed to do better the next year, we worked hard to make the necessary changes. We didn't want to remain stagnant.

It was an exciting time for us. We were young and energetic and ready to take on the world. Christina went on to share some of the things she learned from the time we worked together: *We were embarking on something that was very new that had not been done before. Once we put our minds together and made it happen, it was a real statement to the Baltimore community about how we didn't need traditional funding sources to make something happen. What we wanted to show everyone in Baltimore was that there was a true need out there to be filled and that kids would show up if we met that need. Young people want to be motivated, want to have a reason to pull themselves up, want to see there's something greater out there for them. We learned that young people were hungry for what we were offering and they wanted more, so that's why the conference came back year after year. And for us as leaders of the project, there was so much learning we were doing. Most of us were in our 20s and that's really young in terms of work and professional careers. LaMarr was a little older than I was and so I learned a lot personally from him. He showed me that we could put our minds and passions to work and see tremendous results. That felt really fantastic.*

We were a group of young aspirational professionals, made up of many hues, striving to do something great. And we did. Looking back, the idea for Youth Explosion, which really was beginning to form when I was still teaching at City and which I brought with me into my soon-to-be social entrepreneurship organization Urban Leadership Institute (ULI), was borne out of a question posed to me by one of my high school students. My students saw me traveling to teaching conferences and one of them asked simply, "Señor Shields, why don't we have any conferences for young people like you teachers do?" And the rest was history.

---

After spending two years as a Promise Fellow, I was hired as a program director for Community Impact Baltimore to work in one of the toughest parts of the city, a neighborhood chronicled in Simon and Burn's book "The Corner." Most Baltimore residents avoid the notorious and crime-infested intersection of West Fayette and Monroe Streets, which has a 24-hour open air drug market that fuels the economy of this long-dying neighborhood, but I was ready to get right into the mix and see how I could best be of service.

My responsibility as program director was to train a cadre of youth mobilizers, as we called them, to positively impact the neighborhoods. I loved my job. It was gritty. It was full of drama. It impacted me in ways I couldn't have imagined. I had come from a pretty rough part of Chicago, but Baltimore was different – open air drug markets, heroin highs, men and women slowly dying in broad daylight. This was new to me, because Chicago was a crack town, and it was different for me to witness addicts with heroin highs, who moved and talked so slowly, roaming the streets.

Most of all, I was shocked by the brazen openness of it. I had never before seen a drug dealer throw out testers to current and future clients in the middle of the day for all to see. It reminded me of being in a Sam's Club or Costco, where you walk around shopping while testing stations are set up with promising new foods, luring you in to first taste and then buy. The drug dealers seemed to throw out the most testers around the first of the month, when folks would be getting their welfare checks or as they say in Baltimore, their "independence cards." What an oxymoron.

In spite of all the sadness, destitution and destruction I saw around me, I loved this neighborhood and the people in it. I learned so much about organizing from the characters I met. Someone looking in from the outside might have thought there was nothing but chaos happening around me, with the drug attacks on the corners, the vacant lots, the dilapidated houses. But underneath all of the chaos there existed a sense of order in that we knew were doing the right work. There was beauty beneath the ashes.

The residents were concerned, well-trained and organized to fight the drug trade. And they did. There were a number of community associations that decided to merge efforts and resources to deal with the huge problem. And they were not waiting for City Hall to provide support. As a young outsider, I was excited to be a part of the movement to clean up the neighborhood and to change the reputation of Baltimore as a violent and drug-controlled city, as portrayed first in "The Corner" and then eventually in HBO's hit series "The Wire."

Besides mobilizing young people to have a greater impact on their neighborhoods through activism, we were also raising money to send high school graduates to college. I loved it. I thought it was an amazing concept. We were taking care of those most affected by poverty and rewarding them for their intelligence. We would ask local businesses in the community to donate funds for deserving students who lived in Southwest Baltimore, and at graduation time we would provide last-gap funding to those who qualified. The youth mobilizers raised the money and interviewed the prospective scholars.

Through this work, I began laying the foundation for what would become my start as a social entrepreneur – a term I must admit I hadn't heard of until I met my good friend, neighbor, and professor at Rutgers University, Dr. Jeff Robinson. He explained, "What you are talking about doing is called social entrepreneurship." According to ASHOKA, an organization that supports social entrepreneurship, social entrepreneurs are "individuals who propose and create innovative solutions to society's most pressing social problems. They are ambitious and persistent, tackling major social issues and offering new ideas for wide-scale change. Rather than leaving it up to the government or business sectors to meet societal needs, social entrepreneurs identify what is not working and seek solutions by changing the system, spreading messages of hope through their work, and persuading entire societies to move in different directions by beginning to do business differently."

*Cool,* I thought. *I can do that.*

Just as traditional entrepreneurs focus on changing the face of business, social entrepreneurs seize opportunities others have missed to improve communities, to enact positive change, and to create solutions to solve old problems in new ways. I loved it. Dr. Robinson eventually became my business mentor and helped me to shape my own social entrepreneurship model and to hone my approach to my work moving forward.

As my work expanded, so did my brand. I met celebrities who were either doing similar outreach work or whose paths I crossed in connection with the work I was doing. While I was enamored with who they were and what they did, they reassured me that I was the true celebrity – that my work was more important than the songs they sang or the films in which they appeared. By far, the celebrity who had the greatest impact on me was Bill Duke. The actor, director and filmmaker whose credits include "Menace to Society," "Dark Girls," "Car Wash," "X-Men: The Last Stand," "National Security," "Predator" and "Sister Act II" really poured into me during our conversations about celebrity, service, and the importance of giving back. I feel like he helped prepare me for some of the new contexts in which I'd be working and leading.

---

After leaving Community Impact Baltimore, I walked into what I thought was my dream job. David Miller – another teacher who I had crossed paths with at community and educational forums through the years –and I joined forces to found the Urban Leadership Institute (ULI). We were two young teachers who shared some strong commonalities in our stories – both of our best friends were killed at young ages. Curtis had had hopes of attending Morehouse and David's best friend actually *had* attended Morehouse and was killed in Baltimore while home on a college break. For both of us, our losses fueled our missions to provide better tools for those working with Black and Brown boys and to provide strategies to help the boys themselves navigate the system.

We really began to establish ourselves in the world of educational social entrepreneurship and non-profit work. The more we built upon our work, the more we were invited to sit at the tables with city decision makers and the better situated we were to make demands on behalf on young people. As the president and executive director of a growing organization, I really dug into the day-to-day operations of our work.

At the same time that David and I were writing curriculum, contracting with local school districts to implement our curriculum, and traveling throughout the country speaking, I was also overseeing grants, taking care of human resources responsibilities, and leading weekly staff meetings. Our first big break came when we were chosen by Eddie and Sylvia Brown as one of the community-based organizations to run the Turning the Corner Achievement program (TCAP), a five million dollar program designed to help African American middle school students in two different neighborhoods – one in East Baltimore and one in West Baltimore.

David was also funded through the Open Society Institute to develop his "Dare to Be King" curriculum. We wanted to set ourselves apart from all of the other youth agencies in Baltimore and nobody at that time was really writing curriculum, so that was where we focused our energy, dug in deep, and set ourselves apart. Our curriculum positioned us to make a real impact in the school system. We introduced our Train the Trainer model, and people from all over the country came to Baltimore or invited us to their cities to discuss the "Dare to Be King" framework.

The first conference we spoke at was sponsored by Rutgers University and focused on the use of art to reach at-risk youth. We led a workshop about Hip-Hop and were really well received by the audience. From that point, other opportunities to speak and train at conferences started to open up and the demand for the work that we were doing with young men of color started to expand.

One spring day, David and I received a call from the World Trade Center in Baltimore. Nothing ever surprised me at ULI, as we'd get calls from celebrities, pubic officials, school leaders, crazy telemarketers, and the list goes on. But this was a different kind of call. The caller identified herself as Joan Ramirez, a Senior Manager for the Professional Exchanges Program, and explained that in a few short days she'd be hosting a delegation from 10 different African countries. She went on to invite us to the World Trade Center to talk about our work with urban youth and to discuss strategies for youth engagement. After we had gotten over our excitement, we prepared to show up. And show up we did. Neither David nor I had ever been in the World Trade Center. We had walked past it many times while visiting the Baltimore Harbor, but this was our first time setting foot in this amazing structure – the world's tallest pentagonal building.

We checked in at the desk and proceeded to take the elevator to the 10th floor where we were greeted warmly by event staff. They whisked us into a room filled with people who looked like us, all speaking a wide variety of indigenous languages. I remember that some were even speaking French. Sitting there in the room, I couldn't believe that David and I were about take part in an international conversation about working with young people. Just like at the United Nations Headquarters in New York, we were given two sets of headphones and briefed quickly on how to use them to talk with the audience. We learned that the headphones would automatically translate everything for us. I think I was more intrigued by that device than by actually speaking to the audience. And I loved learning that even with language barriers, so much of our non-verbal language really is universal. I also realized during the delegation that the struggles and hopes of our children are universal. David and I had an opportunity to ask a lot of questions of these educators, government officials, and social service leaders from the other side of the world. We asked them what challenges they were facing, what hopes they had for their students, and how quickly they planned to implement changes when they returned back home. And we discovered that many of their hopes and challenges mirrored our own. They talked about young people being disengaged, bucking authority, being influenced by Hip-Hop culture, striving for a better life, and wanting adults to move aside so they could be their own change agents.

The conversation ended, and as I removed the headphones and placed them on the table in front of me, the first thought that popped into my head was: *I wish Señor Hogan and my other De La Salle teachers could see me now.*

My journey with ULI was one of the best times of my life. David and I traveled all around the country speaking to thousands of people. We did it, and we did it well. I had the opportunity to really dig into what it meant to be an urban educator on a large scale and learned so much from every single experience.

What began to happen, though, as David and I moved around the country teaching and training was that my own horizons started to expand with my work. I became aware that there was a huge world out there and that there really was space to do and be anything I wanted. Whenever I started to think that the work was getting mundane, I'd challenge myself to consider how I could keep the content engaging and fresh. Every time I led a workshop, even if I was training on a topic familiar to me, I worked to surprise the audience and really give them an *experience*.

As I was acquiring my voice and finding myself, I found it reaffirming to receive positive feedback from strangers at a time when some of the people close to me didn't really seem to value or share in my larger vision. I remember one day I was speaking in Indiana when an 84-year-old woman came up to me after my training and told me that she was so proud to see a young man so excited about giving back. And on top of that, she told me that I was handsome. Moments like that were all the affirmation I needed to know that I was on the right track.

Another trip took me to Keystone, Colorado to speak at a child welfare conference. I found myself in a picture-perfect resort town about an hour west of Denver. Here I was, in this idyllic setting, surrounded by snow-capped mountains, breathing in pristine, brisk air, and looking around in wonder – trying, yet again, to take it all in and figure out exactly how I had landed myself here. I was there to deliver a keynote address to over 1,000 youth service providers, judges, social workers and foster parents. The child welfare conference coordinators had invited me to speak on the effects of Hip-Hop on youth culture. I had been to Colorado a few times before and was really growing to love the state, with its great vegan restaurants, fresh air, and access to nature.

Not too long before that trip, David and I had been in San Francisco to train a large group of doctors, nurses and other health practitioners about Hip-Hop culture and its effect on young people. The conference, sponsored by Kaiser Permanente, seemed like such an odd setting for our work and it really blew me away that we had been invited to speak there.

I remember that David and I were on our way from the airport to the hotel when a woman asked us if we were Hip-Hop artists. We probably had on sweat suits or something and even though we laughed, we were actually offended. Here we were, teachers and leaders in the field of education, being profiled as Hip-Hop artists solely based on how we looked. Even though this was the very topic we were speaking on, it just didn't feel good to me that day to be stereotyped by that woman.

She didn't ask the white males on the bus who were dressed in similar clothes the same question. That experience helped me to solidify my theory on cultural collisions, where cultures and values clash in ways that feel very much like a head-on accident. To some these collisions may seem trivial, but to folks like me who have become more attentive to cultural cues, these clashes often feel like micro-aggressions of racism toward the one who is being judged, stereotyped, belittled, or otherwise crashed into. Cultural collisions often play out in classrooms when conflict occurs. Educators who lack the appropriate social capital automatically assume that it's just students misbehaving, which often leads to students and teachers crashing into each other due largely to cultural misunderstandings surrounding communication patterns and other modes of expression.

David and I survived the interaction on the bus, of course, and made it to the site where we'd be keynoting the conference. We would soon come to learn that many of the health care professionals at the conference, who were working around issues of youth prevention and education in health care, had little to no training in culturally relevant pedagogy. They were trying to reach the youth in their community, but they knew they needed help. So here we were. As in Keystone, the audience members in San Francisco were familiar with mainstream Hip-Hop music, but not with many of the surrounding cultural contexts. More than anything, they were unsure as to exactly how to engage young people around a phenomenon that youth saw as central to their world.

I remember being honored and humbled that they'd asked us to be the ones to come and train on what was at the time pretty ground-breaking stuff. And at the same time, I remember being inspired by this group of health care professionals who were willing to step outside of their box in order to address the issues they were seeing in the communities they were serving. I was an Ubuntu teacher moving into a brand new arena, and it felt amazing.

Not long after, I traveled to New Jersey to speak at a high school made famous by Morgan Freeman and the movie "Lean on Me." It had been the backdrop for the very vocal principal, Joe Clark, to turn around a failing high school in a crime-ridden barrio. And I asked myself yet again, how did I end up here? How did this little Black and Brown boy from the South Side of Chicago who was counted out by so many end up in a position to speak in the same auditorium where the famous Joe Clark had given speeches to hopeful and hopeless students, not knowing their outcomes nor the directions that life would take them?

As I walked into the auditorium that day, I began to reflect on how I could've easily been one of those students sitting in that auditorium listening to Joe Clark, who back in the day was just a courageous principal who dared to do something different. And now here I was stepping onto that same stage, talking in a tone that echoed Mr. Clark's, providing a similar message to a group of young people who were looking for direction.

"You can't get rid of the pain until you've learned its lesson" is what I told the 500 students who listened to my message that day. "When you are faced with the challenges in your life," I told them, "you have to ask yourself two questions – first of all, what can I learn from this? And second of all, how can I use this knowledge? You see, beauty teaches patience and pain teaches endurance. We need to be aware of how we view ourselves. We need to let go of judgment. We need a code of conduct for ourselves that we and we alone can live by." So as I turned to the teachers and the parents, I shared that the best message I could hope to convey that day was that it's better to live by example than to just call yourself an expert – make sure you get down to living your principles rather than merely talking about them.

Some might look at my life as it unfolded in the years after City and think that I had some sort of a commitment problem when it came to my work, or a lack of focus, but I don't see it that way. I see it all as a part of the journey of becoming more clearly myself and of finding my place in the world. With every leaving I learned, with every new beginning I forged ahead with promise and hope.

# CHAPTER 14

# IT'S TIME FOR SOME PRAISE

*Don't be a hard rock when you are really a gem.*
- Lauryn Hill

The PRAISE College Readiness Program at Johns Hopkins University, formerly the Paul Robeson Academic International School of Excellence, is rooted in the work that David and I did together centering around African American and Latino male achievement in Baltimore City. The program's current emphasis and name change grew out of my desire to focus on helping to increase the number of Black and Latino boys going to college.

Every Saturday for the past decade, a group of young men of color have gathered on a college campus in Baltimore City to attend a program whose namesake was the great Paul Robeson. It always amazes me when I travel to speak and ask crowds of people if they've ever heard of Paul Robeson. The answer is usually a resounding no. Paul Robeson was a true Renaissance man. He was an African American singer and actor who became very involved in the Civil Rights movement. He spoke over 10 languages and graduated with degrees from both Rutgers and Columbia University. He was an international star not only for his acting, but also because of his activism. He was like Denzel Washington, Danny Glover, Harry Belafonte, Bill Duke and Common all rolled into one.

One of our PRAISE board members, Henry, described the program we created with Robeson as an inspiration as a *program for young men to recognize the pitfalls to avoid and the strategies to employ to make it in this world. PRAISE shows them how to transition into manhood without the headaches the generation before them went through. We give these boys opportunities to engage with men from all walks of life and to become more invested in the community.*

Vincent, now a college freshman, entered the program as an eighth grader and shared that he learned *how to become a better man in the community, in my life, and out in the world doing things I'm proud of. I learned how to carry myself in* public and I learned how to study in school so that I could graduate on time and go to college.

Vincent continued: *Through PRAISE, I met different people who were all there to help young Black men like myself. Dr. Shields always helped us the best he could and was a father figure to many of us. He helped us find scholarships and he taught me how to become a better man. In PRAISE we had the five wells of greatness: well-read, well-spoken, well-dressed, well-traveled, and well-balanced. Learning these things helped us dig deeper into ourselves and recognize the potential each of us had to be better. Dr. Shields helped us think about what we wanted to do with our careers and with our lives in general – whether that be sports or business or something else. But he always made sure he found a college for us to go to, even if it wasn't one of the big name schools. Now I attend a small school in Delaware where I play football and study law and justice.*

One of the most important elements of PRAISE has been the mentorship program we set up for the boys and men in the community. Vincent described the importance of the mentorship component when he noted that *To this day, I keep in touch with my mentor, who is a great father figure in my life. It's good to have that male role model because there are some things a mother can't explain to a guy. I have my older brother, and he and I talk a lot, but when I had my mentor, it was basically like having a father. I feel that's needed for any young man, so he knows he has a strong person right there who he can go to if he's in a tough situation. Maybe his mentor has been there before and can help him through it. Or if there's a problem with a boy's mom being sick a lot, then maybe there's that male to help him get through this. For example, my mom's been sick and my brother was working a lot to help her out, so even though my brother is a big part of my life no matter what, he just wasn't around much. But my mentor was there and we talked things out. He taught me how to express my feelings and that if I held things inside then they might come out in negative ways through my actions. And my mentor taught me how important it was to have someone to guide me through the tough stuff so that I could focus on school, go somewhere, and get out of the place I'd been in for a long time. That's what LaMarr had us do as well by taking us out of the country through the trip I went on with him to Puerto Rico. He showed us there's a whole other world outside of Baltimore. A whole other world.*

David and I made a commitment to these young men and to the Weinberg Foundation that provided us with the initial funding to do our work. And on a historic day that I'll remember forever, in the summer of 2006, we graduated approximately 30 boys from our Saturday Academy. They had been with us for a year, as either sixth, seventh or eighth graders, and we had done some amazing things. What was remarkable was that the Weinberg Foundation had actually approached *us* about doing this work with boys. Often organizations have to go out and chase the funding and try to convince the powers that be that the work we're doing matters, and here was the Weinberg Foundation coming to us, saying, "Here. We believe in you. We're going to fund you. Now go get the work done." And get the work done we did.

There's something special about an inaugural class. Many of these PRAISE scholars had overcome so many obstacles – from being too shy, too defiant or just plain out of control to dealing with major life trials. One of the greatest challenges in the early days of PRAISE was working with the parents, many of whom were young, single mothers who were not used to school structures, rules and the high expectations that PRAISE imposed on them and their sons. No matter how these families had come to us, though, the experience changed not only them, but me as well.

The graduation itself was amazing! As we called the names of the class of 2006, parents and other family members cheered. The press was there to witness the well-dressed young men of purpose celebrate an important milestone in their lives. And even though some of them wore shirts that were a little too big, ties that were tied a little sloppily, for the most part, the boys carried with them an awesome expression of accomplishment. I remember some of them sharing that they had been so used to losing, and that this had been one of the first times they felt like they had actually *won* something.

After the conferral of the diplomas, we gave out special awards to those who had gone above and beyond what was expected of them. We gave out recognition for brotherhood, leadership, improvement and character. The coveted Paul Robeson Service Award went to a kid named Nicholas for exemplifying the character of Paul Robeson throughout his time in the program.

Nicholas didn't stop when he won this award, and he later came up with the idea to open a café at the University to raise money for PRAISE. I started taking him with me to speaking events when I spoke locally in Baltimore and he was so excited and really blown away by the responses we'd get from the audiences. He shared with me one day that he had always craved attention, but before PRAISE he only knew how to get it in negative ways – by mocking himself and his weight, by getting other people to laugh more at him than with him. But that he had learned that he could use his intelligence and his gifts to get attention. The right kind of attention.

Our first PRAISE class was the foundation of something that at the time I couldn't even fully comprehend. I knew that I'd really miss that first group because they embodied promise, hope, and what can happen when you take a vision, get some needed support, and are able to make a tangible difference in the lives of those who need it most. What I began to see with PRAISE was that we could, with consistency and high standards, defy the statistics concerning Black and Brown boys in Baltimore City. And that was so exciting to me on so many levels.

We could never have anticipated, because PRAISE had been so easy to fund in the beginning, how difficult the road ahead would be. We were bringing students through the program and doing amazing work, and yet we reached a crossroads where the program looked like it wasn't going to be financially viable, like it wasn't going to make it from a strictly business standpoint. We had a number of trusted advisors telling us to just close the doors, abandon ship, move on. Ironically, at the same time that our funding was cut we had an independent program evaluation done which clearly indicated that in order to most effectively meet the needs of our boys we would need to expand the scope and length of our programming.

Guided by this recommendation, and despite the lack of funding, I made a *promise* to a very special group of boys that I wasn't going to let them go, that I was going to see them all the way through high school to graduation, and once I let them know this, I had no other choice but to stick it out. Getting the boys through was intensely personal to me, and I knew I had to make good on my promise at any cost. See, once our funding had run out, so had many of the adults associated with the program. And the decision to keep the doors at PRAISE open meant that I had to go against the advice of some of those with whom I was working most closely, but my allegiance was to the promise I had made to the boys, and to myself.

And I was determined to keep this promise. I remember distinctly that day so many years ago, after we had received the news about our poor financial outlook and after I had made the decision to stay the course anyway, when I was able to call all of the PRAISE parents and let them know that not only were we not shutting down the program, we were expanding it and this meant their sons were going to be able to stay with us through high school. A lot of tears were shed that day, predicated on the hope that comes with a promise kept and a dream realized.

Even though I was working with a group of boys that had grown used to disappointment, I wasn't going to let them be disappointed on my watch. In education and in life, I think we have to be able to do what we know is right, even against daunting odds. We have to ask ourselves what we'll do when the pressure is on and we have to be able to live with the answer we give.

―――――――

The best testament I think that we can give to the work we do as educators exists in the legacies we pass on. When asked what advice he'd give to young men reading this book, Vincent had the following to share: *One message would be to be courageous and to not let the environment around you hold you back from your full potential. Don't get caught up in the things your friends have. Appreciate the things that you have and that are your own. And make your own destiny. Don't let anybody tell you what you're gonna be or that people who look like us are not gonna make it. You don't listen to that. That's something you block out. You write your own life. You shape your own destiny.*

Another alumnus, Joshua, when asked what advice he would give to his 12-year-old self just embarking on the six-year PRAISE experience, shared that he would tell his younger self that the program was going to be worth it, that it was going to *really turn out as you thought it would be. You'll complete it and look back knowing you did everything you could not to become a statistic.*

The only statistics we focus on coming out of PRAISE are the positive ones. In 2014 we graduated our first class that had been with us for the entire six-year program through both middle and high school. We proudly boast about our 100 percent graduation rate, our 100 percent college acceptance rate, and our 98 percent college matriculation rate. The other two percent of graduates who have chosen not to attend college have entered the military. When we believe enough in the promise of our youth and when we create programs that answer the call, it's amazing – but by no means surprising – what can happen.

―――――――

We don't hit all the marks, though. Those Curtises we're chasing? Sometimes they chase us right back and haunt us with all of the *what ifs* that make us question whether we could have done more, where we missed the call, how the signs slipped right by us.

Just last month, I showered, slowly got dressed, and dreaded every second leading up to what I was about to do that day. I almost didn't go. I almost called the boy's mother and told her that I couldn't make it. But as soon as the thought of calling her entered my mind, I knew I had to get myself together. I had to step outside of myself and my own hurt, anger and disappointment and remember the many times when people had had my back even long before I had deserved it.

I was heading to the courthouse that day to attend the arraignment of one of my former PRAISE scholars who was out on bail for a charge of statutory rape. He had been a model PRAISE scholar during his six years with us. I had even considered hiring him on as a staff member after graduation. He came from a good church-going family. He had supportive parents who loved him and worked hard to provide him with opportunities. He was a diligent student who made so many gains both academically and socially while in PRAISE, who soaked up every bit of knowledge, mentorship and opportunity we threw his way.

And yet here we were, getting ready for his day in court. He would have to face the judge and own up to the fact of what he had done with the victim, who had been 12 years old at the time. And I would have to face him and own up to my own immense disappointment and conflicting emotions. I knew I had to show up for the young man and his family, but I also knew that my own *daughter* was 12 years old. And it was near impossible to disconnect the two.

But then I remembered the story of one of my heroes, Harriet Tubman, who didn't just escape to freedom and then become complacent. Likewise, she didn't boast about what she had done and she didn't focus only on the ones who wanted to escape. She had to remind many of the people that they were in bondage, first. Then she went back to get them, even in the most difficult of personal circumstances. She somehow put aside her own hurt, for example, to help her husband escape when he had been with another woman. She was able to move beyond herself to see her bigger mission. And she could have saved even more than she did if she could have convinced more people that they were living as slaves, and that they deserved the opportunity for freedom.

Programs don't change people; people change people. Because when the money runs out, the spirit of the program has to live on. You see, we're all at risk, no matter our improved GPAs, no matter how much we have overcome, no matter how many statistics we have defied. And we can't take it personally when the ones we've poured into the most fall. We've got to keep it moving, and we've got to remember that it's all of our responsibility to keep going back, to work relentlessly to save our children, and to never give up.

# CHAPTER 15

# OPENING THE GATES

*I'm living out my dreams. Don't dare hit that alarm clock.*
- Big Sean

We bring them through the door like people brought out of bondage. We give them an opportunity that can change the course of their own lives and the legacies of their families and communities. And as we do all this, we're *looking* for reasons to say yes.

Every February since 2009, I've had the privilege of serving as a reader for the Gates Millennium Scholarship program. It still blows me away that a kid like me – who got kicked out of high school, who barely skated through, who had teachers discounting him left and right, who didn't even realize his own academic potential until well into college – is now able to give back through this work. I find it empowering to be given the opportunity to help make the decision to green-light a kid to move to the next level, to be on the giving side of a larger society that so often focuses more on blame and tearing people down than it does on solutions.

Gates Millennium Scholarship recipients are awarded comprehensive scholarship funding to attend any college or university of their choice for up to five years in any discipline. And if they choose to pursue advanced degrees in one of seven chosen disciplines, they are eligible to receive funding through their doctoral programs. I had heard of the prestigious scholarship that is only awarded to 1,000 students nationwide, but to then be invited to help select the scholarship recipients just amazed me.

As Mary Williams, a long-time administrator of the program, described the program's purpose: *We're constantly being reminded that young people need mentoring, academic and social support, and financial resources in order to become college graduates and leaders in our country. The goal of the Gates Millennium Scholarship was to develop a $1.6 billion grant program to remove* all financial barriers to education for high-performing students with financial need so that they can attend college and then can go on to do whatever they want.

Mary explained that the program creates avenues for Gates Scholars to really follow their passions post-graduation because they don't have to worry about student loan debt. Also, the scholars are able to network with other Gates Scholars throughout the country from the time they are awarded the scholarships. *How wonderful is it to start out college with building a family from the beginning?* Mary shared. *The Gates Scholars get to attend a leadership conference so that they go in as incoming college freshmen already talking about graduate school. It's important to have that mindset so you know what you need to do to achieve.*

Mary further spoke about how the program aims to be transformational and not transactional: *We provide mentors, leadership development opportunities, an alumni association that reaches back to current scholars, campus-based leaders, and an alternative spring break event they can attend.*

Mary expressed her belief that I have a strong link to the scholarship program because I understand the value of giving young people a transformational experience, and she's right. She shared that *the transformational component of what we do is LaMarr's favorite part because he understands the powerful impact of the work. Our readers work hard, but it's extremely rewarding because they understand the end result of the work. LaMarr is really passionate about youth being educated.*

The United Negro College Fund (UNCF), for which Mary works, collaborates with the Hispanic Scholarship Fund, the American Indian Graduate Center, and the Asian and Pacific Islander American Scholarship Fund to manage the Gates Millennium Scholarship fund. Every winter for the past six years I've joined an amazing group of fellow educators and community leaders for the annual scholarship read.

Mary described the week-long read as follows: *We bring in people who work directly with young people – educators, counselors, administrators, admissions representatives at schools. We provide training that we refresh every year so we're consistent in our evaluation. The reading is an opportunity to collaborate, and that's a great part of the experience. The entire week they're evaluating applications from 8 a.m. to 5 or 6 p.m. And as they're evaluating, they have their colleagues in the room to dialogue with and to ask questions of and to share the stories of what they're reading in the application essays.*

*The best thing about this is that you're reading into the students' lives and you're contributing to changing not only the lives of those who are selected, but also their families and their communities. There are times when the evaluators might have tears in their eyes as they ask themselves how they can say yes to these students. When we close that week of the read, the readers are FULL. They're full because they see the great talent of students that exists across this country, so many of whom have need. And they know they've had an opportunity to really make a difference.*

For me, the Gates read isn't just about the ability to reward awesome young people through the scholarships, but also about the relationships I've built with fellow readers through the years. There's a camaraderie among the team of readers as we share stories of the personal challenges faced by the kids whose essays we're reading. We shed tears because so many of us can relate intimately to the words on the page, the struggles to overcome tremendous obstacles, and the stubborn hope that we can and will do better, that we're somehow all working together to be a part of the solution.

We're working to combat everything about the "I got mine, now you get yours" philosophy that I have such a problem with because it contradicts the notion that we're supposed to be encouraging and uplifting our youth, not leaving them to fend on their own. And through the scholarship program we're given an opportunity to say, "Here you go. We believe in you. We've made it and we're here to give back and pay it forward. We trust that you're going to use this opportunity to do something amazing. We know you can do it." In turn, the scholarship program teaches leadership skills and requires that its new leaders productively give back to their communities and pass on the blessings that they have received.

As my Gates colleague Ryan noted, our efforts reach far below the surface: *What we're fighting against is deep systemic racism and structural inequality in America. I mean, our country was built in part upon inequality and racism and because of these things you have perpetual effects in communities. That's why you have segregation in housing, educational inequities, and income disparities. Education itself can't solve the problem, but you do want to have interventions that make a direct difference for individuals. I don't ever think there will be equity in outcomes and that's difficult for me to grasp. I mean, in order for this to be possible you'd have to reverse too much, like literally just be inequitable to folks in power. And that's not going happen, nor do I think oppressed people want that to happen. So the best we can do is create opportunities for folks to make a path for themselves. And that's what we're able to do through this scholarship program.*

Ryan went on to explain that a lot of the communities from which Gates Scholarship recipients come suffer from unequal access to educational resources. He shared that *In most cities where there's a large concentration of Black and Latino students, you might have a calculus course, let's say, that's a pre-requisite for a lot of STEM majors in college, but that calculus course is often less rigorous than the same course offered in wealthier, suburban areas. So you don't have kids getting equitable preparation. In order to mitigate these inequities, you have to interject interventions that involve opportunity. Of course, its not solving inequality, but it's allowing students to focus on their studies and not have to worry about the finances. I mean, for the recipients of this very competitive scholarship program, that's just amazing.*

---

In addition to being a part of the African American Gates Scholarship read each year, I have also had the opportunity to travel around the country as part of an outreach team, hosting events that encourage eligible students to apply for the scholarship. At these events, we would speak with potential applicants about the details of the application process, as well as provide reasons why they deserved to pursue the scholarship and illustrate the ways in which it might change their lives. One of the Gates team members would deliver the logistical details about the scholarship program, and then I would get up and encourage the young people to apply and to realize their own greatness.

What I did, essentially, was talk to the prospective Gates Scholars about how far they had come, remind them that they had worked so hard to remove the labels that had been placed on them because of their race, gender, or socioeconomic status, and then talk to them about how their phenomenal academic records were a part of their legacies that could never be taken away. And then I shared that a path to higher education could add value to this lasting legacy.

Ryan talked about how he would deliver the basic content of the program and then hand the mic over to me to, in his words, "really push them in other ways." Ryan shared that *the most important piece LaMarr communicated to the young men was a sense of caring deeply. He literally said he loved them. So for some kids it might be the first time they're hearing this, especially from a stranger. He treated them as whole human beings, and I think he was fully conscious that every student in that room could be whatever he or she wanted to be. When you look at the media, there are all these deficit messages about our minority youth that are unwarranted. LaMarr made learning cool and he helped create a community that said, "These are your friends here. They're all doing well. Let's stick together." He was conscious of the messages young people received, from* their own communities even, and made sure they understood that their identity wasn't a deficit for them. I like the fact that he dismissed any doubts the young people had about whether or not they could make it. I think he thought a lot about structural inequalities and racism that tend to perpetuate inequitable outcomes, and he was masterfully able to disrupt these harmful narratives through his words – he was able to help the young people come to understand they really were brilliant kids.

Ryan was able to more eloquently reflect on my sense of purpose in this work than I could have when he shared that *I think he sees himself in a lot of students he wants to uplift in a lot of ways. I think he understands that a lot of these folks can be whatever they want to be – whether that's a neurosurgeon or a president or a judge. They just need to be loved and lifted in ways that other students have opportunities to be loved and lifted. That intersects with his purpose. Everyone has a purpose and I think every project LaMarr takes on is a project to uplift people.*

---

One day, I was at one of my favorite vegan restaurants in Washington, D.C. with my friend Candace having a conversation about a recent trip I had taken to Florida Memorial University to speak with over 300 potential Gates Scholarship applicants, young men with high GPAs and so much promise. I was sharing with her that I was always blown away at the amount of Black brainpower in these rooms, full of young men with aspirations of becoming brain surgeons, engineers, chemists, pilots, teachers and lawyers, among other pursuits.

And I shared with her how, standing up there on stage, I'd say to myself, *Where is the press? Maybe if someone opens fire in the auditorium it will bring the media out.* But I could never focus on who wasn't in the room. I had to stay focused on who was – and I needed to remember that *I* knew how smart *they* were and they knew how smart they were. And I shared with Candace that I pictured guys from KAOS, younger incarnations of ourselves, sitting in the audience as I spoke. I imagined talking to them about the scholarship and all it could offer. And I imagined Curtis standing up and asking how much it would cost to attend Morehouse and I imagined Andre asking if the scholarship would cover graduate school at the University of Michigan and I imagined Kerroy wanting to know if he had enough community service hours to apply and Derrick wondering if there were any current Gates Scholars at the University of Louisville. Because even though we acted like wild boys, the guys in KAOS were about school. And several of us would have been eligible for the Gates Scholarship back in our time. And so with every kid that I've been able to say *Yes!* to through this scholarship program,

I've said a silent prayer of gratitude in honor of Curtis, Andre, Derrick, Kerroy and all of their unrealized dreams.

So I was in this vegan restaurant discussing all this with Candace when a young gentleman overheard me make mention of the Gates Scholarship and approached my table and said, "Excuse me sir, my name is Justin and I'm a Gates Scholar and I just wanted to thank you right now."

Justin went on to share that he was a sophomore in college majoring in political science and told me how much the scholarship had impacted his life. And I responded that that was great to hear, and that I loved that we had met in a vegan restaurant. Here he had come from Memphis, the barbeque capital of the world, and he was dining in a vegan restaurant. I told him that the scholarship must have changed his eating habits in addition to his mind. We both laughed. And I was just blown away in that moment and so humbled and grateful for the opportunity to do this work.

# CHAPTER 16

# THE MISSING PEACE

*Don't wait for the world to recognize your greatness.*
*Live it and let the world catch up.*
- Puffy aka P. Daddy


*We: sij T-we:m (All of us together)*
- Tohono O'odham Nation


From the outside, everything in my world was going well in the year 2011. ULI was in full swing, PRAISE had been established for a number of years, I was involved with the Gates Scholarship Program, I had a beautiful family with a wife and three children, and life was good.

And yet I was feeling a strong desire to expand my work, to go in a different direction, to serve communities beyond urban youth with backgrounds very similar to my own. I began to verbalize my unrest, but not everyone received my desire to expand positively. Many people thought that I was selling out, and told me as much. It brought to mind Malcolm X's trip to Mecca that I referred to earlier, where he saw Muslims of every hue, whereas previously he had only come into contact with the Black Muslims from the United States, and how many people had questioned his decision to go to Mecca in the first place, let alone return from the trip talking about new ways to affect change, new horizons to expand.

Now, I'm no Malcolm, but I can remember hearing my pastor, Willie F. Wilson, quote the great theologian Howard Thurman, who said "Don't worry about what the world needs. Ask what makes you come alive, and go do it. Because what the world needs is people who have come alive."

I realized that I hadn't spent more than what many people pay for their first home to earn college degrees from some of the finest institutions across the country so that I could resent my life of 50 hours a week of work.

But that's what had happened somewhere along the way.

After years of working with several non-profits, traveling all across the country, and speaking to thousands of people, my job had become so emotionally draining and had begun to take such a physical toll on my health that it was actually causing me gripping anxiety attacks. I couldn't understand why, because by all outward measures I was doing *exactly* what I had thought I was called to do.

But I was feeling exhausted more often than not and I was scrambling to find scraps of happiness in unhealthy places. When I took the time to listen, my inner monologue sounded something like this: *You know you're not doing what you love. Your life lacks a deeper meaning and you have no idea what you're passionate about anymore. So what in the world are you going to do with your life?*

See, I wanted to do more, but I had no idea which path I wanted to take. Even though externally it may have looked like I had it all together, I was feeling confused, stuck, and – worst of all – embarrassed by my lack of direction. I was treading water and the water kept rising higher and higher until I began to have trouble breathing.

As the months continued to pass, I became more and more aware of the sense that I was wasting time. I saw my life passing me by, leaving me only with regrets and "what ifs."

I finally felt the need to be brutally honest with myself about my unhappiness, and I embarked on some serious soul searching. I asked myself some tough questions, including the question of what it would be like to be authentically me. I discovered that my unhappiness was rooted in my lack of passion and I slowly began taking control.

I knew that I was going to have to make some sort of major shift in my life, some sort of leap of faith, but I had no way of knowing at the time what that would look like. I never worried about making the wrong choice, though, because I knew that I didn't want to be unhappy any longer and that my happiness was more important to me than any paycheck or sense of security.

---

And then I had a divine encounter in Chicago that led me to Arizona on a trip that changed everything. I had received an invitation to speak in Chicago at the 100th anniversary of a conference for the International Association for Truancy and Dropout Prevention. When I first learned where I had been invited to speak, I couldn't help but think, *Dang! People have been dropping out of school for a long time!* My focus that day was on using Hip-Hop to engage urban youth, a topic that I had been training on frequently throughout the country at the time.

It was in Chicago at that conference that I met April Ignacio. When she first introduced herself to me, I thought she was Latina. April, I would soon come to find out, was from the Tohono O'odham Nation in Arizona. She had beautiful tribal tattoos and loved Hip-Hop music. We hung out one night after the conference and just had a blast. We connected almost immediately. She was really stern and smart and understood her culture and her people deeply. She was keenly astute about issues of racism. I came to find out that she had children who were older than my children were at the time and I quickly came to look up to April for her wisdom and insight on the ways of the world.

At some point during the conference, she asked me if I had ever spoken on a reservation. I hadn't at the time and told her as much. I knew I loved learning about different people and their cultures and rituals, though, so I was excited when she went on to tell me that every year her reservation brought speakers out and that she would love to invite me to come and speak.

I eagerly accepted the invitation and not long after, I boarded a plane to Arizona. Before leaving Baltimore, I had been given a poem by one of my colleagues at Johns Hopkins that really put things into perspective. The poem by Brian Vallie, "Indian Holocaust: A Poem for Columbus Day," contextualized for me the experience of a group of people who I honestly had had very little interaction with up to that point in my life. I sat on the plane to Arizona just reading that poem over and over again – filled with words about the calculated massacres of entire indigenous populations, about how white people knowingly gave Native Americans blankets infested with smallpox, about the creation of a system of dependence that had stripped Native people of the ability to thrive or even survive, and about conquest, oppression and dominance.

I arrived in Arizona, walked out of the airport, and realized that I had landed in what *had* to be the hottest place on earth. I just knew the devil was about to tap me on the shoulder at any moment – not because I had done anything wrong, but because it really *was* hot as hell. Once I had gotten over the shock of the heat, though, I realized that I was feeling, for the first time in a long time, a deep sense of inadequacy. I questioned whether my message would be strong enough, whether it would resonate with people who looked differently than me and whom I knew so little about.

April picked me up from the airport and drove me out to the tribal casino, which sat about 30 minutes from the reservation itself and where I'd be staying for the duration of my visit. She shared with me that the Tohono O'odham Nation was a federally recognized tribe located in southern and central Arizona. With over 28,000 members, it had the second largest tribal land base in the country, which was also historically one of the most impoverished regions in the U.S. I listened to her and thought to myself, *And I thought the Chicago projects were poor!* Once we arrived at the casino and I settled into my room, April let me know that she wanted to take me around to meet a host of different folks in the community before my talk. On the drive from the casino to the reservation, April blasted Biggie and Tupac as we drove by small ranch-style homes and more cacti than I could count. I was intrigued by these unusual-looking birds with really long beaks, which I later learned were use to draw out liquid from the cacti and from deep beneath the dry sand. The entire drive, my mind just raced, wondering *How are they going to receive me?*

As we drove up to the reservation, or rez, I remember a very ominous-looking border patrol officer being stationed at a checkpoint right at its entrance. I thought that it was odd to see a U.S. government official checking Native Americans into their own land. Because we were so close to the Mexican border, there had been some issues with "coyotes" – people who helped smuggle emigrants from Latin America across the U.S. border – sneaking Mexican immigrants onto the reservation. That was apparently why the border patrol had set up shop at the reservation's entrance, but April confided that – as I would have expected – the reservation was less than thrilled with the patrol's Gestapo-like tactics.

We drove to a downtown area where we ate a great lunch at a local café before visiting outside in the plaza square for awhile with some of the locals. I was blown away by how quiet and laid back the entire reservation seemed and by how friendly everyone was to me.

April then led me over to the jail to talk to some of the men who were incarcerated. There, I started to realize that many of these guys were just like the brothers I knew from back in the neighborhoods and barrios I frequented. And yet this jail was a bit different than any I had visited before, and – as far as jails go – I loved it. The jail had sweat lodges and was filled with open spaces. It also had a beautiful industrial kitchen where the prisoners were involved with preparing traditional food. I was impressed that they were able to keep their cultural practices so alive even while locked up.

Then I visited a school board meeting, and that was when I *really* understood that the tribe faced challenges just like those encountered by the minority groups who looked like me and with whom I was so comfortable. As I listened in on the board meeting from the back of the room, I realized that many of the issues – from funding challenges and student involvement to parent engagement – sounded very familiar to me. I also witnessed a disconnect between the school board members and the community members when it came to proposing solutions for how to better engage their youth. I knew from what I had read ahead of time that Native American youth living on reservations can often face an overwhelming array of challenges – from poverty to addiction to abuse – and I knew that the rates of high school dropouts and deaths by suicide on reservations were well above the national average. But actually *being* there, meeting so many amazing people, and seeing some of the challenges the community was facing firsthand was a different type of education than I could ever have received by reading any research report.

Our next stop was the radio station. There I met a few DJs who absolutely loved Hip-Hop music. I felt an immediate connection to them the moment we started talking because music contains within it such universal themes. We talked about the struggle over the promotion of Hip-Hop music at the time and that the elders were resisting it despite the fact that it was infiltrating the rez everywhere. We agreed on the power of music to connect. We also talked about how the kids on the rez loved Hip-Hop music because of their own connection to a culture of strong oral traditions. I thought about one of my favorite films, "Smoke Signals," and one scene in particular in which oral traditions are discussed. When the film was released in 1998, the groundbreaking significance of it almost outshone its considerable strength as a piece of art. This contemporary road movie about two Native Americans who travel together on a journey of both literal and metaphorical significance was the first feature film to be written, directed and co-produced by Native Americans. After seeing the film, and then visiting the rez, I began to experience a sense of clarity. I could see that I was being given an opportunity to explore issues of stereotyping and cultural representation on a different level. I was so used to being on the side of those trying to be understood that it felt momentous to be the one trying to understand.

The DJs really prided themselves on being the voice of the reservation. I asked them what they would say if they could send a message to their younger selves. And I remember distinctly that one of them responded that "It's not where you start, but where you end up, that matters. We come from strong people with a rich history and very grounded roots. I'd tell myself not only to dream big but to think big and not only to think big but to do big."

*Cool,* I thought, *I'm going to use that in my speech!* Finally I arrived at the middle school where I was to speak and by this time I was feeling much more comfortable about not only the environment I was in, but also the message that I was going to deliver and how it was likely to be received. My talk that day was about a dream deferred. Drawing on the Langston Hughes poem of the same name and my understanding that dreams mean a lot in Native American culture, I connected the material in a relevant way to the young people's lives. We talked about dreaming big and I expressed that while I had been really nervous to speak there, I had been strengthened by all of the stops I had made leading up to my visit to the school. And I told the students that it was in their DNA to be fighters, that they came from people who had survived all types of atrocities, lies and misfortunes, and that even though the road ahead of them wasn't going to be easy, they could make it. I reminded them that as Tohono, they had a very strong Native foundation and culture that they should embrace, make their own, and never feel burdened by. I told them that as young people they carried the hope of their entire people within them and they needed to draw strength from that and – in the words of my new friend from the radio station – not only dream big but think big, and not only think big but do big.

I spoke from my heart and that was it. My talk was a hit. I began to see during this trip how my love for people and the callings of my heart were expanding right in front of me. I developed a deeper sense of empathy. I felt pain for the people I met. After my talk, April drove me around some more. During this drive, we had a deep conversation about race. She explained the rez's proximity to the border of Mexico and spoke of the damage that white people had done to her people and the role of religion in their struggles. And we talked about relationships. She shared that if she had ever brought home a Black man she would have been ostracized, but if she had brought home a white man it would have been okay. I remember distinctly the power of that conversation, driving down the highway with the trees and cacti and rolling meadows providing a scenic background for the discussion of issues so deep. *Wow,* I remember thinking, *here's a father who witnessed the destruction of so much at the hands of white people, and yet he'd rather his daughter date someone who looked like the oppressor than someone who looked like me. There's the deep, deep power of white supremacy.*

April talked to me that day about the lasting feelings of inadequacy borne from being oppressed at the hands of white people for so many generations and that this oppression permeated the reservation in such a deep way that it created an energy of powerlessness in certain contexts. She shared that it was very hard to pull young people out of the environment in which they were comfortable.

And then I somehow brought up the topic of being a Gates reader. "Wow!," April exclaimed. "We have a Gates Scholar right here on the reservation! And she doesn't want to leave the reservation to go away to school."

I was a bit dismayed at this news, but not really surprised when I thought about it a bit more. There's a cultural dynamic that many Native American and Latino communities share when it comes to their youth going away to school. So many high school graduates are hesitant to leave because of the strong spirit that keeps them close to home. They're afraid to go away to college and, many times, the cultural values of family obligations and the importance of staying close to their heritage clash with the American ideals of ambition and achievement that attending college often necessitates.

---

I took so much home with me from my trip, but I also left some things behind. I left behind the false belief that my message would only resonate with some and that people who didn't look like me might not receive me well. I left behind the erroneous notion that I belonged only in urban environments, only working with Black and Brown boys who shared a history similar to mine.

On the flight back home to Baltimore from Arizona, I reread the poem that I had read on the flight out and I wept. And then I thought, *Wow! Here I am again in this place I thought I'd never be, listening to stories of people who are so different and yet so similar to me.* I liked the way it felt to be on that reservation and I knew that I wanted to expand my horizons even further. I knew that I had purpose-driven dreams. And I knew that I wanted to continue to listen to and tell the stories of those whose stories aren't often told, like all of the amazing individuals I had met during my trip to Arizona.

I came home with a renewed sense of purpose and belief in my work. I came home with a deeper understanding of cultural rituals and was ready to take my Ubuntu teaching philosophy to a new level. And I must admit, this renewal felt good. Despite some of the chaos I had witnessed on the rez, I again saw beauty beneath the ashes. And I felt hopeful.

I realized that my message was a universal one of hope, truth, fear and frustration and I didn't want to confine myself by only focusing on people who looked like me. I thought that if I had been able to elicit such a positive response from a Native American nation which rarely encountered people with skin as dark as mine, then there must be a whole audience waiting for me out there in the world. My spirit was really saying that I needed to expand and move in a new direction.

---

I returned from that trip to Arizona and told my wife Meshelle that it was time for me to leave ULI, that my heart was calling me to do something different. She was used to me leaving by then, and I'm sure that she had probably seen the signs before I had that a move was coming. So I made a clean break. Not too long after my trip to Arizona, I sat down with David and handed over the books to him. I left him with all the curriculum and programming that we had worked so hard to develop together. I told him that the only thing I wanted to take with me was PRAISE.

And then Meshelle and I sat down and began to brainstorm. She came up with the name the Cambio Group and I loved it. Change was indeed in the air. We talked about creating an arts and advocacy organization where we'd be able to work both individually and collectively to affect change on a new level. We wrote up a plan together and then just went for it.

I remember the day Meshelle and I waited outside the front of the state building together to file our new business paperwork. She looked over at me and said, "We're about to do this." And I said, "Yep," got up, and walked up the steps and into the building. I knew without a shadow of a doubt that even though I wasn't certain exactly where I was going, I was moving in the right direction.

Leaving ULI was one of the hardest decisions of my life. David and I had built a dynasty, and as we had watched so many others go out of business, we had managed to stay focused and driven toward our goals and our vision. We had become brothers in the struggle, similar to my KAOS brotherhood, but instead of fighting in the streets, David and I fought in board rooms and in city hall meetings, against crooked cops and dispassionate leaders, alongside empathetic educators and agents of change. We had in essence changed the headlines. We hadn't had foundations dropping millions of dollars into our business bank account. We had been young, and maybe a bit foolish, but we had been so committed to changing the world. Looking back, it's amazing what we accomplished in such a short amount of time with little more than our hearts, a shared vision, an incredible amount of energy, and some pretty great opportunities. Although David and I still collaborate on projects and support each other's life's work, my stepping away from ULI and stepping out on my faith really did signify the end of an era for both of us, our collective work, and our shared vision of what was possible.

I think there are two ways to determine whether you are following your heart – the first is whether you are following the desires that your heart is calling you toward, and the second is whether you are living *in* your heart. Like really *being in* it. Our society today is largely driven by our minds, our fears and our egos. We do not place as much value and emphasis on passion, love, fulfillment, and spiritual purpose. Rather we focus on external success, money, security, stability and reputation at the expense of the deep calling of our hearts. As a result, we are often too busy trying to get ahead and make something of ourselves in this world to just be still enough to listen.

My heart was calling me not to do something different, but to do the same work in a different way. So I needed to stay faithful to my vision of what it meant for *me* to be an Ubuntu teacher. I needed to honor my calling to expand beyond working only with Black and Brown urban children. And that realization gave me such clarity. I didn't know exactly *where* I was going, but I knew *why*. And I realized that nothing in the world can take away the sense of peace that comes from knowing that you're traveling the path you were meant to travel, with purpose, on purpose, and for purpose.

# PART V

THOUGHTS FROM AN UBUNTU TEACHER

# CHAPTER 17

# THE JOURNEY NEVER ENDS

*The purpose of life is a life with a purpose.*
*So I'd rather die for a cause than live a life that is worthless.*

- Immortal Technique

In Spanish, the word *cambio* literally means change. I have to wonder, though, if I was *really* prepared for the change that was about to unfold in my life. What I do know is that I never expected it to all happen so fast. Although looking back on it now, I wonder why I thought things could have gone any other way. Paolo Coelho, author of one of my all-time favorite books "The Alchemist," said that "when you want something, all the universe conspires in helping you to achieve it." And that's really the only explanation I can give for what began to happen after I left ULI.

The world opened up to me and, for the most part, I was embraced by the broader community in which I began working and learning. I started to receive invitations to speak in very diverse settings – from educational communities to law enforcement organizations to leadership conferences – and with every trip, with every new training I led, I learned more and more about myself and the place in the world where my work fit.

As I began to expand the scope of my work, I noticed that many of the audiences I was now coming into contact with were white kids who held an infatuation with urban culture. And I began to ask myself, *why would I NOT want to pour into these kids who don't look like me? Why wouldn't I want them to hear certain messages from me about urban culture, equity and purpose?*

And I began to really challenge myself. I knew that with so many opportunities to travel around and meet people from all walks of life, it was up to me to live up to my full potential. It wasn't my destiny to just show up at some places, some of the time, for some audiences.

I began to realize at a deep level that despite everything that makes us unique, people are just people. Most all of us want the best for our children. We all want to be respected. We all want to be heard. We all want to be loved, free of judgment. For in the words of Mother Theresa, "If you judge people, you have no time to love them." And what are we here to do if not love?

I began to see how my work was shifting from talking about pedagogy to talking about helping people tap into their own personal gifts. And the more conversations I had about personal development being important in others' lives, the more I realized it was notably absent in my own.

So I started to further expand my horizons, but I also began to dig deep. I read more. I meditated more. I focused on mindfulness more. And I laced up my sneakers and ran more. I stopped listening to music with negative and violent lyrics. I attended retreats. I poured back into my soul. I spent more time with my family and with elders. I listened more and talked less. I did the opposite of "Don't just sit there, do something!" I decided I needed to not do anything and just sit there. Calm my mind. Get myself in line.

---

When I step up in front of a room to speak, I often open up by telling my audience that they're in for a treat, that it's going to be the *best* workshop they've ever participated in. I tell them they're actually not even going to participate in a workshop – they're going to have an *experience*. And then I explain that I'm not going to do anything amazing or say anything too profound, but that I'm going to focus on how I want them to *feel* when they walk out of the room at the end of the hour, or two, or three. Dr. Maya Angelou said that "people will forget what you said, people will forget what you did, but people will never forget how you made them feel." And I remember Dr. Angelou's words when I speak – I focus on people leaving with a great feeling. I focus on them being like, *Wow! What just happened in there? Why do I FEEL this way?*

Then, I dig in. I act as if nobody is around. I dance as if nobody is watching. And I don't have expectations about any of it – except for the feeling bit. I don't care about being the best researcher or knowing the best people or having the best PowerPoint presentation or coming out with the best punch line. And I don't care if people leave the room liking what I've had to say, but I do care if they've *heard* it. I care if they've internalized my message and that they've been able to somehow tap into the greatness that's already inside of them, that's already inside of us all.

When people come up to me after a talk and tell me that they wish they had known that I was going to make them cry, then I know I've done my job. And if I hear laughter erupt in a room during a training, then I also know I've done my job. Because we can find healing in our tears and we can find hope in our shared laughter. That's Ubuntu.

And I want it to translate. Recently, a teacher came up to me after a training and said, "Wow! All this stuff you taught today? I'm going to go home tonight and start using it with my own son. I thought I'd just be learning things about teaching today."

*Good*, I thought as I smiled at her and thanked her. *We're getting somewhere here.* Because at the end of the day, it's *all* personal. We're all connected. And no matter what the topic of my talk happens to be, I need people to feel something at a deep enough level to want to start to make changes where it matters most – with ourselves first.

---

If this journey has taught me anything, it's to be humble. It's never about me. It's *always* about the work. And it's so easy, honestly, when you're standing up in front of large crowds of people, getting positive responses, to start to believe that you're something special. But the truth is that all of us are special and none of us are special. I've written here about my own journey because it's the only path I know so intimately, not because I'm that unique.

I'm not the one who is fighting the hardest battles anymore. It's that mother I met in a parent workshop recently who was campaigning *so* hard for her son to have access to a quality education, even when he'd messed up, even when he'd been wrong, even when he was facing expulsion. It's about her fighting even when she knows it will be an uphill battle, because if she lets go of this fight, then what does she have left to live for?

And it's listening to this mother talk and it's seeing in my mind my own mother when De La Salle Institute asked me to leave. It's remembering my mother's tears and my mother's fight. And it's understanding why I can't give up on this work. Because I had a mother who did battle for me when I didn't deserve it, I can understand the depth of this mother's fight as she stands in front of me. And so who am I *not* to share with her the tools that I know of to help her navigate the system with more grace? Who am I *not* to reach out to her son and equip him to be successful in the best ways I know how? And now, who am I *not* to share my story if, in so doing, I can change the trajectory of even one life? What else could possibly matter more than this?

Last year I was preparing to lead a two-week anti-bullying tour for the second year running, and I was dreading it, because the first tour – traveling around and speaking with hundreds of students in two different schools every day for two solid weeks – had been exhausting. I had been in tears daily and the young people had been in tears. And then I had gone back to my hotel room at night, cried some more, and wondered how I was going to muster the strength to get up the next day and do it all over again. I'm not sure if I was afraid to confront the bullying my KAOS crew had inflicted on others during our own youth, or if I didn't want to address the bullying I had received at the hands of of my teachers and, later, some of my teaching colleagues. Or if I regretted that I still didn't have the answer to my son's question of why people are so mean to each other sometimes. But whatever the reason, I knew I had to get it together.

As I was wallowing a bit in my own dread of the upcoming tour, I started to remember all the young people the year before who had had the bravery to approach the microphone, shaking and in tears, to share their war stories about bullying. I remembered in particular an autistic student who had come up to me as we were wrapping up one day. He thanked me for giving him a voice in front of such a large audience. He told me that he had been afraid of so much, but that I had given him some courage, opportunity and skills. He shared that he was no longer afraid to speak up for himself and others.

I remembered a young lady who had given me a video the year before to use on my next tour. It was a video she had created about secrets, about how she had contemplated suicide, and about how she had made it through the darkness. Here she had trusted me with her story, so who was I *not* to share her story of strength with others? Who was I *not* to get it together to find the strength I needed to do the tour the second year?

Eventually I gathered myself together to answer the call to complete the second bullying tour. And even though it was just as impactful as the first time around, I have to admit that it wasn't quite as emotionally draining. Because I was able to carry with me the strength I had seen in the kids that first year. And their strength gave me strength. The Ubuntu concept of reciprocity is amazing when you feel its effects in action, when you let go of the rigid teacher-student roles and instead commit yourself to doing the work that needs to be done. And then resting and getting right back out there to do it again.

---

Somewhere along the way, I decided that I would get my doctoral degree. For me, the challenge didn't lie in going through the doctoral coursework or even completing my dissertation. The hardest part was deciding to go for it in the first place. In my head I had had all of these conflicting voices rattling around for years – voices of people who said I needed to do it and of people who questioned why I would want to do it and of people who said I could never do it.

Thirteen years prior to starting my doctorate, I met Dr. Freeman A. Hrabowski III, a man who would later become my mentor. An educator, advocate and mathematician, Dr. Hrabowski had begun his term as president of the University of Maryland, Baltimore County back in the early 90s. The first time we met, he told me that Black and Brown men with PhDs were almost unstoppable, that I would be able to go anywhere I wanted to with a doctoral degree. He called me "Boy" during our first meeting, and I remember thinking, *I don't need it. I don't need this damn degree*. I remember thinking that I didn't need *anything* external to me to define my worth, that the young people I worked with didn't give a damn what letters I had after my name. So the very first time Dr. Hrabowski spoke to me about the value of a PhD, I wrote the opportunity off right then and there. I talked myself completely out of going after a doctoral degree before I had gotten even one foot in the door.

Around the same time, I approached a good friend and mentor of mine, who was working as a business advisor at New York University, to ask his opinion about pursuing my doctorate. He asked me, "D, why are you thinking about this PhD thing? You're already *doing* everything that you should be doing without all this degree stuff that I have." And in a way he was right. But I felt like I was always working to prove to people that I could do the work without the schooling, although from the time I first started teaching I did have some solid education behind me. I revisited that conversation with this friend a couple of years later, because I was still exploring the idea of getting my doctorate. But I was trying to figure out how I could do it with a full-time job, a wife, and children. He stressed again that I didn't need the degree to do the work.

Almost a decade after these conversations with people whom I admired and respected, I was doing some research in Anne Arundel Public Schools in Maryland around engaging Black and Latino boys. Nobody else was coming into this county doing this research or this work, and I saw a need to fill. I saw clearly how the pieces of my work and my education fit together, and I felt a strong pull back to school, back to that final degree.

I was reminded that it was up to me to pursue my own dreams, even if I knew that they didn't all make sense to those around me. I had been working on the Ubuntu concept of looking inward for the answers before going to the books. I had been searching inside for so long, and I had been mastering my own experience. But I wanted to learn more and I knew that I was ready.

As part of my journey toward earning my terminal degree, I had to do some research and write my dissertation. Before this book, that dissertation was the biggest experiment I'd ever performed on myself, the longest ongoing conversation with myself I'd ever had. I was really just trying to figure out some of the same shit I'd always struggled with on a different level – about what it meant to grow up Black and Brown in America, about why I had caused so much chaos in my younger years, and about how I had made it through. I felt a need to understand deeply some of what had happened to me so that I could help others navigate what *they* were going through.

So I got the degree, but I didn't want it to change me. Maybe that's why when people introduce me, I want them to talk about the things I *didn't* do right that have helped get me to this moment in my life, not the things that I *did* do right. I want them to introduce me as a young man from the South Side of Chicago. A man who struggled just like everyone else. Who is still a work in progress. But who somehow, some way, made it through. I ask people to introduce me like that and tell them that I'll take care of the rest.

People say, "But you have all these accolades," and I often remind them that none of that has anything to do with what I'm planning to tell people in any given moment. All people want to know is that whatever I'm going to talk about is going to help them in some way. They're sitting there thinking to themselves, *I hope whatever this dude says is going to help me tomorrow with this little knucklehead boy in my class or this trifling administrator who has been on my case all week. I hope he says something useful. I hope he doesn't waste my time.*

When Dr. King spoke about how he wanted to be remembered after his death, he told people not to mention his degrees or that he graduated at a young age. He wanted people to say that he was a drum major for justice. And his words have had such an impact on me, the idea of being remembered for the causes we stood for and not the degrees we earned along the way.

I know that sometimes my education and accomplishments can turn people off because it can seem that I've sold out, that I'm trying to be better than them, that I've forgotten where I came from. And I know that for others, hearing about my degrees excites and inspires them. In some circles it lends an added credibility to my work, makes audience members sit up a little straighter in their chairs and listen a little more astutely. It's like they're just *waiting* for me to say something prophetic. And some days I might and some days I might not. Some days I might sound like an intellectual and some days I might sound like a little thug from the South Side of Chicago. And most often I'll sound like a mixture of the two. Because I'm not where I want to be and I'm not where I came from. I'm still striving. I'm still trying to figure it out. I know that having a terminal degree like a doctorate degree doesn't mean I'm finished with anything. It's just another part of my journey. And the journey's not over yet.

On the flip side, I do celebrate what I've accomplished. Because I want boys who have had childhoods similar to mine to see what's possible. I want to represent opportunity and hope and perseverance and hard work. It's an *honor* for a kid like me who always struggled in school to have made it to this point, but earning my doctoral degree has not been the defining moment in my life. It's just a part of the bigger picture, a piece in the puzzle of who I am, who I've been, and who I'll become. It was hard. It was a lot of work. I recognize that the title of "Dr." comes with a lot of responsibilities and expectations. And sometimes I live up to the expectations of others and sometimes I fall short and sometimes I blow the expectations out of the water. But in all of this, I don't see myself as an expert in anything except my own story. I'm constantly striving to be an authority on myself, and beyond that if I can just ask some good questions, stimulate some meaningful conversation, shatter some deeply held prejudices about what's possible, then I've done my job. I've walked in my purpose.

# CHAPTER 18

# CHANGING THE HEADLINES

*I know I can be what I wanna be. If work hard
at it, I'll be where I wanna be.*

- NAS

So many young men of color make the front pages of the newspapers for the wrong reasons. Instead of receiving their coveted 15 minutes of fame, they are tied to tragic events as victims of police brutality, poor education, law enforcement misconduct, and what many are calling a racially unjust American criminal justice system. The headlines read: "Menace to Society," "Hell Breaks Loose," "Weed, Fights, and Guns: Trayvon Martin's Text Messages Released."

And whenever I see headlines like these, I'm reminded what a shame it is that so many of our men of color are receiving negative press, being targeted and treated unequally. It's unfortunate that so much bleak data swarms our lives – statistics like one in three black men will encounter the criminal justice system at some point in his life, boys of color have the highest suspension, referral and expulsion rates nationwide, and boys of color are more likely to be labeled hyperactive than their white counterparts.

I envision a society where positive headlines like "100 percent of Urban Prep Seniors Admitted to College!" and "Meet the Student Accepted into all Eight Ivy League Schools!" become the norm. I can't wait until the day that headlines highlighting hopeful statistics and stories about the achievements of our young men of color drown out the negative press – statistics such as a 2013 Education Week report that noted that the high school dropout rate for African American males recently hit a historic low; or a Boston Globe article that reported nine out of 10 Black people age 12 or older currently don't use illicit drugs and 93 percent don't suffer from substance abuse issues; or a report from the U.S. Department of Health and Human Services that found seven out of eight Black teenage boys are *not* fathers; or my personal favorite, the National Science Foundation's finding that 33.4 percent of the African Americans who earned doctorates in 2008 had fathers who graduated college.

I envision a society where we talk more about all the work that's being done *right*, instead of focusing incessantly on where we're falling short. We should applaud the work of organizations like the BME Community, which describes itself as "a growing network of all races and genders committed to building better communities across the U.S." and Excelencia, an organization committed to "accelerating Latino student success in higher education by providing data-driven analysis of the educational status of Latinos and by promoting education policies and institutional practices that support their academic achievement." We must emphasize the many other organizations and individuals throughout the country working tirelessly to create programs to counter the increasingly negative representation of Black and Brown boys in the media and broader society, to give our young people positive outlets for personal expression, and to proudly display our cultures through arts and academics.

It's possible to change the headlines if we're willing to dig in deep and do the work. I'm doing the work with and for my own children. My kids have learned what it means to be ambassadors for both country and community. They've expanded their peer network with new friends from Haiti, Puerto Rico, Africa, Costa Rica and the Dominican Republic through my international travel work. They've learned about the power and potential of international exchange from the staff and personnel at the Haitian embassy. And they've discovered ways to enhance their college applications and pursue their lifelong ambitions years before they'll even finish high school. They're used to being around people – people who look like them and who look different than them – doing great things.

I'm especially working with and through my 8-year-old son to help change the headlines. Because the only side of the statistics I want him to be on is the positive side and I know that with consistent focus and hard work it's possible. We may be fighting an uphill battle, we may be swimming up a stream that's still trying to wash us out to sea, but when I look into the eyes of my own son – so filled with hope and promise and wonder – I know that it doesn't matter how weary I become, I'll never stop fighting.

---

Last school year, I worked closely with two groups of high school boys – one that was all African American and one that was all Latino. And even though both were challenging groups to work with in many ways, I also felt so hopeful when I got right down to the heart of the matter. We talked a lot about the young men's feelings that they were being viewed by the school and the larger society based solely off stereotypes and misconceptions. I told them that we were going to work together to change the headlines.

It was out of those two groups that I formed EVOLVE (Encouraging Vigilance and Optimism through Leadership, Valor, and Excellence). The premise of EVOLVE is one of the potential and promise of our youth – the fact that all children have the ability to learn and succeed, that all children can be inspired to achieve and to attain their goals if given the confidence and competence to do so. Through EVOLVE, our hope is that even the most challenging children who come to school with significant difficulties will be able to soar.

I was working with one of those groups of young men one day and played the Jay-Z song "Can I Live." There's a line at the end when Jay-Z raps "I keep one eye open like CBS." We had a conversation about the meaning of the line and what Jay-Z was saying here about the significance of keeping one eye open as it related to trust, or the lack thereof. What did it mean never to be able to close your eyes? Never to be able to trust completely?

A conversation ensued and I asked the young men if there was anyone in the school who they felt like they could trust. You could have heard a pin drop in that room it was so quiet. For five minutes, nobody said a word. I wasn't arrogant enough to hope they'd say that they trusted me, since I had only been working with them for a short time, but I did find it disturbing that they were not able to name a single adult on campus whom they trusted.

So I put on my researcher hat and asked them to consider the connections between their mistrust of their teachers and their learning. And they told me that it was hard for them to learn from people they did not trust.

That conversation echoed what boys have been telling me consistently through the years, and what the research supports: that it's hard for boys to perform academically for someone with whom they feel they have little to no connection. The topic of trust has also been a common theme in the many conversations I've had through the years with my boys from KAOS. We rolled deep because we needed to be with people we could trust. Because the outside world seemed so untrustworthy. That was why we protected each other, why we spent almost every waking hour with each other.

Trust works other ways, too. As teachers, we've often learned to mistrust the very students who so desperately need our trust. All it takes is one disruptive young person to ruin it for the rest of the students in a classroom. We don't want to get burned again, so we tighten the rules and narrow the focus. We develop an attitude that we can't rely on our students to learn independently or to make the right choices. In the lower grades, our response manifests itself as control – it's as though we have to regulate all of the learning activities so that things don't get out of hand, so that the room doesn't get too loud, and so everything stays nice and neat. We leave little room for student-directed learning because we don't trust that our students will do what needs to be done. In the upper grades, the same principles of distrust might look a bit different, but they stem from the same place. We come down punitively on students for the smallest of infractions, we dictate the lines of questioning and the flow of classes so tightly, we watch our backs constantly for fear of some sort of student-led mutiny.

But Ubuntu teaching shows us that there's another way, a better way, to teach and lead and learn. And we can't always describe it, but we know it when we see it. It's that undeniable *feeling* you get when you walk into a true student-centered classroom. You look around and take in the possibility of it all. You hear sounds of authenticity and see images that reflect the students and their growth. There's a level of humanity and cohesion and connection, a sense that students are holding *themselves* accountable. And the Ubuntu teacher is more of a coach – giving students the plays, but not getting out on the field with them.

Trust has its roots and wings in the level of competence we as teachers possess to work with the students who so desperately need our trust. In my professional experience, I have found that while many schools focus on teaching methodology, we're not well enough versed in cultural competency. Countless teachers I come across are simply culturally unprepared to teach boys of color. However, all it takes to move forward is for those teachers to be transparent and say, "I just don't know what to do." Whenever I see this level of honesty from teachers, I always smile because I know we have something to build from.

On the other hand, I've worked with a lot of teachers who, although they look like their students, are culturally disconnected. We cannot assume that just because we look like our students we're going to automatically have trust or connection. If teachers' arrogance or fears prevent them from admitting when they too need support, then our boys are no better off in classrooms where the teachers *do* look like them.

Connection can come in many forms, and even though I know from my experience the deep pain of not having teachers who looked like me and to whom I could relate authentically, I also know that there are teachers throughout the country who do not resemble the students they're teaching, but who are working tirelessly and succeeding at forging meaningful connections. At the same time that we need to advocate for a teaching workforce in which more than two percent of teachers are African American males, we also need to honor and work with those who *are* showing up each and every day to do the work, whatever the color of their skin.

Following my conversation with the young men, I hosted a focus group with some of the teachers in the school. I shared with them what the boys had indicated to me about their lack of trust, that they had questioned why they should trust their teachers when they felt like their teachers talked to them like they didn't matter. And while most of the teachers were receptive to what I had to say, one teacher was not. She held steadfast in her belief that, despite what the young men expressed to be true, the lack of trust between teachers and students was not really a problem. Ironically enough, she was the only teacher of color in the room and she was the one putting up the biggest fight. What was it? Arrogance? Denial? Both? Whatever *it* was, it wasn't serving the boys well.

Fostering strong relationships has become a popular phrase in educational circles today, but I often wonder if we are really asking the young people what *they* need in order to build solid relationships with the adults in their lives and then *really* listening to their responses, whether or not we agree with or even like what they have to say.

---

Most of my career I've worked with older students, so I honestly hadn't thought much about the impact that we can effect on younger children until I started to observe my own son once he turned 5 years old and entered kindergarten. Watching him learn, grow, and ask me increasingly complex questions about the world inspired me to seek out an opportunity to work with younger boys. I call them the Genius Club. It's a program I'm developing with early-elementary-aged boys because I've come to believe that if we're *really* going to start changing the headlines, then we have to start with our babies.

I remember a day last year when I was working with a group of teachers at the school site of the Genius Club. The teachers expressed that they felt so worn down and lost, that they didn't know *how* they were going to begin to reach the boys in their charge. Although it might have appeared to an outside observer that the teachers just didn't care and had given up, what was going on was so much deeper than that. They were attempting to steer a ship without a map, looking for a lighthouse where they saw none.

Honestly, sometimes I can understand why people who look like me can be so abrasive toward white teachers who seem like they just don't have a clue, or don't care, or both. But the more I work with teachers of all backgrounds, the more I learn that many of these teachers really *do* want to engage deeply with their students. They are trying to unpack and move beyond prejudices that they weren't even aware that they held until they first stepped foot in the classroom. And they're asking, pleading even, to be better prepared.

It's up to us, all of us collectively who work in education and especially teacher education, to answer the call and to give the teachers what they need and what so many of them are so desperately seeking. It's also up to us collectively to call each other out when we fall short.

I can't talk about the Genius Club without talking about Christopher, a kindergartener at the school. He was so cute and so little and I just had a feeling that he would benefit from being a part of the group that I was forming. But his teacher, before she even knew anything about the Genius Club or what we'd be doing, made it quite clear to me that she felt Christopher *shouldn't* be in the group, that there was no way that he would learn from the experience.

I chose Christopher anyway and noticed pretty quickly that the kid didn't seem to talk at all. We were a few sessions in and I was just wracking my brain for ways to connect with this boy, to get him to open up, to provide a space comfortable enough for him to say something, anything. And then one day, without any planning at all, a Taylor Swift song came on, and Christopher said, clear as day, "My sister plays this song all the time!"

And I was like, *Wow! Okay. Now we're getting somewhere. I think I've found a point of connection. Music.*

So I returned to the teacher, who I had come to find out was really struggling with Christopher in her class, and shared with her what I thought was my epiphany about how to connect with Christopher, how to get him to speak. And the teacher, appearing very underwhelmed, told me that she already knew that Christopher liked music. And all I could think to myself was *Why didn't this woman tell me this? Why isn't she willing to work together WITH me to see how we might positively impact Christopher's life? What's with the secrets?*

But the thing is, that situation wasn't an isolated one. So often in schools, we find ourselves wanting to somehow hoard the best information, strategies and resources for our own classrooms, our own students. It's as if we want to have a monopoly on the greatness, like we think on some level that if someone else comes in and *also* makes a connection with our students that somehow we've failed. And I often think we do this because we're working in a profession where we get so few accolades, where the victories can seem so few and far between, that we develop a deficit or scarcity mentality that causes us to hold tight to whatever we can.

I know that early on in my teaching career I was guilty of this thought process as well. I was making some amazing strides with my kids and building really strong connections, but instead of sharing what I was learning with other teachers in the building, I often remained on the defensive and kept it all inside the walls of my own classroom.

In this area, like so many others, we have *got* to do better if we're going to change the headlines. We have to collaborate more, be willing to authentically and openly admit when we need help, and recognize that – at the end of the day – we really are all in this together. We have to be willing to foster the Ubuntu quality of authentic and sustainable connections whenever we are able.

---

Another day recently I dropped by unannounced at a school where I'd been working because I wanted to check in with some of the boys in my program there. And almost as soon as I set foot on campus, the principal caught me in the hallway and quickly pulled me into her office, where the school's behavior specialist was seated at a conference table. The principal was visibly distraught and wanted to share with me what had just happened. She recounted a less than friendly altercation with a mom of one of her African American male students and said she needed my help.

I told her she had to start at the beginning, so she pulled out a little booklet from one of her desk drawers. She opened up the booklet, filled with a whole bunch of mess – curse words, crude phrases, pictures – nothing I hadn't seen before. I thumbed through it a bit and saw that the booklet's author had actually divided up the written material into chapters. There was an organization and structure to what I was looking at, and an obvious investment of time.

The principal shared that one of her students, who I knew from my work at the school, was the booklet's author. The behavior specialist described the student as "the one who always wears the *Hustle* shirt," and I knew immediately which kid he was talking about.

I wasn't shocked by what she showed me – I'd seen far worse. So I just turned to the principal, smiled, and said, "Oh, it looks like you've got a little writer on your hands!"

She returned the smile, but then quickly got serious again as she went on to tell me the rest of the story. She had had to call the boy's mother in. She had been nervous to even make the phone call because she and this particular parent had already had their fair share of conflict and confrontation during the school year. But the principal told me that she had mustered up the courage to make the call and that the mother had come to the school with two young children in tow, walked into the office, and upon learning the reason she was called in, said "I can't believe you brought me in here for this fucking bullshit! *This* is why you've brought me in?!"

According to the principal, the mom didn't seem to see anything wrong with the language in the booklet – she said that "this is how we talk in the projects." The principal said that the only thing the mom seemed really upset about was that her son had misspelled some of the words that he'd written.

The principal said she had taken it home with her all weekend – the confrontation with the mother, the boy's little booklet, all of it. She was deeply upset by the entire event and was trying to unpack it all for herself, to figure out where she had gone wrong, what she could have done differently.

She questioned whether the conflict had to do with a poverty mindset on behalf of the parent. She began quoting the long-outdated and hotly contested work of Ruby Payne. And I stopped her right there, looked her in the eye, and asked her "What do you *really* want to say right now? What do you *really* think about what happened?"

Because even though I knew that we were dealing with some deep racial and cultural clashes here, I also knew that this instance wasn't that serious. I had to let her see that she might be digging too deeply into some outdated – and largely discredited – theories of poverty written by another white woman when here she was, living out her own experience, with all the information she needed right in front of and within her to find some resolution and peace.

See, I was looking at this woman heading up a school that has a history of being a place where slaves actually migrated to receive an education, a school where many of her students are the children of the children of slaves. And the cultural collision as she described it to me *was* admittedly upsetting, but I also knew that it likely wasn't as complicated as she was trying to make it.

I'd been working with this principal and her school for awhile, and so I knew her to be a quiet leader who was deeply committed to working through challenges related to poverty and lack of access to resources. I wanted her to be able to get it all out – all of her anger, distress, disappointment and confusion – so that we could work to move beyond the incident and toward some strategies she could use going forward to more effectively engage with parents.

She shared her worry that she had handled it all wrong, her feeling that the mom hadn't valued her concern, and her need for the child to understand that in the school building, certain standards had to be met when it came to appropriate use of language. In the meeting with the mom and her son, the principal had turned to the student and said, "See, in school this is how we do things..." and tried to explain the importance of school-appropriate behavior. But she felt like even though the boy had seen her in the hall later and had given her a big hug, she had still made mistakes. And she felt like she couldn't get on the same page with the boy's mother. At all.

I listened to her at length, and then I asked her what she had *really* wanted to say to the mom that day, but hadn't – for fear of misunderstanding, for fear of being called racist, for fear of something else that maybe she couldn't even name. She wouldn't tell me. She thought I was joking. And I told her to look at my face, that I was dead serious. All I was able to get out of her was that "There would have been some un-Godly words said." I couldn't convince her to say any more than that, even though I told her that maybe she needed to say the words in my presence, to just release it all and let it go. Whatever *it* was.

And then I said that even if she wasn't willing to share with me, I had a few things to share with her. I told her that, from my perspective, the mom *had* been out of line that day. That not everyone in the projects talks like that, and that I bet that the mom knew that. And that, honestly, it had nothing to do with living in the projects – it had to do with that mom, in that moment, making a foolish statement. Maybe *she* was afraid that her son was slipping away from her, maybe she was tired of being called up to the school when her son was in some sort of trouble, maybe she was exhausted from feeling like she constantly had to be on the defensive in the face of white authority. Or maybe she felt like I did when Brother Tim reached out to save me all those years ago at De La Salle – maybe she wanted the help to come from someone who looked like her and her son. Maybe she felt vulnerable. Maybe she questioned why this white woman cared so much about her Black son.

So I let the principal know that I was honored that she had come to me to try to sort things out when she hadn't had to, that she was willing to admit that she didn't know how she felt about the whole exchange. I had to acknowledge her for her willingness to be vulnerable and open to growth. Sometimes the greatest thing we can share with another human is our space and an opportunity to exchange ideas without judgment or fear.

But I knew as I left my meeting with the principal that day that my work was far from over. I exited the office and headed right over to the cafeteria to find the kid in the *Hustle* shirt. I knew we needed to have a conversation. I located him almost immediately and spoke with him for a few minutes about the incident. I talked to him about the work I was doing at other schools, and how the boys enjoyed meeting together in small groups. I then told him that I thought he would be a perfect fit for a new group I was forming at the school. I asked him if he liked winning and said that I was looking for a winner to join my team. He said he was a winner and I said, "Me too!" And that was that.

And then I plotted a way to get the mother back to the school to meet with me. Because I felt like there was a bridge that still needed to be built there as well. It actually happened kind of by accident. I called another mother from the school whose son I was working with and I just asked her if she knew the other boy's mom. As it turned out, the mothers were good friends. So without divulging anything, I asked this mom if she could bring her friend up with her to the school. And she did.

I sat there with the student's mom, knowing that we had some work to do. Because the very first words out of her mouth about the principal had been, "This white woman..." And I interrupted her right there. I said that we just needed to clarify something here. I told her that "this white woman" loved her Black son and was willing to fight for him in his mother's absence. That she wasn't going to get it all right, but that she was working hard. And the mom said that she was angry, that she didn't want this white woman telling her anything about how to raise her Black son. I let her speak and I validated her feelings, but I didn't let her hide behind them. Because in this instance, playing the race card was the easy thing to do. It was a cop out. And we're never going to make the progress we so desperately need to make until we can move beyond our default modes of defensiveness and anger.

What I wanted this mom to understand was that she really needed to look at her own mindset – about herself, her son, the school, and her larger community. And I wanted this principal to understand that everyone needed to work together to help change the mother's mindset in a compassionate and proactive way. And then I had to let the principal know that *her* own understanding that everyone from the projects was going to act a certain way, talk a certain way, react a certain way in a school context, also needed some work.

There's no quick fix to issues of racism, of poverty, of sexism, of all the other – isms that permeate our schools and our larger society. But we have to be able to dialogue honestly. We have to be able to dig deep into the pain and find some hopeful avenues of healing.

---

You see, in my work I love connecting with parents. Of course some of them are crazy and there are times when I wish I could take some of these babies out of their home environments and move them in with me, even though I know my wife is definitely not letting me move any other kids into our house. But I've never met a parent, crazy or not, who didn't want the best for his or her kids. I've met *many* parents who have lacked the skills to advocate for themselves and their children, but a lack of advocacy skills is not synonymous with a lack of care.

Just the other night, I was getting ready to begin a parent workshop when a woman walked into the room, looked around, and immediately asked, "How long is this gonna be?! There's only a few of us in here. You think we're going to go all the way until 8 o'clock?" And I told her that it didn't matter to me if there were two or 200 people in the room, that we were going to do the work that we needed to do. And that yes, we'd probably be there until the scheduled end time. I told her that the fact that *she* was there said a lot about her commitment and that it wasn't my job in this context to get the people to come – it was my job, metaphorically speaking, to feed the people who showed up hungry.

As the evening went on, I discovered through some of what she shared that one of the challenges this woman faced was her self-admitted lack of patience. She was a grandmother raising her children's children and was tired, stretched thin, and didn't have the patience for wasting time.

See, I could have easily become frustrated with this woman right at the beginning of the evening. Or I could have given into the pressure I felt from her combative entrance and rushed through the material I had prepared for the workshop. I could have put forth less than my full effort because the room wasn't packed. Or I could have easily begun talking about how "these parents" just didn't care that much because look at how few had even shown up in the first place.

But I didn't do any of those things. I dug in deep with the people who *had* shown up. I gave them all that I had to give. I helped them understand where their pain was coming from and where they were struggling, and then together we worked through some strategies. We did the work we needed to do together. Two or 200, it doesn't matter. The right people always show up.

---

The evening wrapped up and my mind flashed back to just a month before. My PRAISE team and I were getting ready to launch a new group of scholars, having graduated another group of seniors last year after taking them through the six-year program, and I knew that we needed some help getting the boys off to a strong start. So I put up a call on Facebook that read as follows: *I need 40 men (lifeguards) to help us support 40 amazing young, male scholars in Baltimore. Meet today at the Johns Hopkins School of Education located at 2800 N. Charles Street from 5:30 – 7 p.m. If you are one of my former students, clients, friends, family members, or anyone concerned about keeping our boys alive, I'm expecting you to be in the building. This is not a griping session. It's a solution-based session. They need you. I need you. Bring a friend. Thanking you in advance.*

The call was clear, I thought. So I showed up that evening – no expectations, just the hope that the people who needed to be there that night would show. And I sat there. Alone. And not a single man showed up. Not a one.

Honestly, at an earlier time in my life, I would have been enraged. I would have been beyond frustrated and upset. Of course I was disappointed that nobody had answered my call. But I have come to believe deeply that the people who are meant to be in any given place at any given time will show up. I believe this, but I honestly have to admit that waiting there all alone I could have used some sort of sign that my belief was a valid one. Because I wasn't feeling in my heart that I was meant to sit there that night alone.

Then a young woman walked into the room. I thought at first that she was probably in the wrong building, until I gave her a second glance and realized that she looked vaguely familiar, even though I couldn't immediately place her.

"Señor Shields?" The second she addressed me, I knew where I recognized her from. She was one of my former City students, a young lady who over a decade earlier had graced my high school Spanish classroom as a quiet and studious teenager. I honestly didn't remember much about her immediately aside from her name, but I was *very* curious as to why she had just walked into that particular classroom at Johns Hopkins.

She told me that she had seen my Facebook post and had written down the address and decided that she needed to show up. And it wouldn't be long before I would find out why.

We sat there and she caught me up on her life since high school, that she was raising her son alone, and all of the challenges and triumphs she'd had in her life since her graduation from City. She also shared with me the deep pain that she had endured during high school and that, unbeknownst to me at the time, I had helped her navigate through some of that pain through the way I taught, the lessons I shared, the care I showed. The crazy thing was that she hadn't even been one of my most memorable students – she was quiet and had presented no academic problems. She was one of those kids who most of us would have assumed was doing just fine. But like Curtis, she had a lot of pain that she was hiding beneath the surface. She presented well, but inside she was falling apart. And nobody realized it at the time, not even me.

But here she was, all these years later, answering an invitation that wasn't even intended for her, because she was raising a Black son alone and because, as she said, "I knew how you were as a teacher way back at City and even though I didn't even know what this was all about, and even though I'm not a man, I just knew that anything that you were a part of I wanted my son to be a part of, too."

Ubuntu teaching is about recognizing the cyclical nature to everything we do. There are no accidents. Every single interaction matters. Every single thread has a place in the web. The right people *always* show up, and thanks to the interaction that evening, I'm now working on something that's been on my heart for a while – getting a Junior PRAISE program up and running for boys who are not yet old enough to join the full Saturday program.

———

Because if we can reach them early enough, the headlines are going to change on their own.

My buddy Derrick's son, Masiah, is one of Mosiah's best friends. Masiah and Mosiah are two peas in a pod. At 8 years old, they are inquisitive and intelligent and kind and so full of life.

Derrick shared with me recently a story that speaks to exactly *why* the headlines need to change, and what our role in the process can be.

One day, Masiah came home and asked his parents if he could change schools. He was attending a private Christian school with a great academic record, but one day Masiah told his dad, "I just don't know how much more of this I can take. They're asking me to do things that I just don't think I can do. They're asking me to be quiet ALL of the time, even at lunch. I need a different situation."

Derrick described his son as a *high energy, very vocal kid with a wild personality and some very advanced ideas of the world. He's very clear on who he is. IF he's sitting in a chair in class, then he's going to be beating on the desk. And he'll* probably have one foot on the chair, one up on the desk, and both of his shoelaces will be untied. This is just how he learns.

At the time that Masiah asked to find a new school, he was earning all As academically, but in the behavior department his marks were consistently low. The school had a very strict way of running things and even though there was a strong African American male presence among the teachers, Masiah seemed to be constantly at odds with the older white female teachers in the building.

Derrick told me that they had gone to visit a host of different schools, and Masiah had expressed clearly the one he wanted to attend. When asked why, he responded that they had recess there and he really needed the opportunity to move around. Masiah was required to pass an entrance exam, which he did without difficulty, and Derrick went to visit the school one last time to further explore the culture of the staff. He wanted to be sure that he felt the teachers and administrators were genuinely happy, that it seemed like they *wanted* to be there. And then he met with the guidance counselor. He shared with her the following: "I think you guys have something great here. I am trusting you with God's gift to me – my son. I love who he is, where he is, and where he's going. I love every aspect of his being and I'm trusting you with that. My son has a song in his head and I don't want anyone here to turn off that song or try to change it. You can ask him to turn it down sometimes, because I know he plays that song very loud, but you can't ask him to turn it off. You can ask him to teach you the words, you can ask him to help you understand the song and what it means to him, but you can't turn it off."

———

Several weeks ago I was consulting in a suburban school that had a teaching force that was about 95 percent white. I was there to lead a training on effectively engaging Black and Brown boys and their parents. The principal had warned me before my arrival that the last consultant they had brought in to address the topic of diversity had been a disaster. The consultant, who had been paid to work with the staff on how to better meet the diverse needs of its student population, had divided the audience and uncovered a lot of hostility and anger that she hadn't been prepared to help the staff navigate through.

I knew that my audience might initially be skeptical of hosting another outside consultant, especially since no matter what topic I'm hired to present on, I always manage to address issues of diversity and access and equity. So I took a deep breath and did what I knew I had been invited there to do. And afterwards, I took another deep breath and smiled. Mission accomplished.

After my training, one teacher approached me to say, "Look. I'm white but I've got two Black sons and that last consultant who came in here was the devil!" She went on to share that the most powerful part of my training that day had been when I brought up a panel of boys to speak. The panel was made up of a diverse group of boys – one city kid, one suburban kid, and two private school kids. I had advised the boys ahead of time that they needed to be raw and honest, but also humble. The teachers asked the boys some great questions and I had been so proud of the whole exchange.

It was like this training had solidified everything I believed about what we need to do to change the headlines. If we want to know what's going on with our boys of color, we need to be humble enough to go right to the source. We have to ask *them* about their own experiences instead of theorizing and pontificating about what we *think* they need. And we need to create safe and authentic spaces where honest, open dialogue can take place. If I had come into that training to create a hostile and divisive environment, if I had played the blame game, if I had flaunted myself as some sort of expert, then none of the meaningful work that was done that day could have been accomplished.

When this teacher validated me for having done something right that day, I have to admit that it felt good. But what felt infinitely better was what happened shortly thereafter.

One of the boys from the panel, Daniel, walked up to me. "Dr. Shields, let me ask you something," he smiled up at me. "How long have you been doing this? Because this was just amazing today! It's like I was listening to you talk before we went up there and I was just like, man, you were saying everything that I would say up there and it was just so amazing!"

I often say that even though research and theory are important, I don't care as much about something being research-based as I do about it being De'Quon-based. You see, when we show young men the possibilities of their lives, when we involve them in the conversation, when we validate their experiences, when we provide them with hope, then all of the negative headlines will just slowly begin to fade into the background of a new narrative.

So often we focus far too much energy on the negative headlines, what's *not* going right, on who is not showing up to answer our call. But we have to remember to honor those who are responding. Because no matter what anyone might say, we are really all in the business of saving lives. Together, we can and will change the headlines. The work isn't easy and it won't happen overnight, but I believe that it's possible.

# CHAPTER 19

# BUILDING BRIDGES, CROSSING BORDERS

*Damn right I like the life I live, 'cause I
went from negative to positive.*

- Biggie Smalls

Not too long ago my wife and I were watching an old episode of the TV show "Touched by an Angel." There was a scene in the episode where a character, Darnell, learned what his name meant. He learned that Darnell is actually the name of a weed that looks like wheat, and that if he understood the power of weeds then he'd understand that they can grow anywhere. Curious to glean a bit more about the roots of my middle name, I went online and did some research. I read that my name meant that I could adapt to any environment and be comfortable around people who didn't look or sound like me, that I could bob and weave through life with relative ease. Unlike flowers that need to be planted, the power of weeds is that they can grow almost anywhere.

And then my mind flashed back to just a few months before when I had sat in a geodesic dome in the middle of the southern California desert with a small group of people, talking about what we learn when we're around different individuals and about how so often we run from who we truly are because we don't take the time to really get to *know* all of the deep callings of our hearts. And then my mind bounced back to being a young TFA teacher, feeling like such an outsider sitting in a circle among a crowd of white people, and now there I was all these years later sitting in a similar circle in a different context and being the one leading the charge. But that time, in the middle of that magical desert, the conversations were going so much deeper. I was sitting there co-leading the charge with the sole mission of getting to the heart of the matter. And I felt at home and it felt amazing.

I sat there in the desert and once again thought, *How in the hell did I get HERE?!* And I realized that this part of my journey had really begun over a decade before, when one day I went to visit a friend who ran a non-profit book exchange called The Book Thing of Baltimore. I was perusing the shelves when I stumbled, literally, across a stack of new books – all hardcover – sitting on the floor next to one of the bookcases. I *love* hardcover books, so of course I picked one up and began to read it. The title of the book was "The Courage to Teach," and it was written by some white dude named Parker Palmer who I had never heard of. But once I started reading, I was hooked. It felt like everything that I read echoed what I believed about teaching and learning and my role in the process. I started to realize that there was someone out there not only doing what I was doing in education, but writing about it and placing it in some context.

This revelation of hearing someone put a name to an educational concept that I intuitively believed in had come about once before when in my early 20s I had had the opportunity to meet a man by the name of Dr. Rassias. Dr. Rassias was a seasoned professor out of Dartmouth who, at 70 years old, had had a whole lot more energy than I had even then as a new teacher. I had been invited to a workshop that Dr. Rassias was teaching on his patented approach to language immersion. I watched him share his world-famous method, which serves as the foundation for an entire language center at Dartmouth University that bears his name, and it was like he was talking about exactly what I had always been doing in my classroom but for which I had never had a formal context. When I talked in an earlier chapter about whole body teaching, well that's what I was seeing Dr. Rassias give a formal structure to.

As I'm writing this I'm remembering the scene in the film "Akeelah and the Bee" where Akeelah, the little girl, is tapping her leg, and using rhythm to spell. She's incorporating her whole body and I just love this visual. All subjects have a rhythm, but especially languages. Just like Derrick revealed about the song in his son's head, I think that all students have songs and rhythms that guide their learning. And if we're going to be Ubuntu teachers, we need to learn the rhythms of their songs instead of trying to change the music.

So I walked into this workshop led by Dr. Rassias and realized that there was a *name* to what I'd been doing my whole life. I had never seen anyone else teach language with rhythm like he was, and nobody had taught me to do it in my own classroom – it was just what I had done. The experience really opened my eyes and reminded me of the importance of being receptive to learning from people of all different backgrounds. If I had harbored negative thoughts about people who didn't look like me and closed myself off to learning from them, then I would have missed out on the entire Rassias method and the affirmation it gave me to my own teaching pedagogy. I was the only African American in the class and was by far the youngest teacher in the room. But I didn't care. I had allowed myself to be open and, in so doing, I had met someone who greatly influenced the way I teach because he had affirmed that what I had been doing instinctually made sense.

So I was in the Book Thing of Baltimore reading Palmer's book and I couldn't get enough. Since the books were free, I took every single copy they had in stock right on the spot and started handing them out to as many teachers as would take them. I realized that many of us taught theory and pedagogy, but we weren't necessarily teaching reality. And Palmer's book was *all* about reality. It was a wake up call. And I felt compelled to share.

One of his lines that most struck me was his statement that, "We blame teachers for being unable to cure social ills that no one knows how to treat; we insist that they instantly adopt whatever 'solution' has most recently been concocted by our national panacea machine; and in the process, we demoralize, even paralyze, the very teachers who could help us find the way."

As those of us who teach have learned, we as educators face chaotic situations on a daily basis in schools and often even in our personal lives. If we do not care deeply and are not equipped with effective strategies, a supportive network of administrators, parents, and community members, and the tools necessary to handle the chaotic situations that are bound to occur, then we most likely will fall into a vicious cycle of unrealized potential – that of our students, of ourselves, and of the opportunities that meaningful and effective education can afford to both student and teacher. Palmer's message was a strong one, and I couldn't help but share it with every teacher I knew.

About 10 years after I discovered Palmer's work, I was preparing for a workshop in Georgia and found myself thinking again about Palmer. I wanted to reference him in my upcoming training, so I Googled his name and learned that he ran an organization that hosted retreats. I knew instantly that those retreats were something I had to be a part of, because I really needed to know if I was on the right path with where I was going and what I was doing and the ways in which I had internalized the lessons I had learned from his book over the past decade.

I decided to attend a local retreat in Maryland first, and I knew when I walked in that I belonged there. Even though I didn't look like anyone else in the room and had never been to a retreat of that sort before. But I felt in that moment that I was being invited, not forced, to participate in something meaningful. Because of my deep respect for Palmer's work, I felt that the retreat was going to be a unique and important experience for me. And it was.

The highly personal style of the retreat really laid the foundation for my development of a more intimate relationship to my own calling. The resources were consistently rich and insightful and the readings and guided reflections extended an invitation to reflect on the themes in my life and work in a new way. The retreat leader mentioned that I might want to consider attending one of Palmer's larger retreats in Bainbridge, Washington. So I applied and was accepted. I had never been to Bainbridge, but I was excited about the ferry trip there – the thought of being surrounded by so much natural beauty just filled me with energy and hope. Once there, when I laid my eyes on a vegetarian restaurant I knew beyond a doubt that I was in the right place.

As with the Maryland retreat, everyone was so welcoming that weekend. There were about 30 of us in the retreat group and I was one of just a few African Americans. I remember joking with another brother, a Morehouse graduate, and telling him that I was growing used to being the only African American in spaces like that one and that because he was in the room we'd have to share the responsibility for the weekend.

But see, I was changing. I was starting to feel comfortable in all of these different settings because I was becoming more clearly myself. I was beginning to shed some of the baggage borne of environments with few people who looked like me. During my time with Teach for America, I had struggled with who I was going to be and what type of teacher I was going to become, and to be facing those doubts in an environment that at the time seemed ill-equipped to acknowledge or validate who I was and where I had come from was painful. I didn't like feeling that everything we were learning about teaching and education was being whitewashed when I knew the realities of the communities in which I wanted to go teach and work. And digging back even deeper to my time at De La Salle, when I had *really* been trying to figure out my place in the world, there had been a constant struggle between my need to grow and be validated and many of my teachers and white classmates who had continually reminded me – through both words and actions – that I didn't really belong in their world anyway.

But by the time I showed up in Washington for Palmer's retreat, I was different. And the context had shifted. I knew who I was and what my gifts were. I was coming into my own in terms of my spiritual development. And honestly, by then I could have cared less what the people around me looked like. I wanted to be open to listening deeply to their experiences. I also began to want these white people to hear what I had to say because I knew many of them really had hearts for working in impoverished communities with people of color. And because of the color of my skin, I might get a pass in some places where I knew they would have to prove themselves over and over again. So if I, in some small way, could help them understand my experiences – not as representative of everyone who looks like me, of course, but just as the stories of one man of color who has faced prejudice and pain and anger and self-doubt and has somehow come out on the other side ready to share rather than remain bitter, then in this way, in this context, I knew that I could be of service.

And I had begun to comprehend that the more willing I was to listen deeply to the experiences of others, regardless of their skin color or where they'd grown up, then the better equipped I would be to demonstrate through my actions that we *all* deserve to have our stories heard. That we all have pain points we need to process and work beyond. That we all have something of service to give.

I still hear often from people of color who say that they don't feel comfortable around people who don't look like them because of all the issues surrounding race and poverty and prejudice and pain. And I get it. If you've been reading this story from the very beginning, you should know now that I get it. But I also know that the more comfortable I've become with who I am and the more I've been able to speak with authenticity and honesty about my own experiences, the better I've been able to see that other people aren't the enemy.

The enemy, for me at least, has largely been inside of me all along. And once I was able to recognize that, I was able to start to do some of the deep work that has allowed me to enter into diverse settings with increasing ease. There was a time early on in my career when I was *really* concerned about white folks teaching kids of color. I just didn't think they could do it because I had had seen so few models of good, white teachers in my own education. But then when I *really* looked around, when I took note of who was flocking to the field of education and who wasn't, I realized that *my* perspective needed to shift. And I began to question why I *wouldn't* want to invest in those white teachers who were going to be working, whether I liked it or not in the beginning, with the Black and Brown boys who looked just like me. Why would I not want to be open to recognizing that the world of education is so much more complex than my own isolated experiences, and that unless we're willing to operate from love and embrace the people who are in the trenches day in and day out we're not going to make much progress at all?

The truth is, a lot of people of color – when the doors are closed – may say that those white folks don't know what the hell they're doing with our babies. And sometimes that might be true, but often times it isn't. The reality is that we have to find a way to believe in those we're working with, we have to find a way to respect people even if we don't fully understand them. And I can honestly say from my own experience that the more I love myself, the more I pour into myself, and the more I'm able to deconstruct my own belief systems and the pain of my own past, the easier it becomes to walk into any room with authenticity, to show up completely and unapologetically myself, and say, "Here I am, here you are. Together, we can do this thing."

Whether I'm speaking to an audience of 500 educators about how to meet the needs of our Black and Brown boys, or whether I'm co-leading a SPARK retreat with Marina before a handful of individuals, I'm the same me. Because no matter where I am these days, I'm interested in letting people know that the love-hate relationships many of us have with systems external to ourselves, be they with the educational system, the workplace, or society at large, are really just love-hate relationships with ourselves. My work has gone to the heart of the matter because no matter where I am now, my passion lies in pouring into *people*. Plain and simple. Not pouring into them to make them better teachers or better businesspeople or so that they can show gains in test scores or get some sought-after promotion, but just focusing on their humanity, as authentically and as often as I am able.

We can try to fight systems all day long, we can blame anyone and everyone for our pain, we can call out white supremacy for what it is. But I'm learning that at the end of the day, we have to be able to turn the focus inward. I know sometimes people feel threatened by the idea of looking at themselves rather than seeking solutions outwardly. But my own journey has taught me that the more I deal with my own stuff, the more equipped I am to continue to work out there in the world. In other ways, I think I'm a little *less* threatening in some settings now that my approach has changed. I think that so often I used to walk into a room thinking, *To hell with all these white folks!* And even though I didn't usually speak the words aloud, people felt the hostility in my energy, my spirit.

As I've continued to grow, I've found myself reading fewer books about teaching theory and methods and more books about the nature of individuals, about spirituality and the human experience, about what binds us, about where we can find common ground.

What happens so much in education and the larger society is that we put ourselves in boxes and, in so doing, we often limit our potential. My teaching didn't start to change and grow until I sought change and growth. The heart of who I am isn't much different, but my approach, my message, my audience and my classroom are.

When you're asking people to dig deep within themselves and to be introspective, to take a long hard look in the mirror, it can be quite a challenge. It's so much easier to turn the mirror outward and adopt a victim mentality of blaming others. It's so *hard* for us to welcome discomfort, but that's what we ask kids to do every single day. We ask of them what we are so often unable to do ourselves. We believe that we shouldn't have to participate in our own growth and learning, but the reality is that we *must*. Going deep is admittedly hard, because when we do take a good look inward, we often find that we have some work to do, that we have to let go of some of our limiting beliefs, and that we have to change. For me, part of being an Ubuntu teacher is being willing to go into uncomfortable spaces and be right in my heart.

Sometimes in workshops I do an activity called the Education Blame Game where I show a picture of a variety of different stakeholders in educational communities standing in a circle, pointing fingers at the people next to them. Then I ask participants where *they* see themselves in the picture. And what's so interesting, but not surprising, is that more often than not people don't place themselves anywhere in the circle. Even if they're teachers, they don't see themselves as the teacher in the picture. Because we never think we're a part of the problem. We're so quick to place blame elsewhere.

We're going to have to start to shift the focus in teacher education and continuing professional development away from external measures of success, or lack thereof, and toward matters of the heart. We're going to need to look closely at our own well-being in order to better equip us for the tasks at hand.

Our kids come to us from worlds that can seem so anti-everything. They're used to conflict. They're combative and defensive and we're going to have to be well enough ourselves to be able to handle the charge. When we hold ourselves accountable, we're then better equipped to hold our students accountable. When we hold fast to the Ubuntu principle that it's the people around us who will help us grow as we come into our own, we can see the truth that this principle has for both our teaching and learning.

Then, if we're bold enough we can start flipping the script a bit. One of the projects I've been working recently to develop, The Teacher Exchange, does just this. We have students *mentoring* new teachers on what it takes to make it in the classroom. The very first lesson the students taught was on teacher stress and techniques that teachers could use to better manage their stress. And, of course, it was amazing! We can no longer wait for someone external to ourselves to save us. We've got to step out and figure out what we need and then be bold enough to seek it.

We've got to walk into our purpose. Why are we waiting years and years to discover what it is we're meant to be doing? One of the questions we pose at our SPARK retreats is what do you do well that you would enjoy doing without pay. We challenge participants to think about *who* they are in relation to the work they do. Because we have to learn, somehow, to have the courageous conversations with ourselves first. And then we can work outward from there.

So often we're afraid of failing. We're so caught up in what people are going to think or say about us if we ask a question, or admit that we don't have it all together, or make a mistake. We don't talk enough about the success that comes *after* failure. I've failed so many times, but each time I've found a way to keep going.

And I have no choice but to keep going. Because I need my own children to know that it's possible. I need them to know that they have the potential to be greater than I am, to do bigger things. I need them to know that they can be happy and satisfied, that they deserve nothing less than to walk in their calling. And that they have a responsibility to give back always. That those of us who have been blessed with so much have a responsibility to give back and to never stop doing so.

Once you're comfortable in your own skin, it's easy to make your message consistent no matter the topic, audience or venue. For me, the challenge has been in figuring out how to carry the lessons that I've learned with me without holding on to all the baggage. The task has been to figure out how to be authentically myself as I continue to grow and evolve.

Because I'm still the same person who at 7 years old sat on my mother's bed in our home on Green Street. My mom came to her bedroom door and saw me sitting there with my hand on the television screen, which was playing a Save the Children-like campaign about childhood poverty in Africa and asking for money to help. She then watched me place a penny in an envelope and carefully address it to the address that flashed repeatedly across the TV screen in between images of emaciated children who lived halfway around the world. The voice on the TV said that you could send in a penny a day, and so my literal 7-year-old self sent that penny away to help children who I knew looked like me, who I knew were hungry, who I knew – even as a child– that I might be able to help in some small way.

# CONCLUSION

*Lord, make me an instrument of thy peace.*
*Where there is hatred, let me sow love;*
*Where there is injury, pardon;*
*Where there is doubt, faith;*
*Where there is despair, hope;*
*Where there is darkness, light;*
*Where there is sadness, joy.*

- From the Prayer of St. Francis

I'm climbing mountains. I'm journeying forward. I'm stumbling. But I'm not standing still. I'm still moving, I'm still growing. The trip, God willing, is far from over. But this part of my life that I've been able to share with you on these pages? This part of the journey is coming to a close as I write this, as I make the final decision that I'm ready to share. Let's just say that getting it down, choosing which stories to tell and which to leave out, sorting through the successes and the challenges, the joys and the love and the pain, all of it has been a tremendous experience of growth for me. I've kept a lot of this stuff very close to me for a long time, and it feels good to be releasing it out into the world.

One of the things I hope you will realize if I've done my job here is that this isn't just a book geared toward Black and Brown boys. As a man of color myself, the only experiences I can speak to with authenticity are my own. Growing up on the South Side of Chicago with a single mother, attending De La Salle and subsequently getting kicked out, not getting into Morehouse, getting into the Navy and then getting out as fast as was humanly possible, attending Grambling and founding UAAM, losing Andre, joining TFA, starting to teach, losing Curtis, chasing Curtis always, leaving the traditional classroom, doing community organizing work, founding and then leaving ULI, building PRAISE, starting the Cambio Group, expanding my work on a global scale, and then ultimately going through the rewarding and yet also difficult process of getting it all down in this book – this is what I know, this is what I have to offer.

Somewhere along the line I began to really own the idea that what you chase is chasing you. I began to really believe at a deep level that everything I had experienced in my life was somehow connected to a greater vision and purpose. I don't know where the journey is going to go from here, but wherever I'm headed, I'm hopeful and I'm ready.

I've got some big dreams still to fulfill. I want to expand the scope of my work in other countries. I'd love to replicate PRAISE in other universities outside of Johns Hopkins. I want to inspire more folks to share and tell their stories because I have seen how transformational it's been for me to be able to do this myself. And I want to talk with others about the stories I've imparted here. I want to have deep and meaningful conversations – with Black and Brown boys, with parents, with educators, with law enforcement, with the girls and women who love these boys and the men they will become. I want to continue the conversations with boys who feel hopeless, who come to school every day, put their heads down on their desks, and wonder what they're doing there, where they're going. I look forward to continuing to create avenues for individuals to do the deepest, most difficult work – the work of the heart and soul – through SPARK retreats, through projects like The Teacher Exchange, through continuing to speak and train and teach wherever and whenever I'm afforded the opportunity.

And I can't wait to sit down and go through this book with my own son and my daughters. I'm anticipating with great humility being able to place this book in my wife's hands, because even though she hasn't always understood my journey, she's somehow loved me through it all. And I can't wait to head home to Chicago and hand copies of this book to all of my boys in KAOS, to honor them for holding me up, for being some of the deepest roots of my life, for inspiring me to do this thing in the first place. And I'm looking forward to handing a copy to my mother and thanking her for everything.

---

I'm sitting here thinking about the future, but my mind also keeps turning back. So many moments from my life are flashing before my eyes. I think there are a couple of stories still left to tell, so here we go.

One time early on in my teaching career my friend Kim and I took at trip to Chicago to meet the educator, social justice advocate, and author Jonathan Kozol. Kim's father was the superintendent for Baltimore City and was working with Jesse Jackson on issues of educational equity at the time, so we were given the opportunity through him to attend this event with other educators. We were the youngest teachers in attendance and were so excited to be in the room.

Before the event, I took Kim to De La Salle to meet my former track coach who had since become the high school principal. We laughed as we reminisced that, as a student, I would lie to my mom and tell her I had football practice on Saturdays when really I was going to the school to serve Saturday detention.

By this time I had already written my children's book in which I had included a dedication to Señor Hogan. I walked through the school straight to Señor Hogan's classroom. I knocked. He came to the door. I gave him a copy of the book and then turned to his roomful of students and said, "Whatever this man has said to you or about you, you don't have to believe it." Señor Hogan laughed. I turned and walked away to the sound of student applause following me down the hall.

***

I was just beginning my teaching career at City. I hadn't lost Curtis yet. I was still in survival mode, trying to make my way, hoping to figure it all out.

One day at a gas station near where I was living, I hopped out of my black Jetta to the sound of two little voices calling out, "Hey Mister! We'll pump your gas for three dollars."

I considered their overture for a moment before deciding to engage the children in conversation before I'd give them permission to pump my gas. I asked their names and I remember Keina telling me both her and her brother's names before he could say a word. I asked them about school – what grades they were in and their favorite subjects – before paying them three dollars in exchange for pumping my gas. When they finished, I told them to be careful and drove off.

A couple of weeks later, I ran into Keina and her brother Artie again only two blocks from my house. Truth be told, I was happy to see that they were okay. I asked them if they would take me to their house to meet their mom and they did. She came to the door with huge sunglasses on, which led me to the conclusion that she was probably high. She invited me in and offered me a seat. The house was dark, but not dark enough for me to miss the roaches crawling everywhere. I didn't want to sit down, but I also didn't want to be rude to this woman who had welcomed me into her home. So even though everything inside me cringed at the thought, I sat. The two of us talked for awhile and she agreed to let me mentor her kids.

Weeks later, Keina and Artie came to my house. In my home, I had adopted the African custom of asking everyone to remove their shoes at the door so as not to track in dirt or negative energy with them. This was a new concept to the kids, but they did honor my request to take off their shoes.

Once her sneakers were off, Keina walked around my living room taking it all in. She perused the books on my bookshelves, gazed up at my high ceilings, ran her socks over my hardwood floors, and then looked up at me with her big, brown eyes and asked, "Why don't you have any roaches in your house?"

The moment the words left her mouth, I knew the importance of my answer. The kid from the South Side of Chicago almost blurted out that we didn't have roaches because only nasty people who don't clean their houses have roaches. But of course I couldn't say that. Because I knew from having been inside her home, having met her mom, and knowing a bit about where she came from, that in passing judgment about why my home didn't have roaches when I knew hers did I'd be passing judgment on who she was, whether or not I intended to.

She was a child and what I always try to remember is that children, for the most part, are not the directors of their destinies in the early years of their lives. Just because I didn't live in a house with roaches, just because it would have been easy for me to feel superior, to ride on the wave of all the hard work that I had done to get to a place where I had a career and a nice home, what did that matter to this child? This child who was probably already more than just a little aware of the differences between my home and hers. Why would I drive a larger wedge between us?

So I looked her in the eye and simply said, "I just don't have roaches." And I left it at that.

My answer seemed to satisfy her curiosity, because it wasn't a moment later that she looked at me with the same big eyes and asked, "Now can I act a fool in here?"

That moment, like many moments I've recounted in this book, was small but significant. Because often the ways in which we respond to the little things translate – whether we realize it or not – into the manner in which we design our lives. In that moment, I made a conscious choice to be kind over superior, to take into account the big picture and look beyond the immediate, and to recognize that the question was weighted, even though Keina was maybe too young at the time to realize it.

Looking back on it, it was a defining moment that helped shape not only the course of the time Keina and I spent together, but also the trajectory of my development as an Ubuntu teacher. Because I recognized the reciprocity of it all. The ways in which we're all connected. The reality that Keina and I were living just two short blocks away from each other and yet existing, in many ways, worlds apart.

Keina was 10 years old when we met and was 15 when she died in a car accident. Her time here was so short. A staccato beat in the full measure of life. But for a few short years, I would like to think that I helped to make a positive difference in her world. She and Artie were some of my first true students, even though we never spent a day together in the classroom. And as with all teacher-student relationships, I was able to teach and to learn, to give and receive, to make a difference when I could and where I could and how I could.

Just last year, Keina's brother Artie called me to let me know that their mom was in the hospital. She had had a stroke and he said that outside of their immediate family, I was the one he had thought he needed to call. Even though we'd been out of touch for years. Even though he was grown.

I went to the hospital and sat with Artie and his remaining siblings. They caught me up on their lives over the prior decade. Two of Artie's living siblings were working as exotic dancers, and he was just getting by. And yet there was something comforting to me, even in Artie's moment of pain, about the fact that he had thought to call me, that I had somehow impacted his life all those years ago in some way. That even if I couldn't save Keina, Artie was still there.

---

Just the other week, I was deep in conversation with the current co-director of PRAISE, Kennedy, an incredible father and leader of the young scholars in our program. We began to discuss the topics of fatherhood and writing. And Kennedy shared with me that he has had a long-time dream of writing a book with and about his father, where he could visit his dad and ask him all the questions he never had a chance to ask him as a child. But you see, Kennedy has only met his father once. Kennedy's dad has been incarcerated most of Kennedy's life. As Kennedy describes it, his dad has either been a career criminal or a career inmate his entire life. But now, even if Kennedy were to make the trip up to visit him, the interview isn't going to happen. His dad is dying. He's had a massive stroke. He can't talk and probably never will again. Kennedy feels that even on his father's journey toward death, he's found a way to disappoint his son – to not be there in the way Kennedy needed him to, to not be able to answer even a single question. Kennedy has always dreamt of writing this book, and he's processing the fact that he'll never get to tell it in the way that he had hoped to.

All I know is that boys like Mosiah and Kennedy's son and many of the sons of my brothers in KAOS won't ever feel the weight of what Kennedy has felt not knowing his dad, what so many of my boys in KAOS shouldered with their fathers absent, what I myself felt for so long.

The day my father died I was at an elementary school preparing to speak at a campus-wide assembly. I was behind the stage in the final minutes of preparation and could hear the noise of 500 anxious little people on the other side of the curtain, could feel their energy and excitement. And then my phone rang. And I picked it up and heard my brother's voice on the other end of the line, telling me that my father was dead. I felt nothing. And I sat there wondering how I *should* have felt – should I have been angry or sad or disappointed?

And I contemplated for a single minute, as I saw the principal walking toward me telling me it was time to speak, whether I should go out there and deliver my speech or tell her the news I had just received and go home. I told her that I was ready. I put down the phone, picked up the mic, and walked out onto the stage.

My message that day was about giving and receiving and loss. It wasn't the talk I had planned to give, but it was what poured out from my heart. These were little kids, so I asked them how it felt when they lost something. When I ask young children about loss, they usually talk about how sad they felt when they lost their favorite video game or a treasured book, or how they cried when their dog ran away.

Then we talked a bit about loss. I asked them how they felt when they found what they had lost and how they felt when they lost something they knew they'd never get back. And then we discussed techniques to process and control our emotions, and I walked them through a deep breathing exercise. I looked out into that auditorium at the fidgety little people deeply breathing in and out, many with their eyes half open even though I had asked them to shut them. And my mind was calm and I felt an overwhelming peace.

After I finished my talk, crowds of little kids ran up to the stage, wanting to take a picture together with me. And they were just climbing all over me. They had no idea what was going through my mind as I was trying to register that I was now living without a father. They just wanted me to be available. I felt like I still owed them that. So I smiled and took some photos, gave some hugs, and received some outpourings of love from those little people.

Once they had left and the auditorium had fallen silent, I packed up my stuff and started to reflect on the message I had just delivered. I allowed myself to begin to think about my father, and loss, and the complexity of it all. Sometimes when we lose something, our loss becomes someone else's gain. And in this sense there might be a silver lining. I would find out later that my dad entered the hospital on the day he died for a fairly routine procedure related to his heart. See, 20 years prior to my father's death, he had received a heart transplant. Another person had lost his life at 21 years old and my dad ended up being on the receiving end of that loss. At the time of his own death, my dad was the longest-term heart transplant survivor in the state of Illinois. I wondered on that day of my father's death what good he'd done with his second chance at life, how much he'd been able to love with that heart he'd been given, what I would do with all the unanswered questions I had for him. Sometimes loss contains within it a silver lining, and sometimes loss is just loss. Dark. Empty. Confusing. Void.

I got into the car, broke down in tears, and drove on home to my wife and children.

---

Just yesterday, Mosiah asked me one of his famous questions, a question that I realized in all my years of teaching, nobody has ever asked me. *Baba, why did you become a teacher?* I had to pause for a minute and ask myself the question again. Why did I become a teacher all those years ago? And why have I remained in education, no matter how winding the path has been? I had always wanted to become a lawyer. What had happened?

"Well, Mosi," I replied. "Here's the thing. As a lawyer, I might make $100,000 a year. But what if, as a teacher, I could help make 100,000 *lawyers* in my lifetime?"

That seemed to satisfy him in the moment, but I knew there was more to it than that. If I'm honest with myself, KAOS destroyed so much. We were smart and hopeful, but we were also at times destructive in our younger years. I caused my mother and a lot of other people who loved me a lot of grief. Chaos, by nature, tears down and decimates. At some point I realized, though, that I needed to start building and rebuilding. That the only way I could go back home would be if I had some healing and hope to offer.

I hear my son's voice so loud and clear as I consider how to wrap up this book. As I figure out what the last words will be. Where I want the stories to end. What I've been able to tell and what I've somehow left out. As I wonder whether I've shared enough, or too much. As I question what I missed along the way. And I see his eyes so filled with wonder, looking up at me and asking – *Baba, can you tell me a story about when you were a boy?* So here you go, Mosiah. I haven't gotten everything right so far in this thing called life, not by a long shot. But I hope I've shown you that there is a way.

# NOTES

For the most part, this book adheres to AP stylistic guidelines in-text, with some intentional stylistic deviations in places. The notes section that follows includes many APA-formatted citations for ease of reference.

## PREFACE

**p. xv – I came up with the idea for this book nearly a decade ago:** My wife, Meshelle, helped come up with the title for this book many years ago after having heard me talk so often about the adventures of my KAOS crew during our teenage years. When asked to write about her perspective on how these experiences have shaped me and, by extension, our life together, she had the following to share: *When you marry someone, you have no idea where the journey will take you. Your heart is open and your ideas are lofty, fluid, and laced in notions of living happily ever after. I can honestly say that the word chaos/KAOS never entered my mind until I met LaMarr and he shared on countless occasions the stories of his childhood. Initially, I thought the stories might have been too farfetched to have any merit. But from my first visit to Chicago in 1997 to my most recent holiday there in 2015, I have met, interfaced with, marveled at, laughed with, and come to know and love every member of KAOS and their families. What I have witnessed through the stories they've recounted and what I have seen firsthand is that a band of boys' experiences, challenges, triumphs, and travesties have afforded them life lessons that have impacted not only their lives as men, but also their roles as husbands, fathers, educators, entrepreneurs and fearless pioneers. LaMarr (Darnell) has been a sort of glue that has kept them connected and the fraternal love they share is palpable. Witnessing their brotherhood, and by extension LaMarr's growth, has been cinematic and uncanny at times, affording me a front row seat to the birthing of an Ubuntu teacher. I will be the first to say that there has never been a blueprint for us as a couple, family or sojourners outside of our insatiable love for God. We have had to blaze roads less traveled and at times it has felt like we were in the midst of chaos ourselves, but if there was anyone I'd ever want to forge the unknown with, it would be my husband. I am humbled by the leg of the journey we are now on and am willing to trust the process as we and our family endeavor to live a life of truth, unconditional love and service.*

## PROLOGUE

**p. xxi – *I'm just doing better than what everybody projected:*** Hip-Hop has and always will play a major role in my life. The decision to start each chapter with a quote from a Hip-Hop artist was a very intentional one, as I feel that the messages contained in these lyrics are as strong and relevant as Langston Hughes or Shakespeare. At my core, I'm a lover of language and my love for Hip-Hop is no exception.

Anderson, S. & Brown, C. & Wilson, D. & Haris III, J. &Lewis, T. (2010). My Last. [Recorded by Anderson, S. M. L.] On *Finally Famous*. New York: G.O.O.D. Music & Def Jam.

**p. xxiii – that he wanted to invite the families of the children:** For an article written on the White House visit, check out Brown, D. L. (2010, Feb 6). Students get face time with President Obama after White House tour. *The Washington* Post. Retrieved from: http://www.washingtonpost.com/wp-dyn/content/article/2010/02/05/ AR2010020503599.html?nav=E8

**p. xxix – At the time of my second visit to the White House, I had been reading the Wayne Dyer book "You'll See it When You Believe It:"** Dyer, W. (2001). *You'll See It When You Believe It*. New York: HarperCollins.

## INTRODUCTION

**p. xxxiii – Chaos (n): complete confusion and disorder; a state in which behavior and events are not controlled by anything:** Chaos [Def. 1]. (n.d.) *In Merriam Webster Online*, Retrieved October 11. 2015, from http://www.learnersdictionary.com/ definition/chaos

**p. xxxv – An Ubuntu teacher is an educator:** Although the definition of Ubuntu teaching as it's developed here is our own, it was inspired by a variety of readings and conversations through the years. There is a growing body of writing on the topic of Ubuntu teaching. You might want to check out Caracciolo and Mungai's (2009) book "In the Spirit of Ubuntu: Stories of Teaching and Research." There's also a Teacher Education organization out of Ireland, the Ubuntu Network, that incorporates Ubuntu philosophies into its teacher prep programs (www.ubuntu.ie). And author Ken Brack published an article in Huffington Post (December 6, 2013) entitled "Mandela's Legacy: Teaching Ubuntu" that looks at the foundations of Ubuntu as a teaching pedagogy. Helen Sayers' "Ubuntu! The Spirit of Humanity," a resource book for workshop facilitation and training, also provides some context for how Ubuntu concepts translate to education.

Caracciolo, D. & Mungai, A. M. (Eds.) (2009). *In the Spirit of Ubuntu: Stories of Teaching and Research*. Netherlands: Sense Publishers

Home | Ubuntu Network. (n.d.). Retrieved September 7, 2015, from http://www.ubuntu.ie

Brack, K. (2014) Mandela's Legacy: Teaching Ubuntu. *Huffington Post*. Retrieved from: http://www.huffingtonpost.com/ken-brack/mandelas-legacy-teaching-_b_4398312. html

Sayers, H. (2010). UBUNTU! *The Spirit of Humanity!*. No publisher.

**p. xxxvi – In my more recent work, I've labeled the way I work, live, and collaborate with others the Shields' Way:** A complete explanation of the Shields' Way is available at http://drlamarrdarnellshields.com/shieldsway

**p. xxxvii – Based on what some research claims:** Fingerman, K. L. & Lang, F. R. (2004). Growing Together: *Personal Relationships Across the Lifespan*. UK: Cambridge University Press.

**p. xxxviii – Will Smith said it well when he explained:** To view a segment of the interview with Tavis Smiley where Will Smith explores this concept, visit http://video.pbs.org/video/1869183414/

## CHAPTER 1: From Green Street to South Michigan Avenue

**p. 3 – *Peace before everything.*** God before anything: Def, M. (2009) Priority. On The Ecstatic [CD]. New York: Downtown Records.

**p. 3 – This morning, I look at the two books in front of me:** I'm an avid reader, but the Tao de Ching and A Course in Miracles are two texts that have had some of the most profound impacts on my daily life.

Mitchell, S. (Ed.). (1988). *Tao te ching: A new English version.* New York: Harper & Row.

Schucman, H. & Thetford, W. (1976). *A Course in Miracles.* New York: The Foundation for Inner Peace.

**p. 3 – The day's reading is on how God is in everything I see:** You can find a complete text of the lesson I'm referencing by visiting http://acim.org/Lessons/lesson.html?lesson=29

Schucman, H. (n.d.) *A COURSE IN MIRACLES.* Retrieved August 25, 2015, from http://acim.org/Lessons/lesson.html?lesson=29

**p. 3 – I pick a card from my affirmation deck:** The daily affirmation deck I use is the SPARK Affirmations, available at www.drlamarrdarnellshields.com or www.drmarinagillmore.com. To learn more about SPARK, visit www.spark-retreats.com. Gillmore, M., & Shields, L. (n.d.). Retrieved October 7, 2015, from http://www.spark-retreats.com

**p. 4 – Chicago's Black population soared during the Great Migration:** For more information on the Great Migration, see Bone, R. & Courage, R. A. (2011) *The Muse in Bronzeville: African American Creative Expression in Chicago, 1932-1950.* New Jersey: Rutgers University Press, p. 38 – 39.

**p. 4– fled deplorable living conditions:** Learn more on the Great Migration, Gallagher, C. A. & Lippard, C. D. (2014) *Race and Racism in the United States: An Encyclopedia of the American Mosaic Volume 1.*

**p. 5 – Chicago was already a hotbed for culture clashes:** To access more information on Chicago culture clashes, please see Thrasher, F. M. & Short, J. F. (1963) *The Gang: A Study of 1,313 Gangs in Chicago.*

**p. 5 – Many found employment:** Bone, R. & Courage, R. A. (2011) *The Muse in Bronzeville: African American Creative Expression in Chicago, 1932-1950.* New Jersey: Rutgers University Press, p. 38.

**p. 5 – In the South Side, the Bronzeville neighborhood:** For more information on Chicago urban history see Gates, H. L. (2013) *Life Upon These Shores: Looking at African American History.* New York: Alfred A. Knopf.

**p. 5 – Post-World War II saw an expansion:** Bennet. L. & Smith, J. L. & Wright, P. A. (2015) *Where are Poor People to Live?: Transforming Public Housing Communities*, New York: Routledge, p. 187.

**p. 5 – In 1955, Cook County Chairman Dan Ryan wrote a bond issue:** Smith & Wright, 2015, p. 187.

**p. 5 – The Eisenhower Expressway, originally named the Congress Expressway:** For more information on the Eisenhower Expressway, check out Smith & Wright, 2015, p. 187-188.

**p. 7 – When De La Salle Institute was founded in 1889:** De La Salle Institute. (n.d.). History. Retrieved from: http://www.dls.org/apps/pages/index.jsp?uREC_ID=212701&type=d

**p. 10 – ID wallets with the phone books in them:** A common term to Chicagoans familiar with riding the L, these were small wallets with address books inside that would be sold on the train.

**p. 11 – Harlem Renaissance poet Langston Hughes recounts:** Hughes, L. & De Santis, C. C. (1995). *Langston Hughes and the Chicago Defender: Essays on Race, Politics, and Culture 1942-62.* Illinois: University of Illinois Press.

**p. 12 – The senior Daley was known for various acts:** To learn more on Mayor Daley, Wilgoren, J. (2006, 1, 6) *Corruption Scandal Loosening Mayor Daley's Grip on Chicago.* New York Times. Retrieved from: http://www.nytimes.com/2006/01/06/national/06chicago.html?pagewanted=all&_r=1&

**p. 12 – In fact, in 1966 when Martin Luther King, Jr.:** Learn more from Chandler, C. (2002, 4, 4). *Shoot to Kill... Shoot to Maim.* Reader. Retrieved from: http://www.chicagoreader.com/chicago/shoot-to-kill---shoot-to-maim/Content?oid=908163

**p. 12 – His Gestapo-like tactics:** Mailer, N. (1996) *Brief History of Chicago's 1968 Democratic Convention.* CNN Time. Retrieved from http://edition.cnn.com/ALLPOLITICS/1996/conventions/chicago/facts/chicago68/index.shtml

**p. 14 – A recent study by a University of Buffalo professor:** You can find a discussion of this research and other related studies in the following Huffington Post article: Cadet, D. (2013). Black Boys Considered 'Cool' and 'Tough' While Black Girls Stereotyped as 'Ghetto' and 'Loud' in suburban schools. *Huffington Post.* Retrieved from: http://www.huffingtonpost.com/2013/10/22/black-boys-in-school-black-girls_n_4151328.html

**p. 15 – After giving each other dap:** Giving dap refers to giving each other handshakes.

**p. 15 – As with many lunchrooms in schools across America:** Tatum, B. D. (Ph. D.) (1997). *"Why Are All the Black Kids Sitting Together in the Cafeteria?".* New York: Basic Books.

## CHAPTER 2: KAOS

**p. 21 – *I'm so Chi I'm bashful:*** West, K. (2004). Get Em High. On *The College Dropout* [CD]. New York, United States: Roc-A-Fella Records.

**p. 22 – St. Sabina school, an institution made famous by Father Michael Pfleger, a progressive white priest known for his leadership in advancing causes of racial, social, and economic justice:** Find more information on Michael Pfleger at Saint Sabina. (n.d.). Senior Pastor Pfleger's Biography. Retrieved from: http://saintsabina. org/about-us/our-pastors/senior-pastor-rev-michael-pfleger/rev-pfleger-s-biography.html

**p. 27 – Shaun Harper talks about:** A complete text of Shaun Harper's report on Black male student success in higher education can be found at https://www.gse.upenn.edu/ equity/sites/gse.upenn.edu.equity/files/publications/bmss.pdf. Harper, S. R. (2012). Black male student success in higher education: A report from the National Black Male College Achievement Study. Philadelphia: University of Pennsylvania, Center for the Study of Race and Equity in Education.

**p. 28 – It's an idea common in the catalogue of films – "Dangerous Minds," "Freedom Writers," "The Blind Side," "Fresh," and "Radio," just to name a few:**

Simpson, D. & Bruckheimer, J. (Producers), Smith, J. N. (Director). (1999). *Dangerous Minds* [Motion Picture]. USA & Canada: Hollywood Pictures Home Entertainment.

DeVito, D. & Shamberg, M. & Sher, S. (Producers), & LaGravenese, R. (Director). (2007). *Freedom Writers* [Motion Picture].United States of America: Paramount Pictures.

Johnson, B. & Kosove, A. (Producers), &Hancock, J. L. (Director). (2009). *The Blind Side* [Motion Picture]. United States of America: Alcon Entertainment

Bender, L. & Ostrow, R. (Producers), Yakin, B. (Director). (1994). *Fresh* [Motion Picture]. United States of America: Miramax Films

Gains, H. & Robbins, B. (Producers), Tollin, M. (Director & Producer). (2003). *Radio* [Motion Picture]. United States of America: Columbia Pictures.

**p. 28 – The documentary "Prep School Negro":** Lee, A. R. (Producer & Director). (2012). *Prep School Negro* [Motion Picture]. USA: Loki Films.

**p. 28 – In a panel discussion held after a screening of the aforementioned documentary:** Hear more from the panel discussion at Williams College (2012, March 20) in association with a film screening of *Prep School Negro* by watching the YouTube clip at https://www.youtube.com/watch?v=ut5t_roXjlQ

**p. 29 – In "This We Believe in Action":** Burkhardt, R. M., & Kane, J. T. (2005). An advocate for every student. In T. O. Erb (Ed.). This we believe in action (pp. 63–75). Westerville, OH: National Middle School Association.

**p. 30 – In her TED Talk:** Rita Pierson's Ted Talk, *Every Kid Needs a Champion*, can be found at https://youtu.be/SFnMTHhKdkw.

**p. 31 – The quote "I am not what I think I am…":** This quote has been attributed to a variety of different sources, including Robert H. Schuller, Max Webber, and Johann Wolfgang von Goethe.

**p. 35 – Kanye West's mother:** Welty, M. (2015). Kanye's Mom Wouldn't Let Him Ride the L Train Because People Were Getting Killed Over Sneakers. *Complex*. Retrieved from: http://www.complex.com/sneakers/2015/02/kanye-west-couldnt-ride-the-l-train

**p. 41 – We watched "Mississippi Burning":** Colesberry, R. F. & Zollo, F. (Producers), Parker, A. (Director). (1988). *Mississippi Burning* [Motion Picture]. US: Orion Pictures.

**p. 41 – They represented the HBCUs – the historically Black colleges and universities built by African Americans for people of color to receive a quality education:** U.S. Department of Education-Office for Civil Rights. (1991). *Historically Black Colleges and Universities and Higher Education Desegregation*. Retrieved from: http://www2.ed.gov/about/offices/list/ocr/docs/hq9511.html

**p. 41 – We'd seen Spike Lee's "School Daze":** Lee, S. (Producer & Director). (1988). *School Daze* [Motion Picture]. United States of America: Columbia Pictures.

**p. 41 – I remember Steve talking about Freaknik:** Burns, R. Haines, E. (2015, March 18). Freaknik: The rise and fall of Atlanta's most infamous street party. *Atlantic Magazine*. Retrieved from: http://www.atlantamagazine.com/90s/freaknik-the-rise-and-fall-of-atlantas-most-infamous-street-party/

## CHAPTER 3: Where Do We Go From Here?

**p. 43 – *And just when it seemed that the game is hopeless we arranged some things for a dose of dopeness:*** Mescudi, S. & Omishore, O. (2012) Dose of Dopeness. On *WZRD* [CD]. New York: Republic Records.

**p. 44 – The 783-acre cemetery opened in 1853:** ABOUT US. (n.d.). Retrieved October 8, 2015, from http://historicoakwoodcemetery.org/about-us.asp

**p. 44 – My mother's fiancé is here:** The reason that we don't refer to Curtis' mother's fiancé by name in the book is that at the time of writing, I couldn't remember his name or find anyone who could.

**p. 45 – In that driveway sat Curtis' mother's car, which we recognized immediately:** I can provide no explanation for why Curtis' mom's car was in his dad's driveway that day, why the police didn't confiscate it at the scene of the crime, or how it got from Curt's mom's house to his father's house. All I can recall is what Curt told me about where he found it and my memory of seeing it in his dad's driveway that day.

**p. 48 – In "I Don't Want to Talk about It":** Real, T. (1998). *I Don't Want to Talk About It: Overcoming the Secret Legacy of Male Depression*. New York: Scribner

**p. 48 – If we want boys to talk, it might be up to us as adults:** As adults, I think we should caution ourselves from saying to a young person, *I understand how you feel*, because we really don't, even if we experienced something similar. We need to provide them with tools and strategies to process their anger and grief. For example, helping young people to find outlets outside of destructive avenues can be really helpful – whether it be listening to music, writing, and/or finding allies who can then support them in their process of healing. We have to help our youth find a way not to retell and relive the painful stories in their minds over and over again.

Christenbury, K. R. (2015, March 25). I Will Follow You: The Combined Use of Songwriting and Art to Promote Healing in a Child Who Has Been Traumatized. *Oxford Journals*. Retrieved from: http://mtp.oxfordjournals.org/content/early/2015/03/24/mtp.miv005.abstract

**p. 48 – Alexithymia is the formal term given to this phenomenon:** Find more information on young boys in Erwin, C. (2010). *The Everything Parent's Guide to Raising Boys: A complete handbook to develop confidence, promote self-esteem, and improve communication.*
MA: Adams Media.

**p. 48 – That's why it's important to get boys to journal:** To learn more about the Rose and Thorn game and other resources to engage young people in conversation, visit http://thefamilydinnerproject.org/fun/rose-and-thorn/

**p. 49 – like, for example, by playing the dozens:** As defined at www.urbandictionary.com, playing the dozens is an "African-American custom in which two competitors – usually males – go head to head in a competition of comedic trash talk. They take turns 'cracking on,' or insulting, one another, their adversary's mother or other family member until one of them has no comeback." Dozens. (n.d.). Retrieved October 8, 2015, from http://www.urbandictionary.com/define.php?term=dozens

**p. 49 – there are other techniques we can use to help them feel more comfortable opening up:** Jeffs, T. & Smith, M. K. (2014). Engaging in Conversation. *The Informal Education.* Retrieved from: http://www.infed.org/foundations/engage.htm

**p. 49 – At a very young age, many girls play with dolls:** *Children Understanding the World Through Play* by Mc-Graw Hill. PDF available at: http://www.educationinnovations.org/research-and-evidence/children-understanding-world-through-play

**p. 50 – If you're reading this as a parent of a son, the best advice I can give:** Erwin, C. L. (2006). *The Everything Parent's Guide To Raising Boys.* MA: F+W Publications Company.

**p. 50 – Erwin also notes that allowing young people:** Erwin (2006).

**p. 50 – And I think we also have to remember:** Larson, J. (2008, Jan). Angry and Aggressive Students. *NASP Online.* Retrieved from: http://www.nasponline.org/resources/principals/Angry%20and%20Aggressive%20Students-NASSP%20Jan%2008.pdf

**p. 51 – When young people face incredibly stressful events:** Robinson, L. & Segal Ph.D., J. & Smith M.A., M. (2015). Emotional and Psychological Trauma: Symptoms, Treatment, and Recovery. *Help Guide.* Retrieved from: http://www.helpguide.org/articles/ptsd-trauma/emotional-and-psychological-trauma.htm

**p. 52 – Exposure to trauma can be further complicated:** Council on Social Work Education (2012). Advanced Social Work Practice in Trauma. *Council on Social Work Education.* Retrieved from: http://www.cswe.org/File.aspx?id=63842

**p. 52 – There's even a growing body of research that links:** A recent NPR article highlighted a recent study published in the Journal of the American College of Cardiology that links emotional distress and risk of ailments such as heart disease and metabolic disorders. Aubrey, A. (2015). Childhood Stress May Prime Pump For Chronic Disease Later. *NPR*. Retrieved from: http://www.npr.org/sections/health-shots/2015/09/29/444451363/childhood-stress-may-prime-pump-for-chronic-disease-later

**p. 52 – There are a lot of theories about the effects of violence on our urban youth:** For a couple of theories, check out the following resources.

Tolan, Patrick H.; Gorman-Smith, Deborah; Henry, David B.

Developmental Psychology, Vol 39(2), Mar 2003, 274-291. http://dx.doi.org/10.1037/0012-1649.39.2.274

Schwab-Stone, M., Chen, C., Greenberger, E., Silver, D., Lichtman, J., & Voyce, C. (1999). No safe haven II: The effects of violence exposure on urban youth. *Journal of the American Academy of Child & Adolescent Psychiatry*, 38(4), 359-367.

## CHAPTER 4: It Takes a Village

**p. 55 – *No matter what the name, We're all the same pieces, In one big chess game:*** Ridenhour, Shocklee, Sadler, Rogers. (1988). Rebel Without a Cause [Recorded by Ridenhour, C. D; Drayton, W.; Aswod, L.; Wynn, K.; Griffin, R.]. On *It Takes a Nation of Millions to Hold Us Back* [Vinyl]. UK: Def Jam Recordings.

**p. 55 – In Black Chicago the Disciples gang, also known as the Folks:** For more information on the history of the Folks gang, please see Florida Department of Corrections, Julie L. Jones, Secretary. (n.d.). October 11, 2015, from http://www.dc.state.fl.us/pub/gangs/chicago3.html

**p. 60 – Leo was founded in 1926 by the Congregation of Christian Brothers:** Get more information on Leo at Our Story | Leo High School. (n.d.). Retrieved September 11, 2015, from http://leohighschool.org/our-story/

**p. 63 – A CNN investigation uncovered many public universities:** Get more information on college athlete reading levels at Ganim, S. (2014, Jan 8). Some college athletes play like adults, read like 5th-graders. CNN. Retrieved from: http://www.cnn.com/2014/01/07/us/ncaa-athletes-reading-scores/

**p. 64 – In April of 2014:** Learn more about college athletes' reading levels at Cooper, E. (2014, June 4). The Real Madness: College Athletes Who Can't Read. *The Huffington Post*. Retrieved from: http://www.huffingtonpost.com/eric-cooper/the-real-madness-college_b_5090744.html

## CHAPTER 5: In the Navy Now

**p. 67 – *Wisdom is better than silver and gold. I was hopeless, now I'm on hope road:*** Hill, L. (1998). Lost Ones. On *The Miseducation of Lauryn Hill*. Philadelphia: Ruffhouse & New York: Columbia.

**p. 69 – And the soundtrack to these goodbyes:** Harris III, J. & Lewis, T. (1988). Boys to Men [Recorded by Bell, R.; Bivins, M.; Brown, B.; DeVoe, R.; Gill, J.; Tresvant, R.] On *Heart Break* [Vinyl]. US: MCA Records.

**p. 69 – I took the ASVAB, a test used to predict:** Official Site of the ASVAB Testing Program. (n.d.). Retrieved October 10, 2015, from http://official-asvab.com

**p. 72 – In the book, Malcolm X recounts telling his teacher:** X. M., & Haley, A. (1965). *The Autobiography of Malcolm X.* New York: Grove Press.

**p. 72 – While in Mecca, Malcolm X was exposed:** Malcom X. (2015). In *Wikipedia, the free Encyclopedia.* Retrieved from: https://en.wikipedia.org/wiki/Malcolm_X

**p. 73 – Looking back on it now, the song "All My Life":** Hailey, J. & Bennet, R. (1998). All of my Life. *Love Always.* United States: MCA.

## CHAPTER 6: Grambling: Where Everybody is Somebody

**p. 75 – *They're gonna try to tell you no, shatter all your dreams:*** McCormick, M. J. (2009). Live Free. On *The High Life* [Digital Download]. No Label.

**p. 75 – Eighty-five years before I arrived at Grambling:** Grambling State University - About Us. (n.d.). Retrieved September 13, 2015.
Retrieved from: http://www.gram.edu/aboutus/history

**p. 85 – My message that day was "What Makes You So Strong:"** Learn more on these sermons at Wright, J. & Ross, J. (1993). *What Makes You So Strong? Sermons of Joy and Strength from Jeremiah A. Wright, Jr.* PA: Judson Press.

**p. 85 – a poem by Sterling Brown called "Strong Men Keep A' Coming":** To find the full poem, see Brown, S. (2007). Strong Men. *National Humanities Center,* Vol. III. Retrieved from: http://nationalhumanitiescenter.org/pds/maai3/protest/text11/brownstrongmen.pdf

**p. 86 – And then there was the Taste of Chicago:** For more information on the famous Chicago food festival, visit the official website at http://www.cityofchicago.org/city/en/depts/dca/supp_info/taste_of_chicago.html

**p. 87 – At Grambling, there was always something popping off in the yard:** The yard is the quad or general outdoor gathering place on a college campus, particularly a HBCU. The yard. (n.d). Retrieved October 1, 2015, from http://www.urbandictionary.com/define.php?term=the+yard

## CHAPTER 7: Buen Viaje

**p. 89 – They got money for war but can't feed the poor:** Shakur, T. (1993). Keep Ya Head Up. On Strictly 4 My N.I.G.G.A.Z... Santa Monica, CA: Interscope Records.

**p. 95 – Often referred to as colorism:** For an article that discusses some of the research on the impacts of colorism, check out: Niddle, n. K. (n.d).What is Colorism:The impact of Skin Color Discrimination in the U.S. and beyond. *About News.* Retrieved from: http://racerelations.about.com/od/understandingrac1/a/What-Is-Colorism.htm

**p. 97 – He informed me that there was a warrant out for my arrest:** David Miller, former ULI co-director, created a poster entitled "10 Rules of Survival When Stopped by the Police." You can learn more about the foundations of this work and purchase copies of the poster at http://daretobeking.net

## CHAPTER 8: The Making of a Leader

**p. 99 – Remind yourself, Nobody's built like you. You design yourself:** Carter, S. C. (2002). *A Dream. On The Blueprint 2: The Gift & The Curse.* USA: Roc-A-Fella Records

**p. 99 – To be perfectly honest, I had an issue:** Woodson, C. G. & James, G. G. M. (2014). *Stolen Legacy: Also Includes The Mis-Education of the Negro and The Willie Lynch letter.* Bensenville, IL: Lushena Books & Sertima, I.V. (1973). *They Came Before Columbus: The African Presence in Ancient America.* Random House, NY.

**p. 102 – *One of my favorite movies* "A Bronx Tale":** Kilik, J. & Rosenthal, J. (Producers), De Niro, R. (Director & Producer). (1993). *A Bronx Tale* [Motion Picture]. USA: Savoy Pictures.

**p. 103 – to become a part of the Longevity Project:** For more information on this project, visit http://www.howardsfriedman.com/longevityproject. Book available at: Friedman, H. S. & Martin, L. R. (2011). *The Longevity Project: Surprising Discoveries for Health and Long Life from the Landmark Eight-Decade Study.* New York: Penguin Group.

## CHAPTER 9: Why I Don't Teach for America

**p. 109 – *The mind is a terrible thing to waste. I show love cause it's a terrible thing to hate:*** Martin, C. E. & Elam, K. E. (2003). Peace of Mine. On *The Ownerz* [Vinyl & CD]. Hollywood: Virgin Records.

**p. 109 – Why I Don't Teach for America:** The title for this chapter came from an article written by Sandra L. Korn in the Harvard Crimson. Korrn, S. Y.L. (2013, Oct 23). Don't Teach for America. *The Harvard Crimson.* Retrieved from:http://www.thecrimson.com/column/the-red-line/article/2013/10/23/dont-teach-for-america/

**p. 110 – His name was Thomas "TNT" Todd:** Thomas N. Todd | The History Makers. (n.d.). Retrieved October 4, 2015. Retrieved from: http://www.thehistorymakers.com/biography/thomas-n-todd-39

**p. 110 – all-time favorite Public Enemy song:** Song available from Boxley, K. & Boxley, H. & Ridenhour, C. & Sadler, E. (1989). Fight the Power. *Fear of a Black Planet.* United States: Motown.

**p. 110 – At the beginning of the song:** Fight the Power. (2015). *Wikipedia, the free encyclopedia.* Retrieved from: https://en.wikipedia.org/wiki/Fight_the_Power Todd's introduction to the song is actually a reference to Vietnam deserters. His words are a parody to a slogan for a cigarette company from the 1960s that claimed their smokers would "rather fight than switch" to another brand. Genius. (n.d.) Fight the Power. Retrieved from: http://genius.com/1858100

**p. 113 – Before you start to think I'm crazy:** Learn more about the Central Park Five at Central Park Five - NY Daily News. (n.d.). Retrieved September 4, 2015, from http://www.nydailynews.com/services/central-park-five. Documentary: Burns, K; Burns, S.; McMahon, D. (Directors & Producers). (2012). *The Central Park Five* [Motion Picture]. USA: Florentine Films.

**p. 116 – This is where Parker Palmer's work of touchstones has become so important**: Find more information at Circle of Trust Touchstones • Center for Courage & Renewal. (n.d.). Retrieved October 4, 2015, from http://www.couragerenewal.org/touchstones/

**p. 116 – My life and work also often reference the second of Miguel Ruiz's four agreements:** Ruiz, D. M. (1997). The Four Agreements:
*A Practical Guide to Personal Freedom*. California: Amber-Allen
Publishing, Inc.

**p. 116 – But whatever it is, we have to get to a place where we can begin to engage in some more honest dialogue:** NPR journalist Michele Norris' Race Card Project was founded in 2010 as a way to encourage open and honest dialogues about race. You can learn more about Michele and the Race Card Project at http://theracecardproject.com/michele-norris

**p. 119 – The 3rd Ward:** Stanton, R. (2013, May 1). Two Houston Neighborhoods called most dangerous in U.S. *Chron.* Retrieved from: http://www.chron.com/business/real-estate/article/Two-Houston-neighborhoods-called-most-dangerous-4476367.php

**p. 120 – Part of the answer to that question:** For more information on efforts to recruit African American males into the teaching profession, check out the Call Me Mister program's work at Clemson's Eugene T. Moore School of Education by visiting their website at: http://www.clemson.edu/hehd/departments/education/centers/callmemister/

**p. 122 – It's worth noting that it wasn't just me and my fellow minority teachers:** Get more information on Teach for America experiences at Blanchard, O. (2013, Sept 23). I Quit Teach For America. *The Atlantic.* Retrieved from: http://www.theatlantic.com/education/archive/2013/09/i-quit-teach-for-america/279724/

**p. 122 – In Kopp's book, she even mentions us:** Kopp, W. (2001). *One Day, All Children...: The Unlikely Triumph of Teach for America and What I Learned Along the Way.* New York: Public Affairs.

**p. 127 – Dr. Monique Henderson's recent article:** A full version of this article, which also ran in the Clarion Ledger, can be found at Harrison-Henderson, M. (2015, Sept 27). In Mississippi, best teachers don't go where they are needed most. *Hechinger Report.* Retrieved from: http://hechingerreport.org/in-mississippi-best-teachers-dont-go-where-they-are-needed-most/

## CHAPTER 10: The Castle on the Hill

**p. 129 – *Teach the youth and speak the truth. Show 'em what peace can do when they'll reach for you:*** Rakim. (1999). Waiting for the World to End. On *The Master.* New York: Universal Records.

**p. 129 – City is the type of high school:** Find more information about City College at Baltimore City College. (n.d.). Retrieved December 1, 2014 from http://www. baltimorecitycollege.us

## CHAPTER 11: Broader Horizons

**p. 139 – *Life is your professor. You know that Bitch is gon' test ya:*** Cole, J. (2010). Villematic. On *Friday Night Lights*. New York: Roc Nation & Sony

**p. 148 – We partnered with Taharka Brothers:** For more information on Taharka Brothers' story, you can visit them at http://www.taharkabrothers.com/story.html.

**p. 148 – The president of Haiti:** For more information on the President's speech and our partnership with Taharka Brothers on that trip, check out http://www. taharkabrothers.com/blog/president-martelly-of-haiti-speaks-of-the-taharka-bros-its-work-in-haiti-as-part-of-a-direct-trade-chocolate-inititaive-part-of-the-big-payback.

## CHAPTER 12: Chasing Curtis

**p. 151 – *We get high on all types of drugs, when all you really need is love:*** Kweli, T. & Simone, N. & West, K. (2003) Get By [Recorded by Kweli, T.]. On *Quality* [CD]. New York: Rawkus.

## CHAPTER 13: On Leaving

**p. 163 – *Never looking back or too far in front of me. The present is a gift, and I just wanna BE:*** Dilla, J. West, K. (2005) Be [Recorded by Lynn Jr., L. R.]. On *Be* [CD]. USA: GOOD Music.

**p. 164 – I had been nominated as new teacher of the year and had been honored as a Golden Apple Award recipient:** For more information on this award, please visit http://www.goldenapple.org/golden-apple-awards

**p. 166 – This idea of hybrid teaching:** The Center for Teacher Quality is a national nonprofit founded in 1999. Its vision is to create a "high-quality education system for all students, driven by the bold ideas and expert practices of teachers" and its mission is to "connect, ready, and mobilize teacher leaders to transform our schools. Get more information on teacher quality at CTQ. (n.d.). Retrieved October 4, 2015, from http://www.teachingquality.org

**p. 168 – America's Promise Alliance, which was founded in 1997:** For more information on America's Promise, please visit http://www.americaspromise.org

**p. 170 – a neighborhood chronicled:** To access more information on this intersection, please see Simon, D. & Burns, E. (1997). *The Corner: A Year in the Life of an Inner-City Neighborhood*. New York: Broadway Books.

**p. 245 – According to ASHOKA, an organization that supports social entrepreneurship:** A complete discussion of social entrepreneurship and ASHOKA's work can be found at www.ashoka.org.

**p. 172 – By far, the celebrity who had the greatest impact on me was Bill Duke:** You can find more information on Bill Duke's work at http://www.imdb.com/name/nm0004886/

**p. 173 – Our first big break came:** Read more on the subject at N.A. (2002). Baltimore Money Manager Donates $5 Million to Help City's Poorest Students. *Jet, 101, 12.*

**p. 173 – a Senior Manager for the Professional Exchanges Program:** More information can be found on the Professional Exchanges Program at https://www.wtci.org/professional-exchanges-program/

## CHAPTER 14: It's Time for Some Praise

**p. 179 – Don't be a hard rock when you are really a gem:** Hill, L. (1998). Doo Wop (That Thing). On *The Miseducation of Lauryn Hill.* Philadelphia: Ruffhouse & New York: Columbia.

## CHAPTER 15: Opening the Gates

**p. 185 – *I'm living out my dreams. Don't dare hit that alarm clock:*** Anderson, S. M. (2010). What U Doin (Bullshittin'). *Single.* New York: GOOD Music.

## CHAPTER 16: The Missing Peace

**p. 191 – *Don't wait for the world to recognize your greatness. Live it and let the world catch up:*** Wallace, C. & Phillips, J. & Jordan, S. & Smith, T. & Conti, B. & Combs, C. (1998). Victory. On *No Way Out* [CD]. New York: Bad Boy Records & Arista.

**p. 193 – The poem by Brian Vallie, "Indian Holocaust: A Poem for Columbus Day":** Vallie, B. (2014, Oct 14). 'Indian Holocaust': A Poem for Columbus Day. *Indian Country Today Media Network.* Retrieved from: http://indiancountrytodaymedianetwork.com/2014/10/13/indian-holocaust-poem-columbus-day-157325

**p. 195 – I thought about one of my favorite films, "Smoke Signals":** Estes, L. & Rosenfelt, S. M. (Producers), Eyre, C. (Director). (1998). Smoke Signals [Motion Picture]. USA: ShadowCatcher Entertainment.

**p. 196 – Drawing on the Langston Hughes poem of the same name:** Genius. (n.d.). Harlem ("What happens to a dream deferred?"). Retrieved from: http://genius.com/Langston-hughes-harlem-what-happens-to-a-dream-deferred-annotated

**p. 197 – There's a cultural dynamic that many Native American and Latino communities share:** For a more comprehensive discussion on the topic, check out this film: Brown, E. & Cardoso, P. (2002). Real Women Have Curves. Available from LaVoo Productions, 691 Tenth Ave Apt #18, New York, NY.

## CHAPTER 17: The Journey Never Ends

**p. 203 – *The purpose of life is a life with a purpose. So I'd rather die for a cause than live a life that is worthless:*** Coronel, F. A. (2011). The Martyr. On *The Martyr* [CD, Digital Download]. New York: Viper Records.

## CHAPTER 18: Changing the Headlines

**p. 211 – *I know I can be what I wanna be. If work hard at it, I'll be where I wanna be:*** Nas (2003). *I Can*. On God's Son [CD]. NY: Ill Will Records.

**p. 211 – So many young men of color make the front pages of the newspapers for the wrong reasons:** For a more comprehensive conversation about media representations and their impact on Black boys, check out the comprehensive literature report on the topic published in 2011 by the Opportunity Agenda. A complete copy of the report can be found at http://www.racialequitytools.org/resourcefiles/Media-Impact-onLives-of-Black-Men-and-Boys-OppAgenda.pdf

**p. 211 – *Menace to Society:*** From a Pittsburgh Tribune-Review article. June 10, 2010, p. A1. A report from the Heinz Endowments' African American Men and Boys Task Force provides further context for the issue. N. A. (2011, Nov 1). A Report from The Heinz Endowments' African American Men and Boys Task Force. *Pittsburgh Tribune-Review*. Retrieved from: http://www.heinz.org/userfiles/library/aamb-mediareport.pdf

**p. 211 – *Hell Breaks Loose:*** Philadelphia Daily News Headline. August 14, 2014. Mathis, J. (2014, Aug 14). How the Daily News Cover Changed Overnight – Then Changed Again. *Philadelphia*. Retrieved from: http://www.phillymag.com/news/2014/08/14/daily-news-cover-changed-overnight-changed/

**p. 211 – *Weed, Fights, and Guns: Trayvon Martin's Text Messages Released:*** Caputo, M. (2013, May 23). Weed, fights, and guns: Trayvon Martin's text messages released. *Miami Herald*. Retrieved from: http://www.miamiherald.com/news/state/florida/trayvon-martin/article1951821.html.

**p. 211 – I envision a society where the positive headlines like these become the norm:** The NAACP produced a powerful 30-second video showcasing some of the positive stats on young Black men. The video is available at www.youtube.com/watch?t=31&v=HgVNsCLd8iY

**p. 211 – It's a shame that so many of our men of color are receiving negative press:** The Atlantic's (2015) article "Beyond the Stereotypical Image of Young Men of Color" also provides some more context for the issue. Knight, D. J. (2015, Jan 5). Beyond the Stereotypical Image of Young Men of Color. *The Atlantic*. Retrieved from: http://www.theatlantic.com/education/archive/2015/01/beyond-the-stereotypical-image-of-young-men-of-color/384194/

**p. 211 – *100% of Urban Prep Seniors Admitted to College:*** Full text article available at N. A. (2013, March 29). Urban Prep Graduates All College-Bound For Fourth Year In A Row. *Huffpost Chicago*. Retrieved from: http://www.huffingtonpost.com/2013/03/29/urban-prep-graduates-all-_n_2981203.html

**p. 211 – *Meet the Student Accepted into all Eight Ivy League Schools:*** O'Neill, N. & Vecsey, T. (2015, April 5). Meet the student accepted into all eight Ivy League schools. *New York Post*. Retrieved from: http://nypost.com/2015/04/05/meet-the-student-accepted-into-all-eight-ivy-league-schools/

**p. 211 – such as a 2013 Education Week report:** Find the full article at The Editors. (2013, May 31). As Graduation Rates Rise, Focus Shifts to Dropouts. Education Week. Retrieved from: http://www.edweek.org/ew/articles/2013/06/06/34execsum.h32. html?qs=graduation+rates+2013

**p. 211 – Or a Boston Globe Article:** Jackson, D. Z. (2015, Feb 22). The positive numbers about young black men. *Boston Globe.* Retrieved from: https://www. bostonglobe.com/opinion/2015/02/22/the-positive-numbers-about-black-men/OTcPR1Hhn8YfOyuVoWZxfJ/story.html

**p. 211 – Or a report from the U.S. Department of Health and Human Services:** Martin, J. A.; Hamilton, B. E.; Osterman, M. J. K.; Curtin, S. C.; Mathews, T. J. (2013). Births: Final Data for 2012. *National Vital Statitics Reports, Vol 62, 9.* Retrieved from: http://www.cdc.gov/nchs/data/nvsr/nvsr62/nvsr62_09.pdf

**p. 212 – National Science Foundation's findings:** Mance, A. (2010, May 28). Factual Friday, Good News Edition: Black Higher Ed Trivia for May 28, 2010. *Black on Campus.* Retrieved from: http://blackoncampus.com/2010/05/28/factual-friday-good-news-edition-black-higher-ed-trivia-for-may-28-2010/

**p. 212 – We should tout the work of organizations like the BME Community:** To learn more about the work these two organizations are doing, please visit their websites at www.bmecommunity.org and www.edexcelencia.org.

**p. 213 – and played the Jay-Z song "Can I Live":** Carter, S. (1996). Can I Live. On *Reasonable Doubt* [Vinyl]. U.S.: Roc-A-Fella Records.

**p. 213 – that it's hard for boys to perform academically:** Hoy, W.K. & Tschannen-Moran, M. (1999). The five faces of trust: An empirical confirmation in urban elementary schools. *Journal of School Leadership,* 9, 184-208.

**p. 218 – heading up a school that has a history:** Freetown, the African American community where this school is located, was founded in the 1840s by free blacks. It was one of the largest communities of free blacks during the 19th century. For more information on this community's history, visit: http://www.aacounty.org/PlanZone/TransPlan/Resources/PDF/sap_lakeshore_commHistory.pdf

**p. 218 – She began quoting the long-outdated and hotly contested work:** Ruby Payne's original book "A Framework for Understanding Poverty" was first published in 1995. For a blog article that includes a fairly comprehensive list to some of the critiques of Ruby Payne's work, check out http://larryferlazzo.edublogs. org/2012/01/24/the-best-critiques-of-ruby-payne/

Payne Ph. D., R. K. (2013). *A Framework for Understanding Poverty: A Cognitive Approach.* Texas: aha! Process, Inc.

Ferlazzo, L. (2012, Jan 24). The Best Critiques of Ruby Payne. Retrieved from: http://larryferlazzo.edublogs.org/2012/01/24/the-best-critiques-of-ruby-payne

## CHAPTER 19: Building Bridges, Crossing Borders

**p. 227 – *Damn right I like the life I live, 'cause I went from negative to positive:*** Barnes, S.; Combs, S.; McIntosh, H.; Olivier, J.; Rock, P.; Wallace, C. (1994). Juicy [Recorded by Wallace, C.]. On Ready to Die [CD]. New York: Sony Music.

**p. 228 – to meet a man by the name of Dr. Rassias:** For more information on Dr. Rassias' work, visit Dartmouth College Rassias Center at http://rassias.dartmouth.edu.

**p. 228 – The title of the book was "The Courage to Teach":** Palmer, P. J. (2007). *The Courage to Teach: Exploring the Inner Landscape of a Teacher's Life.* San Francisco: Jossey-Bass.

**p. 230 – Because of my deep respect for Palmer's work:** For more information on Parker Palmer's retreats, visit the Center for Courage and Renewal at www.couragerenewal.org.

**p. 232 – or whether I'm co-leading a SPARK retreat:** More information on SPARK can be found at www.spark-retreats.com.

# GRATITUDE

We have to start by collectively thanking our families and especially our amazing spouses – Meshelle and Andy. There is no way that we could have ever brought this project to be without your blessing, your support, your ability to take care of everything around us while we dug in deeply to the writing and editing and publishing of this book. There were many early morning and late night video conferencing sessions. Numerous phone calls that took us away from our families. A lot of times when we kept this work so close because we wanted to make sure we got it right before we put it out there in the world. There have been sacrifices on your end that we never could have fully understood while we were so immersed in the work itself. The only thing we can really say is thank you. We trust that the impact of the words we've poured over will do the sacrifices you've made – for no reason other than because you love us – worth it.

We also have to thank our small, but powerful, team. Thank you to our wonderful research assistant, Melissa Schaefer, for all of your hard work in setting up interviews, conducting background research, and helping with this project's marketing and outreach efforts. Thank you to our tremendously talented graphic designer, Laura Stephen. We articulated our vision to you and you made it happen. And thank you to our editing team – Carol Hanley, Dr. Monique Henderson, and Carrie Tomko. We couldn't have made it to the finish line without you. Carol, your expertise when it came to crafting a relatable narrative was invaluable. You pushed our writing far beyond where we were comfortable and for that we are ever grateful. And just when we thought we really were tired of editing, you sent a single email that reminded us of the importance of getting it all right. And to Monique and Carrie, thank you for caring enough about the art of writing to make sure we got the little things right. A special thanks to Carrie for getting us through those final very tedious days leading up to publication.

Thank you to everyone who took the time to be interviewed for this project. Your words provided much of the context and backdrop for the stories as they've unfolded here and we could not have done this without your generosity of time. And thank you to Candace Greene for helping to get this project off the ground, for the time and integrity you took with the initial interviews and background research, and for all the work that you put into some of the earliest chapters of this book. You set the tone and laid the foundation for us to build something of which we're incredibly proud. Thank you.

## LaMarr

I'd like to say a heartfelt thank you to following people. To the Creator, who loves me despite my faults and fears. To the ancestors whose shoulders I stand upon – thanks for your sacrifice.

To my wife, Meshelle, who always makes valuable suggestions for my books and keeps me focused. My journey has been a success because you are part of my life. To my amazing children, Hadiya, Sameera, and Mosiah – you are my constant inspiration.

To my mother, Allene D. Shields, who in the words of Abraham Lincoln said, "All that I am or ever hope to be, I owe to my angel mother." To my brother, John Shields, and my sisters, Denise Shields and Kim Shields, for protecting your little brother. To my father, John H. Shields, for doing the best you could with what you had.

To my African American and Latino families – our time is now.

To Bettye Blaize, my wonderful assistant, who works tirelessly without fanfare or recognition – you are an invaluable member of the team and an integral part of any project I undertake. To my staff at the Cambio Group and my awesome team at PRAISE, you are all important extensions of my work. To my KAOS brothers for allowing me to share our unapologetic story.

To Andy, for allowing his wife to share her gifts with me and so many others. Thanks for your patience.

To the brothers of UAAM for keeping my vision alive. To the mighty class of '98 and all the amazing students I taught at Baltimore City College High School, thanks for all the memories.

To Kevin Brooks, David Miller, Derrick Chase, Hank G., Baba Ademola, Andre Turner, Kevin Johnson, Kenya Knalls, Deon Hughes, Eric Berry, Derek Hicks, Kevin Higgins, Rodney Thomas, Laurenton Ghent, Patrice Gardner, Paula, Tony Bolling, and Kenyon Douglass – our work and friendship has lifted me to a higher level.

To Marina who has gone above and beyond to bring this book to life with her research and writing. When we started together, we were just co-writers. Now we are friends. You are an invaluable extension of my work and calling and have stretched my thinking in so many ways. I've forever grateful.

Finally, to all the teachers who said I wouldn't make it – *cállate la boca!*

**Marina**

Thank you to my family who reminds me daily of my purpose. Thank you especially to my husband, Andy. Your love gives me strength. Thank you to my dad for believing in every single one of my dreams as if they were your own. It's because of you that I continue to dream big and never give up on the work that I know I was put on this earth to do. Thank you to my mom for continuing to teach me about wellness through your example. Without your constant reminder that I need to take care of me, I would have not have found the balance and focus that completing a project like this required. Thank you to all of my extended family for loving me without condition. Thank you especially to my nieces and nephews for just being who you are. Everything I do to try to make the world kinder, I do for you.

Thanks to my business partner and dear friend Monique for being a constant sounding board for any and all things related to writing and social justice and equity and education and, well, life. Thank you to Anne, our business manager, for taking care of things behind the scenes, being always in my corner, and making sure that everything runs so seamlessly.

Thank you to all of my teachers, mentors and colleagues who have helped shape how I view the world with a more critically reflective eye. Special thanks to Dr. Robert Denham and Dr. Phil Mirci. Your teachings and examples of how to navigate some of the deepest educational and social inequities with grace and love continue to inspire me in all I do. Also thank you to Keith L. Brown, who first helped me see what social justice ideals looked like in action. The time we spent together on the road taught me what is possible.

Thank you to all the students I've taught through the years who have reminded me why this fight matters so much. From those high school students very early on in my career who were gracious enough to learn alongside my 20-something self to my college students at all levels who, just when I think I'm getting tired and might give up on the classroom altogether, remind me why I'm called back over and over again – thank you for making this work of teaching a challenging and worthwhile ride.

And lastly, thank you to LaMarr for trusting me to travel along this road with you. Lots of tears, lots of laughter, and here we are. It hasn't always been easy, but I am immensely humbled by what we've created together. There are no words to express my deep gratitude. Thank you.

# ABOUT THE AUTHORS

**Dr. LaMarr Darnell Shields** is an author, teacher and thought leader who has dedicated his life to inspiring others to pursue a higher, more meaningful purpose and achieve sustainable value for long-term success. As a former professor at the Johns Hopkins School of Education, his extensive experience as a scholar-practitioner in the field of racial, ethnic, and academic identity among Black and Latino male youth, coupled with his depth of experience with fostering interconnectivity and deep engagement among educators, policy makers, parents, and other change agents, uniquely positions him as a leader in the field. As a member of the National Blue Ribbon Commission on Equity and Achievement, he brings with him an unparalleled level of enthusiasm and complexity to all the work he does. A teacher at heart, LaMarr has a wealth of experience teaching and leading in both K-12 and university settings. He currently resides with his family in Baltimore, Maryland. For more information on LaMarr and his work, please visit www.drlamarrdarnellshields.com.

**Dr. Marina V. Gillmore** is an author, educator and consultant who has built her professional career around working with youth and teaching, training, researching and writing about issues related to equity and access, social justice, belief and value exploration, and self-efficacy. She holds a doctorate in Leadership for Educational Justice and has conducted award-winning research on the experiences of underserved youth in urban environments. Her work as a scholar-practitioner in the field of social justice comes from her passion for and experience with deconstructing the complexities of injustices in our society and her focus on using the power of the personal story to incite deep conversations and transformations centered around how our perceptions and belief systems impact everything we do. Also a teacher at heart, Dr. Gillmore has taught extensively in both traditional and non-traditional settings at the K-12 and university levels. She currently resides with her family in Southern California. For more information on Marina and her work, please visit www.drmarinagillmore.com.

# OTHER BOOKS AND CURRICULA BY THE AUTHORS

**Dr. LaMarr Darnell Shields**

*101 Things Every Boy/Young Man of Color Should Know* (Cambio Books, 2009).

*Rhyme and Reason: A Hip-Hop Tool for the Classroom.* Co-authored with David Miller (Hotep Press, 2008).

*Hands Off: Strategies to Combat Youth Violence.* Co-authored with Sarah Hasan (Hotep Press, 2007).

*Dare to Be Queen: A Holistic and Comprehensive Curriculum for Girls.* Co-authored with David Miller and Mischa Green (Hotep Press, 2005).

10 Steps Out of Puberty (Hotep Press, 1999).


**Dr. Marina V. Gillmore**

*Balancing Act: 31 Simple Strategies for Maintaining your Balance and Sanity as a Teacher.* Co-authored with Dr. Monique R. Henderson (Institute for Educational and Social Justice Press, 2015).

*Inspirational Youth: Transforming Average to Extraordinary.* Co-authored with Dr. Monique R. Henderson and Keith L. Brown (Institute for Educational and Social Justice Press, 2013).

*Motivation, Education, and Transformation: The Change Agent's Guide to Reaching our Youth and Lifting Them Higher.* Co-authored with Dr. Monique R. Henderson and Keith L. Brown (Institute for Educational and Social Justice Press in association with 20/20 Enterprises, 2011).